What They Are

"This really looks like *a su*
users' guide. We've needed one. John Bryan has put together a finely referenced manual. The '99 Most Asked Questions' are alone worth getting. Until now, I thought that sturgeon thing was a myth."
—Harry Kollatz, Jr., *Richmond Magazine*

"This book is the *definitive text for all users of the James*. Don't start a trip to the river without it."
—Ed Tillett, Virginia Wildlife Federation

"*Exhilarating and illuminating, the best outdoor experience I've had from my living room!* A well researched, beautifully descriptive, easy to understand resource for *endless hours of outdoor enjoyment for the whole family*. Whether you're a seasoned river enthusiast, or an occasional visitor this book will give you a greater sense of pride, respect and appreciation for all the river has to offer."
—Sabrina Squire, WWBT/NBC Channel 12 TV

"John Bryan combines the research training of a scholar with the devotion of a lover. You can't really know Richmond—and you certainly can't know the James River on which Richmond was built—until you've read Bryan's remarkable guide."
—Garvey Winegar, *Richmond Times-Dispatch*

"This is *the book Richmonders have needed for a long time!* It's great to know all the things the James River offers us in our own backyard."
—Jerry Cooper, Cooper's Marine, Inc.

"An encyclopedic and engaging achievement!"
—Ed Slipek, *STYLE Weekly*

"This is *a must-read for residents of and visitors* to our 'River City.' John Bryan's lovingly comprehensive guide to the urban James has added enormously to this Richmonder's list of things to do on, around, and for a splendid segment of our historic waterway."
—Melinda Skinner, Native Richmonder

"The James River in Richmond is an amazing resource. In what other state capital can one expect to see a Bald Eagle, Great Horned Owl, and Pileated Woodpecker all in the same morning? Many thanks, John, for sharing your knowledge and prose with us."
—C.R. Blem, Virginia Commonwealth University Professor of Biology and Editor, *The Wilson Bulletin*

"Please *don't miss this book!* I think of Hal Borland, John James Audubon, John Muir and other terrific nature writers every time I read John Bryan's work. Whether you're an outdoors person or like to stay inside, you'll be glad you own this book."
—Robert J. Fagg, Jr. Co-Founder, The Classic Society Book Club

"*From now on you'll be hard-pressed to say you know Richmond if you haven't read Bryan's book.* He combines a contemporary guide to our wonder waterway with a taste of our rich past and a view of the fresh future the James River is bringing to our city. *A joy to read.*"
—Paul Di Pasquale, Artist, "The Headman" and the Arthur Ashe Statue.

"*THE book* for exploring the natural world along the river in Richmond!"
—Ralph White, Naturalist, James River Park System

"Any book by John Bryan promises to be practical, unique, visually excellent, and *filled with canny and special information.* This detailed guide to the James River is as helpful and interesting as anything he's done. I've never read a book that's explored a waterway from so many perspectives."
—Nick Lyons, *Fly Fisherman Magazine,* LYONS & BURFORD Publishers

"John Bryan provides us with fascinating insights into this beautiful waterway—past, present, and future. Just as important, he shows us ways to experience the James River as never before. I know that lovers of nature, history, adventure, or of city living at its best will enjoy this unique guide."
—Charles F. Bryan, Jr., Director, Virginia Historical Society

"This is a long awaited guidebook. It helps us enjoy The Falls of the James in Richmond—a rich source of historic, ecologic, recreational and scenic treasures."
—R.B. Young, Chair, Falls of the James Scenic River Advisory Board

"Compelling and exciting. It's hard to believe that there is this much to do on the James River, but this book has found it all! A really fun book to read with not only tips on what to do on the urban James, but also with very entertaining stories which only John Bryan can offer."
—Robert C. Edwards, Director, Catholic Communications Center

"Richmond's James River is its most valuable natural and recreational asset. It must be made accessible for all to enjoy and protected for future generations."
—J. Robert Hicks, Jr., President, Alpine Outfitters, Former Director, Virginia Department of Conservation and Recreation

The James River in Richmond:
Your Guide To Enjoying America's Best Urban Waterway

John Bryan

Charles Creek Publishing

Richmond, Virginia
1997

The James River In Richmond:
Your Guide To Enjoying America's Best Urban Waterway

By John Bryan

With special articles by Brenton S. Halsey, Charles V. Ware, Ralph R. White, Rob Carter and Jamie McGrath

Published by:

Charles Creek Publishing
Post Office Box 26746
Richmond, VA 23261 U.S.A.

Book designed by Ben Cornatzer.
"Guide to Manchester Wall Climbing" designed by Rob Carter.
Symbols designed by John Bryan.

All maps in this book are copied or derived from maps originally published by the James River Park System.

All rights reserved. No part of this book—except for portions previously published by public agencies—may be reproduced or transmitted in any form or by any means, electronic or mechanical, including photocopying, recording or by any information storage and retrieval system without written permission from the author, except for the inclusion of brief quotations in a review.

Copyright © 1997 by John Bryan

Library of Congress Catalog Card Number: 97-91569

Bryan, John.
  The James River in Richmond : your guide to America's best urban waterway / by John Bryan. — Richmond, Va. : Charles Creek Publishing, 1997. 336 p. : ill. (some col.), maps ; 74 cm. Includes bibliographical references and index. ISBN 0-9656314-3 : $19.95

  1. James River (Va.) —Guidebooks.
  2. James River (Va.) —Description and travel.
  3. James River (Va.) —History.
  4. Richmond (Va.) —Description and travel.

  I. Title.

F232.J2.B7 1997
97-091569

Dedication

This book is dedicated to Janet—who continues to spice my enjoyment of the James River.

Janet's 529-foot fence/mural on Brown's Island—adorned by children at June Jubilee.

Table of Contents

Chapter One: Access to the Urban James—Where to Park	25
Urban River Mystery	35
Chapter Two: The James River Park System	39
Group Programs at James River Park	41
Summer, 1996	42
Things to Do on Belle Isle	45
July and August Notes	46
The James River Park System Visitor's Center	49
Activities Presented by the James River Park System	50
Texas Beach	51
Pumphouse Park	52
October 10, 1995	53
Interpretative Guide to Belle Isle Historic Park	56
January 29, 1995	61
Chapter Three: Floating and Paddling	65
The Nation's Best Urban Whitewater	67
Richmond Raft Company	75
April 19, 1995	76
The Professional Float Trip	77
Coastal Canoeists	81
May 26, 1983	82
Paddling Tips	84
November 27, 1996	86
Paddling	88
The Float Trip	91
Chapter Four: Fishing	99
August 23, 1983	109
Fly Fishing	110
September 26, 1995	112
Mr. Williams	112
January 31, 1982	116
Fred Murray	117
Spring Fish	119
Belle Isle Quarry Pond	122
August 8, 1983	123
October 8, 1984	124
The First Striper	125

Chapter Five: History — 131
    Timeline of Richmond's James River — 132
    A Brief History of Canals on the James — 133
    March, 1996 — 137
    History Surrounding the James River Corporation Headquarters — 138
    November 14, 1995 — 148
    Virginia Department of Historic Resources — 149
    The Falls of the James Atlas — 149
    Found Objects — 152

Chapter Six: Nature — 157
    January 23, 1983 — 158
    Birding With Charlie Blem — 160
    Birds Along the Urban James — 165
    April, 1995 — 169
    February, 1996 — 169
    Interpretive Guide to the Geology Walk — 170
    February 10, 1996 — 177
    Snorkeling in the City — 180
    October 18, 1981 — 184
    Christmas Morning, 1994 — 186

Chapter Seven: Climbing — 188
    Guide to Manchester Wall Climbing — 189
    The Wall — 205

Chapter Eight: More Ways To Enjoy the Urban James — 217
    September 6, 1982 — 217
    Urban Siren — 219
    A Walk on the Wall — 224
    Annabel Lee — 231
    Cross Country Skiing — 231
    April, 1996 — 232
    Jet Skiing — 233
    Water Skiing — 233
    Biking — 233
    Biking Along the Floodwall — 234
    Jogging — 238
    Swimming — 239
    The Pipeline — 239
    Rowing — 240
    First Day of Spring — 242
    December 13, 1984 — 243
    At the Bottom of the Canal—Spring, 1996 — 253
    James River Batteau Festival — 261

June 14, 1983	262
Maymont	263
Passages	264
March 29, 1985	265
Chapter Nine: The Environment, Conservation, Politics, the Future	267
The Breeze Along the River	267
Disaster Zone: Ecology of a Floodplain	269
In River Time	275
20-Year Projection for Park Needs & Development	276
James River Association	278
Alliance for the Chesapeake Bay	279
Falls of the James Scenic River Advisory Board	281
Center for Environmental Studies	283
Volunteer Projects in the James River Park	285
The Honorable Becky Norton Dunlop	287
August 23, 1981	288
Brenton S. Halsey	289
Virginia Canal Museum?	290
Mayo's Island	291

Appendix

Your 99 Most-Asked Questions About the Urban James	293
Take the Urban River Challenge	303
Resources	306
Index	320

Acknowledgements

I would like to acknowledge here the following persons who offered suggestions and provided material for this publication or helped in other tangible ways—both direct and indirect: **Whit Baldwin** for providing a helicopter trip above the river; **Charlie Blem**, Virginia Commonwealth University Biology Professor, for showing and telling me about birds, and editing; **Charlie Bryan**, Director of the Virginia Historical Society, for telling me about the importance of history; **Rick Busch**, Assistant Director for the Wildlife Division of Virginia's Department of Game and Inland Fisheries, for telling me about animal life on the James; **Rob Carter**, Virginia Commonwealth University Professor of Communication Arts and Design, and **Jamie McGrath** of Henrico County School Board Construction and Maintenance, for showing and telling me about climbing and providing the detailed section on climbing; **Cindy Donnell**, Virginia Commonwealth University Associate Professor of Music, for showing and telling me about rowing; The Honorable **Becky Norton Dunlop**, Virginia's Secretary of Natural Resources, for talking with me about the river and providing other assistance; **Bob Edwards**, Director of Communications for the Catholic Diocese of Richmond, for being my steadfast urban fishing buddy; **Bob Fagg**, Virginia Commonwealth University's Director of Annual Giving, for editing; **Greg Garman**, Director of Virginia Commonwealth University's Center for Environmental Studies, for written materials and information about fish; **Brenton S. Halsey**, Chairman Emeritus of James River Corporation, for written materials and telling me about the river; **Ralph Hambrick**, Virginia Commonwealth University Professor of Political Science and Public Administration, for telling me about paddling; **Chuck Hamm** and **Greg South** for honest and valuable fishing information through the years; **Bob Hicks**, Director of Development for Goodwill, for talking with me about the river; **Marc Hirth**, former head of the Richmond Riverfront Development Corporation, for telling me about the project; **Patti Jackson**, Executive Director of the James River Association, for consultation; **Marc Kalman**, General Manager of Richmond Raft Company, for telling me about rafting and providing a ride and photographs; young **Hank Krohn**, an honor-roll sixth-grader over near Charlottesville, for enriching my and Thomas' urban James outings; **Fred Murray** of Maymont, for telling me about Maymont, fishing, and other information; **Joe News**, Richmond Recreation and Parks, for telling me about fishing; **Terry Oggel**, Virginia Commonwealth University Professor of English, for editing; **Geoff Platt**, Executive Director of Maymont, for telling me about Maymont; **Steve Salpukas**, photographer for *STYLE Weekly*, for consultation and for his good intentions to provide his wonderful photographs for this book; **Paul Timmreck**, Virginia Commonwealth University's Vice President for Finance, for his thoughts on fishing; **Keith Trevvett** and **Richard Morton**, Assistant Buyer and Manager of Alpine Outfitters, for consultation; **Bill Trout** and **Jimmy Moore**, co-authors of the *Falls of the James Atlas* (along with **George Rawls**) for talking with me on Batteau Day at Pumphouse Park; **Charles Ware**, Conservation Chair of the Coastal Canoeists, for telling me about paddling and providing written materials and photographs; **Ralph White**, Naturalist for the James River Park System, for supplying photographs, written materials, interviews, and wise insight; **Alex Wise**, Director of Historic Resources for Virginia, for telling me about history; **R.B. Young**, Chair of The Falls of the James Scenic River Advisory Board, for talking with me and providing written materials; and of course **Janet** and **Kelly** and **Thomas** for their time and support.

Symbols

These symbols, used throughout this book, represent activities which are available on the urban James River. Next to each symbol on this list is one good place to enjoy that activity.

Biking
The loop around Belle Isle.

Birding
The Floodwall Overlook at 2nd and Hull Streets.

Canoeing
Huguenot Woods.

Children's Activities
James River Park System Visitor's Center.

Climbing
The Wall on the south side of the Manchester Bridge.

Cross Country Skiing
Trail from the James River Park System Visitor's Center.

Fishing
Mayo's Bridge.

Fly Fishing
Northbank (Texas Beach).

Geology
22nd Street area of James River Park System.

Hiking
Buttermilk Trail from 42nd Street to 22nd Street.

History
Great Shiplock Park trail around Chappel Island.

Jogging
Tredegar Street, across the Footbridge, around Belle Isle.

Kayaking
Pipeline Rapids.

Motorboating
Ancarrow's Landing.

Nature
Belle Isle.

Projects
James River Park System Visitor's Center.

Rafting
Richmond Raft Company.

Rollerblading
Floodwall Walk—eastern half.

Rowing
Virginia Boat Club just downstream from the Annabel Lee.

Swimming
Pony Pasture.

Trees
42nd Street area of James River Park System.

Tubing
Pony Pasture to Reedy Creek.

Wheelchair Access
Footbridge and Belle Isle, with some assistance.

Wildflowers
Area surrounding James River Park System Visitor's Center.

Wildlife
Northbank (Texas Beach).

Warning—Disclaimer

Much effort has been spent in making this book as accurate as possible. But there may still be mistakes—typographical as well as informational. This book should be used only as a general guide to enjoying the urban James River—and not as the ultimate source of advice or information.

This book's purpose is to introduce the reader to Richmond's James River and to provide entertainment. The author and Charles Creek Publishing shall not be liable or responsible for any damage or loss caused to any person or persons by the information contained in this book.

If you are not in agreement with this disclaimer, you may return this book to the publisher for a full refund.

About The Author

John Bryan has enjoyed urban rivers such as Nashville's Cumberland, Atlanta's Chattahoochee, and Washington D.C.'s Potomac. During the four years he lived in New York City, he caught Hudson River stripers and bluefish near his 116th Street apartment from a blow-up raft purchased at Macy's.

John likes to fish, paint fish, and write about fishing. His articles have been published in such magazines as *Sports Illustrated* and *Field & Stream*, and his artworks have been reproduced in such publications as *Fly Fisherman* and *Gray's Sporting Journal*.

In early 1994 John conceived and began work on this book, and by the time he finished in December of 1996, he had learned that he has much, much, more to learn about the urban James River.

A native of Nashville, Tennessee, John moved to Richmond in 1981 to be the Director of Development for Virginia Commonwealth University's School of the Arts—a position he continues to enjoy. Janet, his wife of 23 years, is an artist and an adjunct instructor at VCU. Their two children, Kelly and Thomas, are 13 and 12 and are in the 8th and 6th grades at Binford Middle School.

Author at abandoned building near the Floodwall.

13

Wheelchair Access

There are many views of the James River which are wheelchair accessible—from the mausoleum in Hollywood Cemetery to the Annabel Lee docking area. But there are also wheelchair accessible locations to experience the river.

Belle Isle has the best access. It's a long haul, requiring some assistance, but worth it. One prime spot is the ramped dock on the Belle Isle Quarry Pond. It offers good fishing in this pond which has been stocked by the Department of Game and Inland Fisheries. Another location is a concrete ramp at the western end of Belle Isle. Depending on the water level, the ramp actually touches the James River just below the First Break Rapids and just above the Hollywood Rapids. The ramp is to the right of the picnic area at the western tip of Belle Isle.

First Break Rapids at the western tip of Belle Isle.
➤

The Floodwall Overlook on the south side near the Manchester Bridge is reached by parking at 7th and Semmes, and from there with some assistance (no steps) you can take the path down beneath the Manchester Bridge and then onto the Floodwall. The Floodwall Overlook at 2nd and Hull Street is also wheelchair accessible. Then you can curve beneath Mayo's Bridge and onto the paved walkway downstream along the Floodwall.

On the south side of the Huguenot Bridge, just upstream from the Huguenot Woods area, is an old bridge abutment which, although littered with natural debris, is accessible with some minimal assistance. It's a good place to look out at the woods across the river.

Viewing the river at flood stage from the Floodwall.

Ancarrow's Boat Access Area is another accessible area. Adjacent to the boat ramp, on the downstream side, is a (sometimes soggy) concrete overlook where you can watch the river, fishers, and boats.

Directly across the river is the Annabel Lee docking area which is accessible to wheelchairs. This area usually has other people there, and in the warmer months is usually productive for fishing.

Wheelchairs can access Brown's Island from the upstream end along Tredegar Street [blocked due to construction as this is written].

The Pipeline Overlook at 12th and Byrd Streets [closed for construction as this is written] offers handicap parking and an easily accessible view of this part of the river.

Finally, Ralph White reports that a mountain bike trail which is also class 3 wheelchair accessible will be built from the 22nd Street area to Belle Isle in 1997.

Handicap parking area just west of Huguenot Woods.

The Urban James River

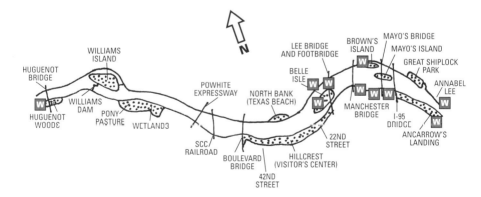

W Wheelchair Access

Letter From an Eighth-Grader

I'm writing this for any kids who might have this book. My name is Kelly Bryan and I'm an eighth-grade girl at Binford Middle School in Richmond. My dad says he started taking me to the James River when I was a baby in one of those baby backpacks. But about the earliest I remember is when he would take me and Thomas with buckets and little shovels to play in a quiet, sandy area. Thomas is my sixth-grade brother. He goes to Binford too. That's a picture of us on the cover. I told my dad not to use it, but he did anyway.

Biking on Belle Isle. ⟶

If you're in middle school—and probably in elementary school or high school too—there are lots of things you can do on the James River here in Richmond. One of my favorite things is birthday parties. Two years ago my friend Giles had her party there, and we rode bikes on Belle Isle. My mom and I have ridden there a lot.

Another thing you can do is science projects. Thomas and I made leaf notebooks there when we were in about the first grade. But now our science projects are harder, and there are a lot of ways we can do them along the river. Thomas is doing one now about birds. He takes his binoculars and looks at them. The ones on the water are a lot easier to see than the ones in the bushes and trees.

Footbridge to Belle Isle.

If you want some good ideas for projects you can go to the James River Park Visitor's Center and just look around. They have a lot of displays of things you see along the river. They also have classes and workshops where you can get great information.

One thing I had to do for a class at Binford last year was a community service volunteer project. Although I had a good time volunteering at the Belmont Library, next time I'm going to do a volunteer project along the river. James River Park has a list of a lot of volunteer projects you can do, and they'll help you on some of them.

One thing my mom and dad and brother and I like doing is walking on those trails along the river and especially on Belle Isle. If you've never walked across the Footbridge that hangs below the Lee Bridge, you ought to do it. The first time it's scary, but now I can even ride my bike on it.

It's fun wading in the shallow areas of the river, but I got scared once last summer when my dad took me and Thomas wading with him out in the middle of the river. All he likes to do is fish, so while he fished, Thomas and I just explored. We all waded from the Boulevard Bridge upstream to that railroad bridge. The river was really low and it got over our heads only a couple of times. Thomas and I wore life jackets.

I didn't get scared until we started back downstream. At first it was fun, because we could just float along and drift with the current. But then we got to this place where the water was fast, I scraped my legs on rocks and Thomas got stuck against a big log. The river was pushing against him and he couldn't float around it. My dad had to come over and get him loose. But he didn't get hurt or anything, and we got back okay.

James River Park is a great place for picnics. My mom says she used to push me and Thomas in our double stroller there and then put out a blanket for us to play. I'm not yet old enough to go there without an adult, but when I get in high school I want to go there with friends. The river is really pretty and you can go out on the big rocks and just talk and listen to music.

My grandparents live in Nashville, my aunt and uncle live in Norfolk, my mom and dad used to live in New York City, and my mom has had an art grant to live in Paris. I've visited all four of those cities, and they all have rivers. But their rivers just look like plain rivers. They aren't anything like the James River. On our river you can do lots of fun things.

If you're a kid in Richmond, you should learn about the ways you can enjoy the James River. You probably won't ever see another river like it in any other city. We are very lucky to live here.

Poet—not Kelly—at the western tip of Belle Isle. Hollywood Cemetery and James River Corporation in background.

A Letter to the Reader

Twenty years ago my friend Wimberly Brown, Professor Emeritus of History for the University of Georgia System, told me he had accepted an invitation to present a 20-minute lecture for the garden club in a rural south Georgia town. He smiled and shook his head as he told me they had suggested a topic which, for him, was going to be difficult. They had asked him to speak for 20 minutes on the topic, "France."

Likewise it is impossible to shoehorn the urban James River into a manageable book. But, even though this book has bitten off more than it can chew, it has, nevertheless, bitten it off. It will be up to you to chew.

One hundred years ago the importance of the urban James River was almost totally commercial. It provided a seaport, a power source, a raw materials source, and a waste site.

Today the importance of the urban James is almost totally recreational. **Our priority is to preserve its beauty, its flora and fauna, its artifacts, its water quality, and its ambience.** Things which didn't matter a hundred years ago are now of primary importance to our public and corporate leaders and to Richmond's citizens. The river is Richmond's most important amenity.

Why? It is of course because of all the individual activities discussed in this book: paddling, birding, climbing, fishing and so on. But it is for a much broader reason too. Those activities—taken in aggregate—plus the river's visual beauty, make Richmond an attractive place to live. (There

have been published accounts of people moving to Richmond simply because of the availability of whitewater paddling.) And as people and businesses move to Richmond, virtually everyone prospers.

Our urban James is indeed the nation's best urban river. It really is. No other river comes close. How do you measure something like that? Try my Urban River Challenge later in the book.

My thought is that as a Richmonder I have three big responsibilities regarding the urban James River. First, I need to continue to learn more about it (so, for example, when the out-of-town candidate asks our search committee what activities are available here for his children, I can talk enthusiastically about a hundred different opportunities in the James River Park System). Second, I need to make opportunities to tell others about the urban James (so, for example, my neighbor's children will have already heard my precautions about tubing in the James before they innocently set afloat). And third, I must step forward and be counted as I see opportunities to preserve the river and make it even more enjoyable (as did R.B. Young and friends 25 years ago when an expressway was seriously proposed for the river's southern shoreline).

In putting this book together I have learned that there are hundreds of sung and unsung heroes who share the credit for giving us the gorgeous urban river we have today. David Ryan's beautiful 1975 book, *The Falls of the James*, produced a dawning of public appreciation for the urban James River. Newton Ancarrow was a wellspring of appreciation, study and sheer enjoyment of nature on and around the river. Volunteers R.B. Young and The Falls of the James Scenic River Advisory Board have studied and provided advice on virtually everything that has any effect on the urban James. Bob Hicks has had many roles in shaping public and private use and appreciation of the river. Brenton S. Halsey has steadfastly championed the river's beauty and ambience amid corporate and public considerations. And of course Ralph White's allegiance to our river's beauty and welfare is ever strong and energetic and poetic.

Five months from now—May 24, 1997—will mark the 390th anniversary of Christopher Newport's "discovery" of the falls of the James, his arrival at what is now urban Richmond. In his ship from Jamestown he rounded the

bend just downstream from where the Annabel Lee now docks, and viewed a riverscape which looked like England's own Richmond on the Thames. He proceeded upstream as far as the rocks would allow and stopped in the vicinity of Mayo's Island.

He and his crew—which included John Smith—viewed a clean river which was rich with vegetation and was a natural magnet to fish and wildlife and birds and of course the Algonquin Indians. There was no mechanized industry, no ocean trade, and no dumping. Today, 390 years later, our urban James has come full circle and probably more closely resembles its discovery day than ever before.

If you haven't yet done so, select at least one aspect of our river and embrace it—first to enhance your own quality of life, and second for those of others.

—*John Bryan, December 24, 1996*

A note about spelling:

Although my resources differ, I was able to make decisions on most spellings in this book: Floodwall instead of Flood Wall, Footbridge instead of Foot Bridge, Mayo's Island instead of Mayo Island, Visitor's Center instead of Visitor Center.

However, it was necessary for me to allow original sources to differ on a few words. Pumphouse Park is also referred to as Pump House Park, and the Great Shiplock is also referred to as the Great Ship Lock. Finally, I had to use batteau as well as bateau, and batteaux as well as bateaux. Authorities were adamant regarding all of these spelling variations.

The Unique Urban James

So what makes Richmond's urban James River all that special? Of course all urban rivers are unique. They're all different. Each has its own attractions. There are probably a lot of urbanites who claim that their own urban river is the best.

But I propose that the urban James is the best of all of America's urban rivers. There is a fabric of contributing factors—a fabric woven with man-made fibers, with natural fibers, with fibers of history, and with bright fibers of luck.

First the luck. Luck of course had nothing to do with the fact that Christopher Newport had to stop at what is now Richmond during his upriver exploration of the river. The tide ends at Richmond. The rocks and rapids begin at Richmond. Richmond was a natural end-of-the-line sea/river port. But luck did contribute to the fact that so much of our urban shoreline is today public land. How in the world can a river city undergo 300+ years of development and not have all of its shorelines wind up in private hands? Of course a lot of wisdom and generosity and energetic leaders contributed to Richmond's public lands, but it's luck that allowed those qualities to shine so long on our river.

The natural fibers of our river's fabric are strong and unmatched. The urban James is situated at a fortuitously precise spot. First, the fall line runs right through the middle of town—14th Street to be exact. If you stand on the 14th Street Bridge and look down, you'll see tidal waters on one side and freestone rapids on the other. You'll see a deep and dark anadromous soup on one side, a clear green mountain-fish splash on the other. **You'll cast your line and catch largemouth bass and ocean-run stripers and Atlantic eels on one side; smallmouth bass and redbreast sunfish and occasional trout on the other.** You'll see bass boats and ocean boats on one side, kayaks and tubes on the other. You'll see people enjoying the river on both sides. All right in the middle of urban Richmond.

The river's north-south position is also fortuitously precise. Look at any map. An inch farther north and the too-cold winter temperatures would eliminate any chance of catching a winter fish. An inch farther south and the not-cold-enough winter temperatures wouldn't allow the fish to settle into that two-month "winter pattern" which we fishers find so challenging and gratifying. An inch farther north and the kayakers wouldn't be out there in January and February. An inch farther south and the kayakers wouldn't get the joy of donning their full winter paraphernalia. The urban James is positioned to sparkle in each season.

History is part of the river's fabric whether or not you're a historian. Belle Isle, smack in the center of the urban river, just on the other side of the beautifully suspended foot and bicycle bridge, is sprinkled with Civil War prison camp remnants. The informative signage adds a flavor and a context to your visits to the huge island, and you can't help but respect and revere and preserve this public retreat.

Upstream there is Pumphouse Park; the original stone buildings still stand, and you are there with them at the river's edge. Back before there was a railroad, mules pulled canal boats alongside the Pumphouse and up- and downstream through the many miles of the Kanawha Canal. When you walk along the canal and pull fish from it there is a flavor, a context, a reverence which hallows these urban waters.

There is Great Shiplock Park, there is the Canal Walk, there are many dozens of things from long ago—even an occasional arrowhead—which add richness to the texture of the urban James.

The brightest colors in the weave of the urban James' fabric are supplied by nature. Set up residence with your binoculars at the window of Richmond's tallest skyscraper and focus on the river below. You will see Bald Eagles flying and nesting. You will see deer among the James River Park's acreage. You will see beaver and muskrat and watersnake and Great Blue Herons. You will see a hundred species of birds, dozens of wildflowers, River Birch trees, Beech trees, and giant Sycamores. You will see migrant and local waterfowl—diving gulls and bobbing ducks. You will watch fishers pull leaping smallmouths, tugging largemouths and toothy walleye. You will see the silent sleek silhouettes of huge gar, the football shadows of fat carp, and you will swear—will positively swear—that you see the return of a lone sturgeon. And, if you were to maintain your binocular vigilance for an entire season, you would see a long-rod fisher lift a single brown or rainbow or brook trout from these non-trout waters.

The breeze along this river touches the best urban waterway in the nation.

A Special Note

After this book was completed, the author looked for an organization to help provide free copies of the book for use by school children. He met Ed Tillett, new President of the Virginia Wildlife Federation, who embraced the idea. The Virginia Wildlife Federation and Charles Creek Publishing have now together provided more than 1,000 complimentary copies of this book to libraries, schools, and resource centers throughout Richmond and surrounding areas.

The Virginia Wildlife Federation's priority interest is education, and its mission and policy are stated as follows:

The mission of the Virginia Wildlife Federation is to promote and educate the public of the need and the methods of conserving wildlife and the related natural resources.

The conservation policy of the Virginia Wildlife Federation is to devote its energy and resources to support for science based management of all natural resources and to the principles of good stewardship and use of resources within their sustainable capacity, and to encourage activities which:

1. Preserve healthy, self-sustaining populations of all species of Virginia wildlife, restore them where they have been degraded, and manage them to protect the natural balance and diversity of the wildlife community.
2. Preserve self-sustaining natural forests and all species of native vegetation, restore them where they have been degraded, control invasive non-native species, and protect the natural balance and diversity of the plant community.
3. Preserve a clean, healthy atmosphere for the support of Virginia's flora and fauna and restore it wherever it has been degraded.
4. Preserve water resources to provide habitat and life support to Virginia's flora and fauna and restore them wherever they have been degraded.
5. Conserve soil resources, the life supporting surface of the land, capable of providing habitat to Virginia's life systems and restore them wherever they have been degraded.
6. Conserve non-renewable mineral resources through reduction of waste and degradation, using renewable resources wherever practicable and tempering all uses with respect for the life they support.
7. Conserve Virginia's natural geological features as critical habitat for many species and providers of valuable qualities of life for people.
8. Conserve watersheds as basic resource units by treating each one as a unique natural community, and restoring all that have been degraded.
9. Promote land use practices which consider all life systems in all developments which alter the land, affect the life it supports or impact the resources it contains.
10. Teach people, the first order of life on earth, to be responsible, ethical stewards and respectful managers of all natural resources.
11. Consider America's natural resources to be as important in Virginia as its own and support their conservation as a priority second only to Virginia.
12. Treat the natural resources of other nations as interrelated extensions of the resources of America and Virginia, and encourage global conservation.

Virginia Wildlife Federation, 1001 East Broad Street, Suite LL5, Richmond, VA 23219

Chapter One:
Access to the Urban James— Where to Park

The following is a list with brief descriptions of all the places you can legally and publicly reach the James River between Bosher's Dam and Ancarrow's Landing. This list is a result of my driving down every road and street and lane on both sides of the entire length of the river. Although a detailed city map may appear to have other places that look like access areas, the following list is complete. One word of advice: there are some stretches of the river which you can drive alongside but which have very obvious No Parking signs. Don't park there regardless of how much you're tempted. It's private property and you could be ticketed or towed. **The days of parking on private property where nobody cares are over.**

Riverside Drive.

SOUTH SIDE

Huguenot Woods

When you cross the Huguenot Bridge from north to south, take the first right down the hill, turn left onto Riverside Drive, and then take a right where it deadends at Southampton. Southampton deadends into a little parking area for maybe four cars—handicap parking only. The river is straight ahead. Turn right into the main parking area which holds perhaps 35 cars. You can launch a boat here (no ramp), hike, ride a bike, and walk through the woods. The hike is along a well-marked path through the woods which circles along the river and then into the woods. The parking area has a gate with a lock and is closed after dark.

Huguenot Woods parking.

Oxford

Just downstream from the Huguenot Woods parking area is a tiny parking area where Oxford meets Riverside; there's room for perhaps six cars. A path into the

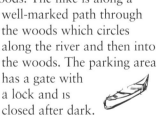

woods leads from this parking area. The path connects with the path which leads from the Huguenot Woods parking area.

Riverside Drive

Between the little Oxford parking area and where Stratford meets Riverside you can park on the north shoulder of Riverside Drive on the grass, single file, making certain your tires are completely off the road.

Pony Pasture West

This is a tiny parking area (five or six cars) on Riverside just west of the Pony Pasture parking lot. Make sure your car is completely off the street.

Pony Pasture

This is a huge parking area (180 cars) off Riverside Drive with restroom facilities, water fountain, and a James River Park System building. The sign says the building is open in daylight hours during the summer. This parking

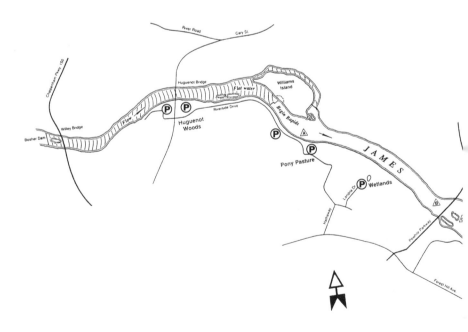

area is closed after dark. This is perhaps the most popular of all the James River Park System areas. There are jogging/walking trails, excellent birding in a variety of habitats, wildflowers, swimming, fishing, and a beginner's whitewater paddling route. **The rocks and rapids make this one of the most scenic areas of the river.**

James River Park System building at Pony Pasture.

The Wetlands

Landria deadends at The Wetlands—one of the nicest areas of the James River Park System. There is room for about eight cars, and there is no parking from 10 p.m. until 6 a.m. The paths in The Wetlands area are through meadows and woods and include three blinds from which to see waterfowl on a small pond. **The Wetlands is a good birding area and is also excellent for persons interested in identifying trees, wildflowers, and animal tracks.** There is also good fishing from the shore. You can take a bicycle into The Wetlands along the graveled path, but it's not appropriate during damp weather.

James River Park System

Ⓟ Parking Area

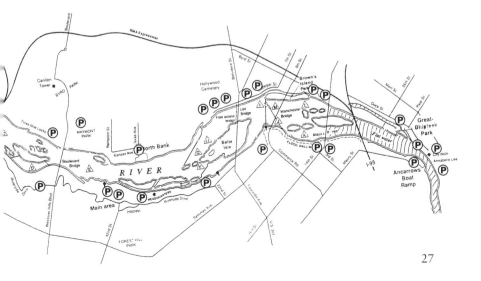

Boulevard Bridge

If you must fish under the Boulevard Bridge on the south side, and want to park as close as possible, you have to park on Riverside just off Westover Hills just upstream from the bridge. Then you have to walk down to the bridge and hike down the hill on the upstream side. Don't park too near Westover Hills; you'll see the No Parking signs.

42nd Street

Just west of the intersection of 42nd and Riverside is a James River Park System access parking lot. It holds 34 cars, and is locked after dark. From this lot you can walk down to the river on an established trail which includes a concrete and steel overpass over the railroad tracks. Paths lead alongside the river in both directions. It's easy to cross over rocks onto the islands which parallel the shoreline. This area is popular for swimming, picnicking, fishing, sunbathing, and rock-hopping. It is also a natural wonderland with a variety of trees and wildlife. In the fall you'll want to sample the Beech nuts and Hickory nuts. Photographers will enjoy the river here with its **abundance of boulders and rocks and ripples and rapids and quiet pools.**

42nd Street East

About 50 yards east of 42nd and Riverside is a little parking area which will hold a dozen cars. It's just a roadside indention, and the sign says there is no parking after dark. This area has a path leading down towards the river.

Hillcrest

At the intersection of Hillcrest and Riverside is a parking area with two brown signs reading: "Headquarters James River Park System" and "Reedy Creek Canoe Access." The loosely graveled parking area will hold 25 cars. From the parking area you must go through a fence gate and across railroad tracks to enter the James River Park area. Although the river is straight ahead, you will need to take the trails to the right or left to access the river. The Visitor's Center is just down the service road to the right, and behind it is the Canoe Access. Wooded trails parallel the river in both directions, and lead almost to the

Boulevard Bridge upstream and almost to the Lee Bridge downstream. Along the way there are several paths that lead to the river and to shoreline islands. **There is good access for fishing, swimming, and picnicking.** The paths are not ideal for jogging or biking (although are used for both), and are not wheelchair accessible.

22nd Street

Just west of the intersection of 22nd and Riverside is a sign which says "Main Area James River Park." There is parking for 67 cars. This lot is blocked from the river by a fence and railroad tracks, and you must walk either west or east (upstream or downstream) as you exit the lot. To the east are uphill steps which lead to a footbridge across the railroad tracks and then down to the river. To the west is a narrow, twisting, wooded trail which leads to the Hillcrest area. These walkways are not ideal for biking or jogging, and are not wheelchair accessible.

7th Street

At the intersection of 7th and Semmes is a parking lot for the Floodwall. It has three handicap parking spots and 18 others. (This is at the south side of the Manchester Bridge.) From this lot you can take the path to the Floodwall Overlook and also down below the Manchester Bridge and up onto the Floodwall Walk. Good birding, biking and jogging.

2nd Street

At the intersection of Hull and 2nd there is a parking lot for 18 cars plus two handicap spots in a lot with a brown sign reading "Floodwall Walk Western Half." This is immediately on the south side of Mayo's (14th Street)

Bridge. **From this lot you can go up on the overlook (wheelchair accessible) and have a marvelous view of the river and the city's skyline.** You can also take the paved path upstream to the Floodwall Walk (not wheelchair accessible from here) or take the paved path which circles beneath Mayo's Bridge (wheelchair accessible) and walk or bicycle downstream along the Floodwall.

Southern States

At the intersection of Hull and Manchester is Southern States. They allow fishers to park in their lot on the side next to the road—room for only two or three cars. Excellent access to the Floodwall and to Mayo's Bridge. Biking, hiking, and fishing along the Floodwall here is excellent.

Ancarrow's Boat Access Area

Follow Maury Street to its end and you'll arrive at this huge parking area with a wonderful concrete ramp into the river. There is room for at least 50 cars with trailers. There is a portajohn, trash cans, and paths along the river in both directions. This area has the only boat ramp on the portion of the river covered by this book. **Fishing is excellent, especially in the spring, both from the shore and from boats.** But the nature of the area is equally abundant. There is a rich, wooded path upstream along the river which goes all the way to the I-95 Bridge, and there is also a meadow which supports wildflowers and birds. If you hike upstream along the river, you'll arrive at the I-95 Bridge and will be mesmerized by the giant deposits of driftwood beneath it. Please don't take any; leave every bit for others to enjoy.

Ancarrow's Landing provides an excellent concrete launch ramp.

NORTH SIDE

Annabel Lee

Go southeast from downtown on East Main and turn right on Water Street. You'll see a huge concrete docking area. This area is used for docking the Annabel Lee, and until recently there was plenty of room also for fishers. At this writing some of the potential fishing area is fenced with Keep Out signs, but there is still room to fish. There is parking for at least 50 cars.

Annabel Lee Downstream

There is a gravel road going downriver from the Annabel Lee. Richmond Raft Company is located a few dozen yards down this road. Even though the property along the road is private, there are a few places where people park and fish. The shoreline is steep and the water is deep.

Water Street "Ramp"

Follow Water Street about 200 yards upstream (towards downtown) from the Annabel Lee, and on your left you'll see a little turn-in area with No Parking signs. This is near where Ash Street meets Water Street. In spite of the No Parking signs, people park and fish here, and there is room for five or six cars. The "ramp" is concrete with wood on top and is five feet above the water, and not a launch ramp. The ramp has room for only one group of three or four fishers, but there is also a concrete platform to the left and above the ramp from which three or four others can fish.

Behind these vehicles is a small fishing platform.

Great Shiplock Park

Another 200 yards upstream on the left is Great Shiplock Park. This area has fishing, biking, and hiking.

There are 23 parking spaces including one handicap space.

The area, including the trail through the woods on Chappel Island, has several descriptive signs of the history of the area. (The bike/hike trail which circles Chappel Island is not maintained regularly, and you will likely encounter numerous obstacles such as fallen trees.) Fishing and bird watching are excellent at Great Shiplock Park.

The Great Shiplock sometimes provides good crappie fishing.

Floodwall Parking, Northside [Note: At publication, this area was closed and undergoing new construction.]

Heading upstream on Canal Street, take an immediate left onto Virginia Street after you cross 14th Street. There are two areas to park here. First is the big gravel lot on your left. You can then walk towards the river, through the railroad track break in the Floodwall, and then walk the railroad tracks (past the No Trespassing sign) out to the island and climb down. Walking the tracks to the island is dangerous and illegal, but some fishers do it anyway. Or you can turn right before you get to the tracks and go down on the metal catwalk over the pipes. This catwalk is interesting as it takes you upstream above the river.

The better place to park is after you drive on past the gravel lot and turn right into the paved lot next to the Floodwall. There is room for perhaps 60 cars. You can then walk through the doors in the Floodwall and follow the path down to the river. Kayakers routinely put in and take out here because of the proximity of the Pipeline Rapids.

Pipeline Overlook *[Note: At publication this area was closed and undergoing new construction.]*
Drive on through this paved lot and through the Floodwall, then take an immediate left and you'll be at a lookout area with four parking spaces plus an additional handicap space. You can also reach this spot by going down 12th Street and taking a left on Byrd.

Brown's Island

View from Brown's Island.

The entrance bridge to Brown's Island is at the end of 7th Street. There is room for perhaps 25 cars to park along 7th Street. Brown's Island is the site for a number of festivals and activities. **The island is a good place for picnics, strolls, and looking at the river.** However, unless you are willing to climb over a fence and down a steep hill, there is no access to fish/swim/paddle in the river from Brown's Island. The upstream end of Brown's Island is wheelchair accessible, and has a river overlook out on a walkway.

Footbridge
Turn right onto Tredegar Street where 7th Street dead-ends at Brown's Island, and go 1/4 mile to the "Parking for Belle Isle" lot. It holds 60+ cars. This is where you park to take the Footbridge over to Belle Isle. At this writing I noticed some broken window glass in that parking lot, so this suggests that you shouldn't leave anything visible in your car which anyone might want to steal. The Footbridge and Belle Isle are wheelchair accessible with some assistance. Both provide

The parking area for the Footbridge to Belle Isle.

wonderful views of the river. **Belle Isle provides a smorgasbord of virtually every way you can possibly enjoy the urban James River.**

Reynolds Take-Out

Just downstream from the above-mentioned lot is a boat access turn-in. You can park here just long enough to remove your boat from your vehicle. There is no ramp, just a sort of bumpy and rocky concrete path. This is a flatwater area which is good for fishing and swimming.

This boat access area, just across the street from Tredegar Ironworks, provides good swimming and flatwater fishing.

Oregon Hill

Where Laurel Street meets Oregon Hill Parkway there is a nice overlook of the river with a few benches and a sidewalk. Park on Laurel or in two pull-off areas which each hold one or two cars.

Hollywood Cemetery

There are nice views of river in this historic cemetery located at 412 South Cherry Street. You'll need to circle around inside until you locate Waterview Avenue. The best

parking and viewing area is at the large mausoleum on Waterview. There is excellent birding here as well as many older trees and a variety of wildflowers.

Riverview Cemetery

You'll find this cemetery where Harrison Street meets Randolph Street, and there is one spectacular view of the river behind the large stone cross bearing the name Hopkins. There is good birding here, as well as a variety of trees and wildflowers.

View from Riverview Cemetery.

Northbank

This is the section of James River Park at the end of Texas Avenue. There is parking for approximately 50 cars. From the parking lot you can take a sloping trail down to the river. I am told that cars in this parking lot are routinely vandalized. (See the "Texas Beach" article in this book.)

Parking lot at Northbank, also called Texas Beach.

Maymont

Where Pennsylvania and Hampton Streets intersect is one of the two entrances to Maymont. Although Maymont is on the river, it does not offer access to it.

Maymont is one of the city's finest amenities.

There is always free admission to this formerly private estate which includes bison, deer and elk, bobcats, bears, Japanese and Italian gardens, waterfall, wonderful trails, a nature center, a mansion, and much, much more.

Pumphouse Park

If you're on the north side of the river, you reach this wonderful area by turning right onto Pumphouse Drive just before you cross the Boulevard Bridge. Go a couple of hundred yards and you'll see the Pumphouse on the left. Park along the street. There's room for at least 25 cars on each side. Parking is allowed during daylight hours only.

Pumphouse Park provides rich history, abundant natural beauty, and hiking trails along the canal.

Street parking at Pumphouse Park.

Urban River Mystery ≈

Whatever was attached to the end of my line was not a fish. It was dead weight. It came slowly towards me from the deep water as my rod bent double and my hands wound the reel's handle. It was a dark and cold and rainy February day in Richmond.

It was only then—on that murky winter afternoon—that I mentally voiced what I had intuitively known for years: no telling what lies at the bottom of this urban river. No telling what waits down there to be snagged by a fishing line. **In just a few moments I would reel in something truly amazing, but something I would be able to talk about with only a very few persons.**

Four years in the mid-seventies on the shores of our nation's most urban of rivers—New York City's Hudson—had hooked me on the special joys of casting a line into urban waters. While standing there adjacent to non-stop sixty-mile-an-hour Riverside Drive traffic and watching rats scamper freely across the boulders at my feet I pulled in stripers and bluefish. I was always alone there at 116th Street; I guess nobody else cared to dodge the traffic to get there. Although surrounded by ten million people, I was alone. It was my remote mountain trout stream, my isolated Caribbean bonefish flat, my deep-in-the-woods private bass pond. I pulled some strange things from that river, but nothing as provocative as what had attached itself to my line almost 20 years later in Richmond.

I looked up at the James River's Lee Bridge there above my head. It slashed a diagonal bar across the Constable portrait of rain clouds in the background. Grays were everywhere: dark grays, light grays, blue grays, brown grays—no yellow grays or orange grays. Cold colors. As I continued to reel in the dead weight I watched the sounds of invisible cars as they crossed the bridge.

My imagination produced a sack of money being tossed over and landing in the water at my feet. I wouldn't turn it in. I'd take it and run. Surely people toss all sorts of things while crossing Richmond's urban James.

I wondered which of the city's six bridges would get the most tossing action—I was probably standing under it.

As a summer adolescent visiting one of Seattle's urban waterways I experienced my most powerful urban river hookup. After catching a couple of smallish bullheads from the tiny shoreline eddy where the Carney boys had directed my line, I decided to cast out into the middle to find something big. It arrived immediately and stripped the line from my reel. It was my first time to hook a boat—a fast boat. It was a clean hookup on the stern of the boat; the driver didn't know. My line vanished in five seconds.

You find fast boats in the urban James, but only downstream from 14th Street where the river abruptly changes from a falling freestone smallmouth habitat to a sluggish, murky, tidal estuary. Above 14th Street are the canoes and kayaks and tubes. Nobody swims below 14th Street; **everybody—I do mean everybody— swims and does everything else imaginable above 14th Street.** Up here the water looks shallow and healthy and blue-green. Down there it looks deep and dingy and brown. Up here is a river full of giant boulders on which people picnic and sunbathe. Up here is the James River Park System shoreline with woods and trails and trash cans and benches. Up here is where you get all kinds of people moseying around.

Whatever was at the end of my line, it was heavy and solid. It was not a branch. When you hook a branch it sort of planes off to one side as you reel it in through the water. This thing was probably the size of a breadbox. Something smaller would catch less water and therefore produce a lesser angle in the line. I felt certain, for example, that it wasn't a gun. **Thomas found a gun once when we were kicking around in a nearby dry sandy area.** It was old and rusted, and the police officers didn't seem all that excited to receive it from us. It was just a .22 pistol.

Nashville's Cumberland River probably has its share of guns thrown from the bridges that traverse it downtown. I grew up there. Shelby Park and Fort Nashborough are a couple of my riverside memories. Back then you didn't do too much recreation along the banks of the dirty old Cumberland. You don't today either, but Opryland has a fancy shuttle-boat service that'll take you all the way from downtown to Opryland. When Janet was a child she fell in over her head at Shelby Park. A fisher pulled her out. She claims to remember lying on the bottom and seeing his arm reaching down for her. She says her father gave the man ten dollars.

I shot imaginary Indians while peeking down on the river from between Fort Nashborough's real-life Lincoln Logs. Bang! Bang! I'd slaughter them as they scampered up the steep river bank trying to attack our Cub Scout troop.

I really thought the thing at the end of my James River line was probably either a small stump or a big hunk of old tire. My track record included both. I would have never in a million years guessed **what was in the briefcase that now reached the top of the water at the end of my line. A briefcase! Money? Drugs? No, but those were among my guesses.**

During my four years in Georgia I made some visits to Atlanta's urban Chattahoochee. On a good day it's a lot of fun. But on a bad day, when they're releasing water from the dam and the river's high, it's no fun. On a good day you can lounge James-River-style on the huge mid-river boulders and eat a pretty good sandwich. And you can catch trout! Trout in Georgia! The water released from the upstream dam is plenty cold enough, and they periodically stock it with trout—some of them big. But, like the urban James, the urban Chattahoochee attracts all kinds of people. I got scared off one day by some motorcycle guys. **Why is it in your fantasies—when you're looking in your home mirror reciting DeNiro's "You talkin' to me?" or Travolta's "Look at me," you can easily whip the bad guys, and then when you get your chance in real life you wimp out? Next time, though . . .**

Back to the urban James beneath the Robert E. Lee Bridge. It was a briefcase—one of those old soft leather briefcases with a zipper. I edged it over to the shore at my feet, reached down, lifted it, and sat it on a rock. Water gently oozed from various orifices. It was coated with river-slime and mud. It had been submerged for a long time—months, maybe years. And it smelled funny. I leaned down and sniffed, and it smelled even worse. Probably just algae combined with deteriorating leather.

I looked all around and couldn't see anyone watching me. The zipper unzipped easily, and I used two sticks to sort of open the mouth of the briefcase. On top of something plastic there were two bricks. **This sunken briefcase wasn't an accident.**

Sometimes you'd see joggers carrying briefcases across the Victory Memorial Bridge in Washington D.C. They'd jog to work, but wouldn't toss their briefcases over into the Potomac. At least I never saw them toss any briefcases during any of my week-long conferences there. That was back in the seventies. I'd go up for a week each year, jog every morning, go to workshops all day, stare into the Potomac near the Kennedy Center during breaks. I saw a small bass swim by once when the river was particularly low and clear. Nowadays the Potomac is the bassiest urban river in the world. The underwater vegetation is back and the entire food chain is fat and sassy. Nowadays I go up once or so a year and fish from a bass boat alongside the Kennedy Center and downstream in front of Mt. Vernon and catch big largemouths and an occasional smallmouth. I've never caught a briefcase from the Potomac.

The bricks were standard rectangular red bricks. Old, but nothing special. Two of them. Obviously they were in there just for the weight. I removed them and then poked my stick at the plastic bag. Whatever was in the bag was solid, but was not hard. But it was not soft either. It was malleable, pliable. Like a bunch of bundled money. Maybe it was money! Maybe I'd be rich! Maybe I'd buy a conversion van and a Ranger boat and fish the Bassmasters circuit next year. I made the calculations quickly: let's see, $40,000 for the van, $25,000 for the boat, $25,000 for tournament expenses. Do drug dealers often deal in $100,000 increments? Sure they do. All the time. At least that's what the movies tell you. That must have been what happened: a drug dealer decided to go straight, give up the business, and throw away his dirty money.

But that wasn't what was in the bag. Far from it. Not even close. Only one very good friend of mine would later explain the precise state of mind of the briefcase thrower—a state of mind which is not uncommon, but which is almost always very secret and very personal.

In the bag were books—soft-leather-covered books. Black leather books with ultra-thin pages. Three of them. And one Polaroid photo. The photo was of a group of eight college-age guys wearing white robes. They stood there in a row smiling, posing for the camera. The books were *The Book of Mormon*, *The Pearl of Great Price*, and *The Doctrine and Covenants*—tenets of the Church of Latter Day Saints, the Mormons. My good friend knows all about Mormons and he was intrigued by my catch. He said the thrower had almost certainly made the very painful decision to leave the church, to abandon his faith, to depart from what had been the foundations of his life. He said the white robes were sacred and secret garments worn in special ceremonies in the Temple. Certainly, my friend said, the thrower must have gone through terrible emotional agony. And finally he figuratively ended that part of his life by tossing it all into the river's depths.

I didn't save the books or the briefcase or the photo—all were in bad shape. The smell had just been the result of normal decay. I've thought about that catch several times since then. When you see people along the urban James you sometimes don't know their reasons for being there.

Chapter Two:
The James River Park System

This wonderful urban park system, located in the center of the half-million-person Greater Richmond, includes shorelines and islands along the south bank, Belle Isle, and a small area on the north bank—almost 400 acres in all. The Park System's focus is of course the James River, but also available are non-river interests such as biking, hiking, history, birds, flowers, picnicking, and just enjoying nature. There are many areas of the Park System—such as at the top of the hill on Belle Isle—where you totally extract yourself from everything except nature. You can even find panoramic views of the woods and the river which offer no hint of mankind's "progress," no hint of industry, no hint of the hustle or bustle which surround you.

Ralph White, Naturalist for the James River Park System.

There are rules and advice for those of us who use James River Park System. The Park Rules state that the following are prohibited: glass containers, alcoholic beverages, metal detectors, weapons (firearms, bows & arrows, slingshots, etc.), and motorized bikes. Rules also state the following: leashes required for all pets; no open fires or camping; fishing licenses required; and plants, artifacts, and wildlife are not to be removed. This last part includes rocks, shells, driftwood, leaves, and all other natural objects. The Park System closes at dusk.

Leashes are required.

There is some very important advice for the James River Park System. Most important is for swimmers and waders. Always wear shoes; there is danger of foot injury from broken glass and metal artifacts. Also, stay away

Main Area

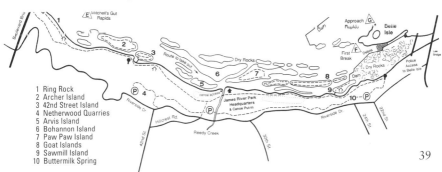

1 Ring Rock
2 Archer Island
3 42nd Street Island
4 Netherwood Quarries
5 Arvis Island
6 Bohannon Island
7 Paw Paw Island
8 Goat Islands
9 Sawmill Island
10 Buttermilk Spring

from rapids. The river can be deceptively strong and can cause injury from scraping or hitting rocks. Lives can be lost from foot entrapment, undercuts, and hydraulics. Foot entrapment occurs when your foot becomes lodged on the bottom when you are being carried downstream. There is sometimes no easy method of rescue. There have been occasions when foot entrapment victims have been rescued by means of a rope held by two persons in quiet water on each side moving upstream. An undercut is when water flows under rocks or wood and then exits on the other side. Often an undercut is large enough for a person to be swept into, but not large enough for an exit. Each rescue is problematic depending on the exact nature of the undercut. Hydraulics are caused when rapidly flowing water drops in a certain way so that it churns backwards at the bottom of the drop—thus not allowing a person to be swept out. **Hydraulics are especially prevalent beneath the dams along the urban James.**

If you are ever caught in swift water, float face-up with your feet at the surface pointing downstream. Near the surface your feet are not prone to be entrapped in rocks.

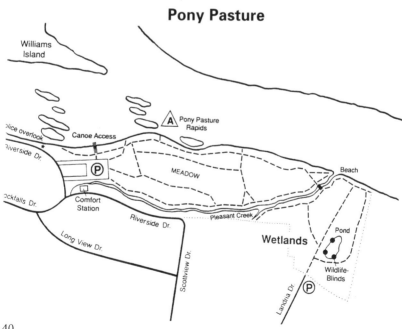

Pony Pasture

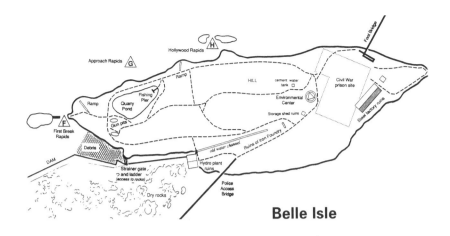

Belle Isle

Pointing your feet downstream allows you to push away from rocks as you get to them.

Life jackets must be worn whenever the river level reaches five feet at Westham Gauge. River level information is obtained by calling (800) 697-3373. When the river level is nine feet or higher, it is closed to anyone who does not have a special permit.

The James River Park System headquarters and Visitor's Center is reached by parking at the area near the intersection of Hillcrest Road and Riverside Drive and walking a short distance east along the Park's road. The telephone number is (804) 780-5311.

Group Programs at James River Park

[*The following information is taken from a brochure published by James River Park.*]

The James River Park System offers a wide variety of historical, natural, educational and recreational resources for use by individuals, families, school and community groups. Below is a list of naturalist-led group programs offered through the Visitor's

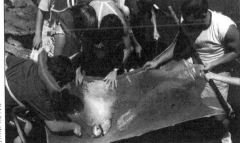

41

Center which is located in the Main Area of the Park at Hillcrest and Riverside Drive. Scheduling is on a first-serve basis and preregistration is required. Programs are offered Tuesday through Saturday, Spring through Fall, and Monday through Friday in Winter.

Most programs are entirely outdoors, so participants should be dressed for the weather. Due to the participatory nature of most programs, it is best to schedule single classes that are age specific. Group leaders must participate in the programs and supervise student activities. Groups are encouraged to include adult chaperones. Call the Visitor's Center at (804) 780-5311 to register or for more information. Special arrangements can be made to suit groups and individuals with special needs.

You may choose to lead your own program in the Park. **The Park is open to the public seven days a week during daylight hours.** The Environmental Education Center on Belle Isle can be reserved by teachers and community group leaders by calling (804) 780-5943. Maps and self-guiding brochures on topics such as Park Ecology, Geology, History, Wildflowers, Birds, Snorkeling and Fishing are available on request from the Visitor's Center. If you plan to picnic, remember, glass containers and open fires are not permitted in the park. **Plants, animals and artifacts are protected by law.**

Summer, 1996 ≈

by Ralph White

On the floor of the Pony Pasture restrooms on the last Saturday in May there was evidence of an insect Armageddon. Covering several square yards were thousands of caddis fly corpses. Exactly why they died I'm unsure; I suspect they are all exhausted males—detritus from the night's entomological fraternity bash, for I think all respectable females would have made their last flights over water.

Caddis flies are medium-small (1/2"), brown, flying insects with nondescript wiggles on their wings, and very distinct long, thin antennae! They spend most of their time as aquatic larva—underwater caterpillars attached to the tops of rocks in fast, shallow water. You don't see them at first. They are hidden in fragile net-homes that look like tiny tatters of old nylon stockings. (Sometimes they are visible by the hundreds in one spot—on the concrete walkway through the river upstream from the Boulevard Bridge.)

INDOOR PROGRAMS
(*at the Visitor's Center all year*):
Snake Study: A hands-on examination of snakes of the James River Park. Discuss snake senses, habits and behaviors and learn to distinguish poisonous from non-poisonous kinds. 30-45 minutes, limit 25 students.
Turtle Talk: A hands-on study of turtles of the James River Park. Examine scales and scutes, skulls and shells. 30-45 minutes, limit 25 students.
James River Park Slide Show (*Off-site, September to March*): A 30-minute slide presentation through a "bit of wilderness in the city." Emphasis on unique land features, history, and visitor uses including park programs, recreation and volunteer opportunities.

OUTDOOR PROGRAMS
(*nature walks offered all year*):
Signs of the Seasons: An outdoor, sensory exploration of the seasonal changes occurring in the park: from buds and bark to flowers and seeds, wildlife homes and food sources. You may request a particular

But you will often find them attached to your arm or leg when you slide over a rock in the river when tubing.

These underwater spider webs filter the river for bits of organic debris like pieces of partly eaten insects or the waste pellets from other insects upstream. It's not that disgusting; we eat the waste products of yeasts in beer and wine. In any case, **these adults lie in nearly mute testimony to the power of light and warmth.**

They grew wings and got out of the primordial soup as the photoperiod increased so they could have sex. It works that way with many creatures. After the fury of mating is the measured laying of eggs and then the gradual decomposition and reprocessing back into nutrients, the ultimate metamorphosis.

You can find caddis flies in smaller numbers on the walls of the Visitor's Center in the evenings of early summer or on any structure with lights along the river.

focus such as birds, trees, adaptations, etc. Best with 20 or fewer students, 1/2 to 1 1/2 hours.

Floodplain Ecology: What are the effects of the James River on the land, plants and animals in the park? Investigate the adaptations of plants and animals to this changing environment and discuss human uses of and impact on this special area. Includes hands-on water quality testing. Middle school and up, best with 20 or fewer students, 1 1/2 to 2 hours.

History Tour of Belle Isle: A 1 1/2 to 2-hour walking exploration of Belle Isle and its history with emphasis on the role of industry in developing Richmond. Sites of interest include: the Vepco hydroelectric power plant, Old Dominion Iron and Steel, the site of an infamous Civil War prison, an old quarry site and excellent views of Hollywood Rapids and the downtown skyline. Middle school and up, wheelchair accessible.

Walk on the Wallside: Introduction to the pedestrian walkway that runs along the Richmond Floodwall on the southside. Magnificent views of the rocks, rapids and Richmond skyline. Tour highlights Richmond history and water-powered industry, river ecology, geology and wildlife observations. Middle school and up, 1 to 1 1/2 hours, wheelchair accessible.

MORE OUTDOOR PARK PROGRAMS
(*best spring to early fall*)

Insect Investigation: With net, magnifier, bug boxes and insect guides in hand, survey the meadow, collect and observe the diversity, adaptations and behaviors of bees, beetles, butterflies and other beautiful beasties. Grades 2 and up, limited to 24, 1 1/2 hours.

Water Wonders: Using dip nets, hand strainers and pond guides, collect, examine, identify and then release aquatic animals found in the Belle Isle Quarry Pond and in river potholes. Discover how animals are specifically adapted to survive in the water and learn about the interrelationships among plants, animals and the environment. Grades 2 and up, limited to 15, 2 hours, late spring and early fall.

Fishing Fun at the Quarry Pond: An introduction to catch-and-release fishing at the Belle Isle Quarry Pond. Baitcast rods and worms provided along with basic fishing techniques and an examination of fish anatomy and behavior. Grades 2 and up, limited to 15, 2 hours, wheelchair accessible.

Frog's Eye Tour of the Park: Explore the waterways between the islands and the creatures that live there. This summer program emphasizes river safety and requires participants to get wet. Life jackets provided and ability to swim is necessary. Grades 2 and up, limit 15, 2 hours, face masks and snorkels available for advanced groups.

Geology Exploration: Investigate the impact of weather, plants, floods and humans on the granite rock of the Fall Line in Richmond. Measure and analyze the diameter, circumference and volume of potholes and quarry sites. Observe life forms and study water chemistry in these areas. Middle school and up, 1 to 1 1/2 hours.

Things to Do on Belle Isle
[*Written by Ralph White and originally printed by the James River Park System*]

Go on an exploration . . . a modified scavenger hunt (but remember that all items are protected in the park). This is a "find it but leave it here for others to discover too" kind of experience.

Find three birds common to the river area. Use the birding guide available through the Department, or try this: Look for a big bird on the rocks with very long legs, a long straight bill and a long neck that it tucks into an "S" when it flies (Great Blue Heron). Find a big dark bird high in the sky whose wings form a sort of "V" and who seems to be knocked around a lot by the wind (Turkey Vulture). In calm water look for pairs or families of birds floating together; males have green heads and females have brown (Mallard Ducks).

Find three trees that are special to this area. Find trees along the river that have very shaggy bark (they hardly ever grow away from the water) (River Birch). Look for trees with bark of different colors—mostly white—but also

July and August Notes ≈

by Ralph White

As the temperatures rise the water level in the James River falls. Some of the loss is due to evaporation, but most is from transpiration—roots sucking up water and leaves releasing it through their pores. It is how plants grow of course—they split apart water and carbon dioxide and create sugar and oxygen. You gotta have sun, but there's plenty of that in summer.

This massive surge of plant growth fuels a similar increase in animal life. On land it is the insects that most immediately affect the human species. **Aphids, weevils, plant hoppers and other sap feeders will be sucking nutritious juices from tender leaves.** Their liquid waste can be an annoyance for several weeks to people who park in the shade of certain broad-leaved trees.

In the natural system nothing goes to waste. Leave the sticky film on your car and it turns black with fungus that is metabolizing the sugars which remain. Were this to drop on leaf litter in the forest, land snails and millipedes would feed on the rich growth. And the growth would be still richer as the leaves themselves would add more nutrients.

An interesting way to watch sap recycle up close is to find aphids on tender goldenrod leaves, blackberries or wild roses. They'll often be accompanied by ants. Ants protect the aphids from predators (like Lady Bugs) and actually move them around from one good site to another. In what might appear an obsessively maternal concern they even stroke them with their antennae to encourage them to drink and defecate more. The resulting "honey dew" is processed aphid waste.

Plant juices that are purposely released attract the most, and most beautiful insects. Flowers produce nectar for this purpose. Butterflies sip nectar at flowers after first tasting the quality and sensing the quantity with their feet. You can watch butterflies do this in most flower gardens, but several wildflowers are particularly good attractors: Bull Thistles (or any thistle) and Milkweed are my favorites. Pull up a folding chair, put on a hat and sunscreen, and watch the action! Remember though that it takes a minute or two for things to settle down. Give yourself five minutes by the clock for a good look. Mid-morning on a sunny day is ideal. I suspect you'll see four or five species of butterflies and 15 or 20 different kinds of creatures.

green and often with patches of brown. The bark falls off in hand-sized pieces from up high (Sycamore). Locate scraggly trees with very big leaves (often bigger than your head) and either purple flowers in the spring or jingle bell type seed pods in the fall (Princess Tree).

Find three kinds of vines on the trees. One kind has little "hairs" holding it to the bark (Poison Ivy). One kind hangs down between the tree trunks and has little "corkscrew fingers" on the tips of the branches to help it hold on to things (Wild Grape). One kind is colored green and has sharp thorns and also has "corkscrew fingers" called tendrils (Green Briar).

Find three colors of insects. Most of these will be away from the river. Yellow (Shorthorned Grasshopper), Black (Field Cricket), White (Cabbage Butterfly). On a day without wind you may also find mosquitoes (look for their babies wiggling in shallow potholes) and gnats (look for them in groups flying around the head of the tallest person—they don't bite) and craneflies (they look like giant mosquitoes but they don't bite and they sometimes do pushups).

Find three kinds of shells. There are small white "clam shells" (Chinese Freshwater Clam—no one knows how they got here, but they're very common); medium to large, thin, black shells with shiny insides (American Freshwater Mussel—Native Americans used to eat them but they're not very common anymore. Hint: check the east end of the island); small, dark snails curled up like a soft ice cream cone (River Snails). Give yourself bonus points if you find two other kinds of snail shells.

Find three old buildings. There is a hydroelectric power plant with three metal grates to let water through to turn the turbines and make electricity. It's made of cement. There is a fence to keep you off of it. There is an old storage shed in which to keep highly flammable liquids like grease and oil and cleaning solvents. It's made of stone and the dirt is piled up around the sides to keep it from ever exploding sideways. There is the first steel frame structure in the Old Dominion Iron and Steel Company, of which all that's left is the framework.

Find the remains of three historic structures. Look for the supports to the old Lee Bridge. (Hint: They're not on the island, but you've already seen them.) Look for the foundations for the machinery that hauled rock out of the quarry and which hauled the quarry railroad cars. (Hint: Some are made of concrete, some of rocks and some are made of a mix of both.) Find the rock wall that made up the side of the "canal" (mill race) that carried water to the old water-powered iron mill. (Hint: It's well hidden but visible below you off the trail.) Give yourself three bonus points for finding the Civil War gun pits. (Hint: There is a boardwalk along one side.)

Find three easy landmarks off in the distance. To the east is the Manchester Bridge (9th Street Bridge) with lots of traffic. To the south are the River Tower Apartments (14 stories tall). To the north is Hollywood Cemetery with lots of big grave stones. Take a two-point bonus if you look to the west and identify the remains of part of the old dam that once connected to Belle Isle.

Find three places where the rock has been changed. Find where flooding has caused rocks and pebbles to grind curved shapes into the granite rocks. Locate where men have cut out rectangular chunks of rock for making walls and foundations of buildings leaving squared-edged pieces behind. Find finger-size holes drilled into rocks where either floating fish traps were attached or quarrying equipment was attached (best during low water). Earn a bonus point for finding an iron ring anchored into the rock (also used in holding fish traps or quarry equipment).

OTHER THINGS TO DO

Go on a History Tour using the Self Guiding booklet.

Go fishing in the Quarry Pond. Equipment is sometimes available from the James River Park Visitor's Center by prearrangement.

Write a poem about a thing in nature: one word to name it, two words to describe it, a short statement saying what it is doing, and one word saying how you (or it) feel.

The James River Park System Visitor's Center

A passing cold front has left the October 21 Saturday sunny and brisk and windy. The gravel parking lot at Hillcrest and Riverside contains only three cars—sparse for a Saturday noon. The lot's Oaks—growing right out of the center of the lot—still have green leaves; they'll cling throughout the winter.

I exit the lot, walk across the railroad tracks—making a mental note to bring Thomas and put out some pennies to be flattened—and then go up and down the wooden steps that cross the fence. I take the gravel road to the right towards the Visitor's Center.

The road crosses the Reedy Creek outflow, and I look down to my left to see the silted creek rush to join the James. It rained last night; perhaps the gray silt isn't so heavy in dry times. Sycamores stretch across this final stretch of the creek.

Learning session inside the James River Park Visitor's Center.

The Visitor's Center appears on my left. It's a gray wood building overlooking a little backwater stretch of the river. The sign directs me around to the ramp at the right of the building, and it takes me to the building's top-floor rear entrance marked "Office." The view is gorgeous: **Willows, Sycamores, Birches, all idyllic in their framing of this little sliver of river that flows here.** A Mallard and a Suzie—a lone fall pair—float and preen in the shallows. The only disturbance here is the defined silt line presented by the Reedy Creek outflow. I wonder if fish feed along that line; they used to long ago in western Tennessee at the spot where Blue Creek entered Duck River.

The Visitor's Center is small inside: a single multi-purpose lobby type area. But it is rich in what it offers. There are recycling containers for aluminum, glass and fishing line. I see beautiful photographs of the park mounted around the walls, including color photos of poison ivy and poison oak. There is a small aquarium with a snapping turtle; a big one covered with paper with holes through

49

which you can spy mussels, sunfish, turtles, minnows, catfish and more; and a couple of others with snakes.

There are specimens on a shelf: twigs from Green Ash, Box Elder, and Cottonwood; pieces of granite and other rocks; antlers, a stuffed gar, snake skins, mussel shells, a hornet's nest, old horseshoes and railroad ties; and taxidermied owl, fox and otter. This room has brochures and rules and instructions and directions and maps.

Outside again I see a noisy Blue Jay crying from Cedar branches. At the kiosk back near the parking lot I see posters listing and describing snakes, acorns, Pine cones, birds, butterflies, insects, water safety instructions, weather tips, and schedules for nature tours and programs.

Handrail at the Visitor's Center.

The Visitor's Center and its surroundings present an appropriate and descriptive introduction to the urban James.

Activities Presented by the James River Park System

James River Park has an ongoing series of explorations and learning sessions. The following is a list of some of the sessions which have been offered:

"Art at the River: Botany Binders"
"Autumn Colors at Belle Isle"
"Belle Isle Exploration Walk"
"Birdwatching for Everyone"
"Fall into Winter"
"Floating the James"
"Floodwall Walk"
"Frog's Eye Tour: Small Group Water Explorations"
"Great River Clean-up"
"Innertube Float"
"Living History Reenactments of Civil War Prison Camp"
"Migrating Monarchs, Darting Damsels and Buzzing Bees"

"Riverside Nature Walk: Ecology of a Floodplain"
"Snorkeling in the City: 30-Minute Mini Trips"
"Thanksgiving for the Birds"
"A Walk on the Wallside"
"Wheelchair Birding on the Floodwall"
"Wildflower Walk"

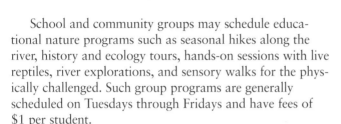

School and community groups may schedule educational nature programs such as seasonal hikes along the river, history and ecology tours, hands-on sessions with live reptiles, river explorations, and sensory walks for the physically challenged. Such group programs are generally scheduled on Tuesdays through Fridays and have fees of $1 per student.

Contact James River Park for a list of upcoming activities by calling (804) 780-5311.

Texas Beach

The "North Bank" area of the James River Park System is commonly known as Texas Beach because its access is at Texas Avenue and its shores have sandy beaches. This is the most secluded and least visited part of the James River Park System, and it deserves special mention for three reasons.

First, the nicely paved parking area receives regular visits from persons who steal things from cars. So don't leave anything of value visible in your car. Some people claim to leave their cars unlocked and their empty glove compartments open.

Second, the walkways, stairs, and paths into and through the park here are rarely patrolled by law enforcement officers, so it's a good idea not to be alone.

Third, nature here is undisturbed compared to other areas of James River Park. The paths through the woods are choked with under- and overgrowth. Mammals such as squirrels, rabbits, raccoons, muskrats and even deer are live and well here. And a rich variety of birds inhabits the trees and shores.

View of the isolated shoreline at Texas Beach.

From the parking lot you'll walk 75 yards down a well-marked path which leads to railroad tie steps down the hillside and then onto a 75-yard steel and concrete bridge which crosses the railroad tracks. On the other side of the bridge and down its stairwell you'll enter the woods and find a couple of trails. Take the one to the right and then straight ahead, and in 200 yards you'll reach the river. Depending on where you exit the woods, and depending on the depth of the river, you may have to slosh through some swampy areas and you may have to cross a small backwater creek to actually reach the river.

JOHN BRYAN

The trail leads upstream along the river for about a mile towards the Boulevard Bridge. You'll end up below Maymont. The path passes Foushee's Mill, an ancient gristmill that got its power from the river.

You'll likely feel isolated from civilization at Texas Beach. The lushness of both flora and fauna combined with the unpopulated shoreline and the picture-postcard shallows and riffles suggest a pre-Columbian era.

As John Maloney states in his May 23, 1995 STYLE WEEKLY article entitled "A Walk on the Wild Side," "There's room for privacy, unlike the south bank of the river, which is often overwhelmed by the summertime masses. It's the Pony Pasture without the parking hell. It's Belle Isle without the crowds and the Lee Bridge overhead. It's there if you're willing to take the road less traveled."

Pumphouse Park

It's February's final Sunday morning and I take a right into Pumphouse Park just before I get to the Boulevard Bridge from the North side. I keep to the right following the road past the Pumphouse—remnants of the canal on the left, woods on the right. The road deadends at the top of the hill and I u-turn back towards the river and park along the road next to the Pumphouse.

The trees have no foliage and through their branches I watch a gray CSX train with yellow borders moving south alongside the James. Three huge blue pipes exit the hill

October 10, 1995

by Ralph White

Crickets chirping softly in the clear-sky evenings, damp spider webs sparkling in morning meadow dew, geese honking overhead in the afternoon, Great Blue Herons stalking through the golden mesh islands of Water Willows—this is the Falls of the James in late October and November. The more frequent northerly winds mean blue skies and puffy white clouds. While the wooded shoreline glistens in shades of yellow, green and tan there are brilliant highlights of red and orange where Virginia creeper or poison ivy have burnished a tree. Cool breezes, shimmering colors, no crowds, no mosquitoes—this is the time to visit the park along the river—"a little bit of wilderness in the heart of the city."

---

and enter the Pumphouse below me. Water cascades from the Pumphouse from the backed-up canal water. I spot an orange and green life vest amid the flotsam.

This is a huge stone Pumphouse—part Gothic looking and part Greek looking. Windows in the Gothic part are now plywood. The 78-window-paned arches in the Greek building are still intact. Old stone steps—blocked by a fence—leading down to the Pumphouse have weeds and small trees growing from between them.

There is a kiosk and a sign: Pumphouse—Three Mile Lock Park. The sign and kiosk give information about the 19th Century Pumphouse and the 18th century canal. And there is the advice that small children must be carefully attended. **I read that people used to attend dances in the second floor of the Gothic building—an area referred to as the Pavilion. Now the entire building is of course long abandoned.**

There is a red bridge—iron and concrete—which I cross over to the Pumphouse island. The river is high and muddy today. Little trails split off into the woods. The bridge crosses the canal and in its mud I see raccoon prints.

I walk over to the Pumphouse itself and stand alongside the old canal—the original stones still intact. The plywood has been ripped off one of the large lower windows of the Pumphouse. **I lean over and look inside. It's cavernous and spooky.** Various cups and bottles testify to current human inhabitants inside. It's probably dangerous being here by myself—maybe not. Behind and below me I see two turtles slither off rocks into the canal. I wonder if there are fish in here; the water should be deep enough.

Graffiti has struck down here—most of it unreadable.

Small trees have taken root among the stones of the old lock. The root of a Locust tree has grown and lifted a 500-pound block of stone eight inches above its original perch.

Water in the Pumphouse Canal flows smoothly, probably five miles an hour. I walk alongside on the plateau where the mules used to pull the boats. The Sycamore tree to my left still has a handful of leaves and many balls awaiting new spring foliage.

I arrive at the concrete platform where the Kanawha Canal merges with the Pumphouse Canal. On the platform someone has carved "Lock Keeper's House, 1786." The Pumphouse Canal is about eight feet wide and 10 or 12 feet deep. At the upstream tip of the concrete platform—which is pointed like the bow of a ship—I can see the Kanawha Canal as it leads upstream along with the railroad tracks. Spring birds whistle somewhere above and beyond. Two more turtles attract my attention as they slide into the river.

A canopied trail leads on up alongside the canal. In a hundred yards it stops at a chainlink fence which has No Trespassing signs on it. But footprints lead around the fence, and I too decide to trespass. I now walk into the forbidden zone and am suddenly at the railroad tracks—live tracks. I step onto and over them and am at the river's edge. The James is wide and high here, up among riverside trees. I will have to come here to fish when summertime shallows arrive. Upstream I see the railroad bridge where Thomas and I have often waded.

Back on the tracks I check my pockets for coins and take all I have—maybe a dollar's worth—to deposit on the tracks to be flattened. Perhaps I should put them a hundred steps up ahead so as not to be noticed by others who cross here. I count my steps: one, two, three, four, five, six

. . . I stop at 25. And I am startled by an impending noise from around the curve. A big noise. I leap from the tracks and scramble up the five-foot embankment. The train arrives in five seconds. Not a slow train. A 30-mile-an-hour train. A big CSX train. I try to count the cars—approximately 100. There are blue boxcars, black coal cars, bright yellow fluid recycling cars, solid white tanker cars, 10 cars hauling sawdust, Union Pacific boxcars, one labeled Cargill Corn Syrup, 10 more coal cars, no caboose.

Now I climb down and lay out the coins—25 steps up-track from the pathway. I see that my sneakers are both untied.

There are other people here now, and on the way back to the car I pass them. At the concrete Lockkeepers House platform I pass a retirement-age couple wearing Reeboks and green Moose Creek National Park sweatshirts. They have a tiny terrier with them. The man is balding and wears glasses.

I pass a psychiatrist with a big black soaking wet Labrador carrying a green tennis ball. I know he's a psychiatrist because he's wearing Reeboks, beige pants, beige shirt, has wire glasses, fuzzy gray uncombed hair, fuzzy gray beard, and displays a big smile.

I notice bicycle tire tracks for the first time. The Oaks still have their leaves too. **A bean tree still supports five-inch fall pods. Fifty-foot Pines still hang with three-inch cones. A Beech tree still pokes hundreds of Beech pods.**

Three cars have now joined mine parked on Pumphouse Road. One is a maroon GrandAm with VCU decals. I wonder if it belongs to the psychiatrist.

There is another man standing near the Pumphouse. He has bright white pants, dark black skin, and a bright blue plaid shirt.

This is the first non-rain, non-snow weekend of 1996. A wonderfully vocal Chickadee serenades me from way up high as I climb into my car. On the way home I take the shortcut through Byrd Park—not to save time, but for the look at Shields Lake to see how many trout fishers are lining the banks this Sunday morning: two, four, six, seven, eight, nine, . . . 25 people there already.

Interpretative Guide to Belle Isle Historic Park

Thomas Bryan at the top of Belle Isle.

JOHN BRYAN

[*The following is taken from a brochure written by Ralph White and printed by the City of Richmond in April, 1993.*]

From a Native American fishing village to a 20th century steel plant, this 54-acre island in the heart of Richmond shows the social and economic history of Virginia's capital city. **Massive cliffs, crashing rapids and stone ruins all beckon you to 300 years of changing land use.** Welcome to Belle Isle, one part of the James River Park System.

This guide is designed for use starting at the footbridge at Tredegar Street on the north shore under the Lee Bridge. The tour can also be taken from the south shore at 22nd Street by walking across the rocks when the river is not high. Start the tour then at Stop #9.

NOTE: While visiting the park, please observe the following rules: Glass containers are prohibited. All plants and animals are protected by law. Please do not litter.

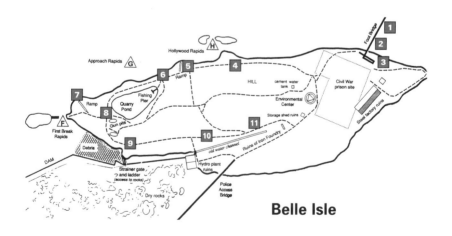

Stop #1 - Belle Isle Footbridge

From your vantage point on the footbridge the panorama of the mighty James unfolds. At moderate water levels, class IV rapids beckon the expert canoeist upstream, while downstream, flatwater pools up behind the VEPCO levee and Manchester Dam. For the past two centuries the river has been dammed up to provide power for flour mills and iron factories. Now channels have been blasted into these dams to provide passage for spawning fish and whitewater boaters.

Stop #2 - Belle Isle Footbridge

From the top of the bridge ramp the split level shape of Belle Isle is evident. The mass of granite on the right gave the site its first name, Broad Rock Island. There is a large quarry at the upstream end.

The flat land ahead was the site of an early 19th century race track. Run by James Bell, it was a rough and rowdy gambling place. The island became known as Bell's Island. When he left, it is said that the good ladies of Richmond retrieved its reputation with the more refined French spelling, Belle Isle, meaning "the good island."

To the east are the remains of the turn-of-the-century metal working factory. Old Dominion Iron and Steel Company made heat exchangers and high pressure steam vessels. About a dozen buildings once covered this plain, but today only the first and last remain. A small bridge provided car access until Hurricane Camille in 1969.

During the Civil War the northeastern four acres of the island were used as a prisoner-of-war camp for northern enlisted men. (The boundaries of the prison are marked by a wildflower meadow.) **Twenty thousand prisoners passed through the camp, and at any one time there may have been as many as eight thousand.** To prevent riots or escape by prisoners, cannons were placed on the hill and along the shoreline, but most men died from dysentery and disease. The fear of northern raids to free the prisoners was so great that the camp was closed and the men moved to Andersonville. Nothing now remains of the notorious tent city. (The Environmental Education Center, adjacent to the old prison site, can be scheduled for use by visiting school groups or rented by private organizations.)

Stop #3 - Dirt Trail to Eastern Tip

A rough trail leads to the far downstream tip of the island. Look for red tape on the trees by the metal framework. Beavers make no dams here because of flooding. Instead they hollow out dens in the river bank. The entrances are always under water.

In the mud are the thin oval shells of American freshwater mussels, a food used by Native Americans, and the more rounded, thumbnail-sized shells of the Oriental freshwater clam that only showed up in the James in the early 1970's. Examine them, but please leave them all for others to discover.

Stop #4 - The Main Loop Trail Along the North Shore

Upstream a small road leads along the shore to the rapids. (Note: A 200-foot section of trail is often very rough after flood damage.) William Byrd described these rapids as "louder than a scolding wife's tongue." The rapids are known as Hollywood Rapids, named for the historic cemetery located on the north shore just opposite. There is no denying the force of the water. Several canoes a year are destroyed here.

Stop #5 - Flat Rocks Along the River

There are several good places to watch rafts and kayaks from the flat rocks along the river. Footing is uneven and damp areas are very slippery. It is obviously unsafe for small children.

Notice in the rocks there are places with drill holes. Some were once used to anchor fish traps and perhaps small floating grist mills. Some held guy wires for cables used in rock quarrying. Still others anchor the cables used today to define whitewater boat race courses held in the spring.

Stop #6 - The Quarry Pond

A hundred yards or so up the road is a pond and steep rock wall. Granite once extended perhaps as far as the water. Stone cut here was used in constructing an early dam and the foundations of an early iron plant on the other side of the island. The quarry was probably abandoned when they hit a spring. It is about 20 feet deep at the western end. (On the east there is a long slope that had tracks and a rail car that was pulled up with a winch. The car remains and sometimes during summer droughts the top will appear.) In late October there are lovely reflections of leaves and rocks in the pond, which can be viewed from the wheelchair accessible fishing pier.

Stop #7 - Western Tip of the Island

At the westernmost tip of the island is a view of First Break Rapids—a hole in the Belle Isle Dam where boaters like to surf the hydraulics. Behind each wave the water actually runs upstream for a few inches. Properly placed, a canoe or kayak can remain stationary riding these. The technique is called surfing.

Belle Isle Quarry Pond from above. Hollywood Cemetery in the distance across the river.

Stop #8 - On Top of the Quarry Cliff

Heading back to the main trail, you will notice a steep footpath that leads up a jagged cliff beside the quarry. On top and just behind the cliff are two large pits. During the Civil War there were cannons and ammunitions here to protect against northern raiders. (Another gun emplacement was located on the south shore just west of the Lee Bridge.)

Stop #9 - Continuing Along the Main Trail

Just beyond the picnic tables is a cement walkway. This goes over the old water intake for an old hydroelectric power plant. A metal grate on the upstream side acted to filter out leaves and small sticks which might damage the turbine blades. (Notice all the logs and debris today.) The metal structure on rails was a cleaning machine. The teeth ran up and down the grating removing debris. The debris was placed in troughs that ran beside the walkway and washed out onto the rocks. Logs would have been hauled out by hand. (Note: This is also the access route across the rocks to the 22nd Street parking lot.)

Stop #10 - Heading East Along the Main Trail

Continuing east on the roadway you parallel a big pit with perhaps a tiny stream. It is called the raceway and once led water to the power plant. The raceway wall on your right was first made of granite, then made higher with concrete.

In a few hundred feet, there will be a nice view of the remains of the VEPCO hydroelectric power plant. Built in 1904 and decommissioned in 1967, it is in serious disrepair and is not open to the public. Please keep off! It is of historic interest, however, because of the way water was used. It traveled straight ahead through the three gates in front of you, and made a right angle turn to level out under the building. A drive shaft came straight up from the turbine, made a right angle turn through the gear box and went horizontally into the building where each generator was located. (Modern systems have the generator directly on top of the turbines connected by a short shaft.) The generators from this plant are still in use in Peru today.

Stop #11 - Continuing East Along the Main Trail

You will catch a glimpse of the ruins of the Ole Belle Isle Iron Rolling, Milling and Slitting Manufactory—an early 19th century plant run by water power and slave labor. Surprisingly, slaves did not sabotage production. Their lives here were better than in the fields. They came to work in the morning, slept in town and had a little pocket money. Their owners were paid a yearly fee by the iron company. Immigrant craftsmen from England and Germany provided the technical skills. It was famous for making horseshoes, nails and spikes. During the Civil War, captured northern soldiers supplemented for slave labor and made copper pots and bowls.

Below you on the right is a stone millrace which funneled water to power the trip hammers, furnace fans and cutting machinery of the Belle Isle Rolling, Milling and Slitting Manufactory. Look for holes in the wall where the energy of moving water was trapped. Ahead and on the right is a brick wall with gracefully curved doorways. The building was designed for horse-drawn wagons. It is all that remains of the factory which moved to the eastern end of the island at the turn of the century and changed names to the Old Dominion Iron and Steel Company. The factory continues today as Dominion Steel in Chesterfield, Virginia and is the oldest continually operating metal plant in the United States.

This concludes our tour of Belle Isle. **Although Belle Isle's industrial days are over, its value to the city is perhaps increased. It permits urban dwellers to find, near the city's heart, moments of seclusion and peace and at the same time it provides some of the best fishing in the state, excellent and challenging whitewater and a superb view of the Richmond skyline.**

January 29, 1995

A thin, wispy chirp slices the chilly air on Belle Isle. Thomas and I look up into the bare trees. Just the faintest hint of a chirp, it's somewhere just above us. It must be small.

It's January 29 and 31 degrees and snowy. It's that seemingly dead time of year. Yesterday we made our annual pilgrimage to Bassarama. Wall to wall plastic worms and high performance bass boats and a parking lot full of pickups and conversion vans. And

the new citation certificates of the Virginia Department of Game and Inland Fisheries. Two dozen different certificates with gorgeous watercolor fish painted by Michael Simon—the best exhibit at Bassarama. I would have displayed them front and center, but instead the Game and Inland Fisheries booth was relegated to the farthest corner of the farthest exhibition building.

The chirp—really just a high-note whisper—sounds again. Is it a Chickadee? It's been a decade since Janet and I memorized birds and their sounds on our feeder on southside. Maybe a Sparrow or a Junco. Thomas and I point our faces upwards into the trees each time we here it.

We arrive at the quarry pond and the chirping stops. Or perhaps my attention is just diverted from the chirps to this green, clear, enigmatic little body of water. With the snow accenting the surroundings, this pond looks untouched, unvisited. Last spring I saw its bass for the first time. Big ones swimming slowly, confidently along the shoreline. Then drifting out of sight into the depths. I would cast and let my lure fall to the bottom out in the middle. I guessed it was at least 30 feet deep. Today I do the same with a tiny yellow grub. Maybe if I jiggle it slowly on the bottom a big one will eat it.

We are on the floating dock and Thomas scrapes the wooden railings for snowballs. One by one he lofts them into the pond. On the south bank of this pond, to our left, is a vertical rock cliff maybe 30 feet tall. It seems higher from here. At the top we see movement among the trees.

Bikers. Two of them on mountain bikes. They appear to be within inches of the edge of the cliff, pedaling the

Thomas Bryan on the dock of the Belle Isle Quarry Pond.

bikes along the snowy path. They disappear and then reappear lower at the north end of the pond. Then they pedal alongside the south side of the pond and come close to us as they pass the dock. Two men, college age, one with a helmet, one with a baseball cap. We watch them as they pedal into the trees. The one with the helmet has dark, wet mud all over the seat of his pants. Thomas laughs.

We leave the pond after 15 minutes of no bites and after the rails of the dock are bare. We see young love in the distance. A tall man—college age—with short blond hair and wire rims and a black overcoat and gloves, embraces a short woman with a red coat and dark hair and gloves. She wears designer snow boots. They hug and kiss briefly through the thick layers of clothing, and then they hold hands and proceed along the trail. **Young love. Holding hands with gloves on. Smiles.**

Thomas and I pass them and say hello and again enter the chirp zone. This time we see it. "Look Thomas," I point. "Right up there at the top of that tree." The little bird jumps to another branch just as Thomas looks.

"I see it," he exclaims. "It's little."

"Yeah, and I can't tell what it is."

The angle allows only a dark silhouette. I can't make out any colors. At first I think it's a Chickadee, but then after a few more flitty jumps and what I think is a glimpse of brown color I decide it's a Sparrow.

"Dad," Thomas says with a question mark, "what walks on three legs in the morning, two legs during the day, and three legs in the evening?" His elementary school has just completed its annual World's Fair celebration, and Thomas' country was Germany. But one of his friends had Egypt.

"I know that one, Buddyboy," I respond. "That's the riddle of the Sphinx."

"Right," he answers.

"But I've got one for you," I say with a raised eyebrow. "There is a fork in the road up ahead and two men are standing there. One fork leads to a bad city and one fork leads to a good city. One of the men is from the bad city and everything he says is a lie. The other man is from the good city and everything he says is the truth. But you don't know which man is which. What one question can you ask them that will tell you which way to go to get to the good city?"

"I'd just call their moms."

"No, you can't call their moms. You have to ask them one question to figure out which is which."

"Which way to the good city?"

"No, that wouldn't work, because each one would point to a different fork, and you wouldn't know which is right."

Thomas looks puzzled and he doesn't say anything for several steps. Small Sycamores grow to our left between us and the rapids. The sign warns that people have died in these rapids. Class III, IV, and sometimes V rapids depending on the level of the river. The whole area is filled with smallmouth bass.

"What's the bad city like?" Thomas asks.

"Everything's bad there."

"You mean like smog and pollution and stuff like that?"

"Yeah, I guess so."

"I think I'd just go to the bad city," he concludes. "You get to eat junk food and there are no parents."

The appearance of the kayakers makes us forget about the cities. Nine of them in two groups. On this chilly day in this icy river! We see them from the suspended footbridge. **They negotiate the rapids and paddle beneath us. One of them tips over and rapidly rights himself.** They may be dressed warmly, but I can see that their faces are exposed, and I can see that at least one of them has just dipped his face in the river. But they all appear to be laughing heartily.

Then there are the dogs. Three of them. All on leashes, but only one being held. The other two run crazy. The owner walks along in ignorance or defiance of the No Dogs sign. We almost always see illegal dogs over here. Thomas still has scars from the Oh-he-won't-bother-you unleashed dog that mauled him when he was three. Kelly still has nightmares from the Oh-he-won't-bother-you unleashed dog that jumped on her and pushed her in front of a car in the Fan. The car stopped in time.

The big yellow one runs and leaps in our direction. Thomas moves around behind me. He's running a hundred miles an hour, his tongue bouncing, his wide eyes focused on me. The owner walks on a hundred feet behind. I stop and brace myself. I grip my fist around the butt of my folded fishing rod.

The dog splashes through a snow-mud puddle 20 feet from me and continues towards me. I have a hundred muddy paw prints on shirts and trousers from Oh-he-won't-bother-you dogs from previous outings. Here come some more.

The dog reaches me and leaps upwards to greet me with outstretched tongue and paws. "He's okay!" hails the owner. Is she talking to me or the dog?

I deftly make a matador pivot and the dog misses. He misses me! Not even a toenail! Miraculously he doesn't make a second effort; he bounds away back to his owner.

If he had made contact his owner would have likely done what all owners do. She would have called him back with a sharp "No!" and then said "Sorry" to me with a casual greeting. I almost never respond. I just look them in the eyes without smiling. I need to do something different; this method hasn't stymied the phenomenon.

At the car Thomas makes the final snowballs of the day. He scrapes them off the hood and throws them towards nowhere in particular. He forms one of them around the hood ornament and decorates it with red berries he picked along the path.

Chapter Three:
Floating and Paddling

The urban James River—from the Huguenot Bridge to the Annabel Lee—has some wonderful paddle and float stretches, but there are also some dangerous areas which should only be attempted by highly experienced experts.

Unless you are an expert, AVOID THE FOLLOWING AREAS: Williams Dam, Hollywood Rapids, Pipeline Rapids. Unexperienced people have died in these areas.

Also, when the river level reaches five feet at Westham Gauge, life jackets are required by law, and when it reaches nine feet the river is off limits. Call (800) 697-3373 for river level at Westham.

JOHN BRYAN

There are some exhilarating, but not too dangerous, stretches anyone can enjoy. From Huguenot Woods (south side, beneath the Huguenot Bridge) to Pony Pasture is flat and slow, but you will need to exit the river on the right side and walk around Williams Dam. The Pony Pasture area has some Class II rapids through which children and adults float and paddle throughout the summer. You will see people floating through and then carrying their tubes upstream and floating through over and over again.

From Pony Pasture to Reedy Creek is the most popular stretch. This stretch takes about four hours to float—or much more if the wind is out of the east—and has gorgeous scenery including an occasional Bald Eagle. Be sure to go with someone who knows the route. The Class II Choo Choo Rapids can surprise you and be somewhat dangerous to the inexperienced. Further downstream you'll want to stay to the right and after the Mitchel's Gut Rapids you'll need to go behind the shoreline islands to locate the Reedy Creek exit.

You should follow some general rules. STAY AWAY FROM DAMS when possible. This includes Williams Dam as well as other small dams and levees along the river. AVOID LOGJAMS. The river's current can easily pin you beneath a log in a manner that rescue is difficult. WEAR SHOES. The James River has old metal artifacts and new

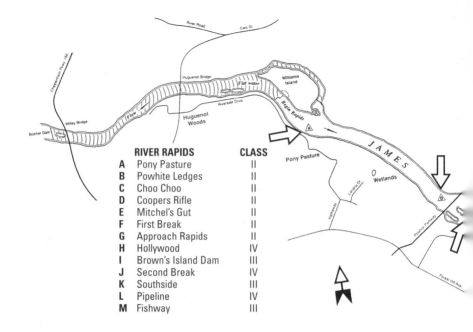

RIVER RAPIDS		CLASS
A	Pony Pasture	II
B	Powhite Ledges	II
C	Choo Choo	II
D	Coopers Rifle	II
E	Mitchel's Gut	II
F	First Break	II
G	Approach Rapids	II
H	Hollywood	IV
I	Brown's Island Dam	III
J	Second Break	IV
K	Southside	III
L	Pipeline	IV
M	Fishway	III

broken glass. FLOAT FEET-FIRST AND FEET-UP DOWNRIVER. If you are in the river without your tube or boat, you must float in this manner to avoid injury and foot entrapment. With your feet pointed downstream, you can push off rocks as you reach them. And with your feet up near the surface, they cannot easily become lodged between underwater rocks. DO NOT USE ALCOHOL. Alcohol impairs judgment, slows reactions, and increases the possibility of injury.

RALPH WHITE

James River Park System

)))) Flatwater
△ Rapids

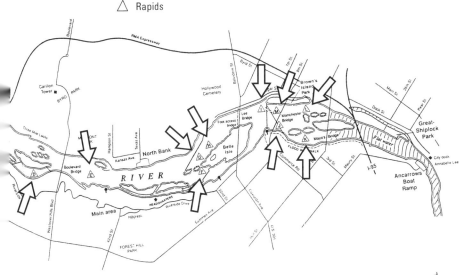

The Nation's Best Urban Whitewater

by Charles V. Ware
[*Originally published in the September/October 1992 issue of* American Whitewater—*updated and slightly modified for this publication.*]

WHAT RIVER:
- has an average flow of 4,500 cfs;
- is free-flowing, and has discharged as much as 330,000 cfs;
- has, in its most popular whitewater boating section, twice the gradient of the Colorado River in the Grand Canyon;
- contains five Class IV or better rapids within a four-mile section;
- provides a home for Osprey and Eagles, and has hosted national bass fishing tournaments;
- has three national presidents buried on its banks;
- has a ten-lane, high-speed shuttle route;
- and runs directly through the center of a major east coast city (and state capital)?

Charles Ware on the Urban James.

SOME HISTORY

Meteorologists have speculated that the 1969 Hurricane Camille produced more rain, in one spot, within a 24-hour period, than has fallen on Earth within recorded history. Nelson County, Virginia was devastated by this natural disaster, and more than 100 of her residents died in massive floods which swept the Tye and Piney Rivers, tributaries of the James River. As the flood crest passed Richmond, it released a great river from the constraints which had been imposed by hydropower dams and diversions. A century's worth of sedimentation, debris accumulation, and vegetative overgrowth in formerly dewatered channels of the James vanished overnight. Hydropower dams were breached, and the James was released from its normal imprisonment within diversion canals.

Richmond grew from an Algonquin trading village at the foot of the falls of the James, to an industrial seaport. George Washington, and others, envisioned Richmond as the terminus of a transcontinental canal system extending to the Rocky Mountains. His James River and Kanawha Canal Company constructed the first of America's great canal systems westward towards the Blue Ridge. Although a water link was never completed to West Virginia's Kanawha River, and thence the Ohio, the canal carried ore to Richmond's foundries, and grains to her mills for export abroad. Immediately prior to the Civil War, **Richmond was America's third wealthiest city, the leading port for grain exports, and among the top in manufacturing.** More than 11,000 industrial workers toiled in factories along the banks of the James by 1861.

War's destruction and postwar economic stagnation saw Richmond eclipsed by other cities, including many in the South. Ironically, Richmond thereby escaped the fate of America's "rustbelt" industrial centers, and has enjoyed a modest renaissance in today's post-industrial America. Factories along the James are being converted into residential condominiums, have been transformed into headquarters facilities for multi-national corporations, and in the instance of the old Tredegar Iron Works, developed into a museum.

Another component of the modern transformation of the James was the implementation, in the late 1960's, of wastewater treatment for municipal and industrial wastes. The James River received raw sewage, in and below the

City of Richmond, until a system of trunk sewer connectors was completed in 1974. Almost miraculously, anadromous fish, such as herring and striped bass, returned to the Falls of the James, and in less than two decades fish have returned in such great numbers that, on any given day, many scores of fishers may be seen along the riverbanks. Richmond even hosted the national BASS Masters Classic in 1989, 1990 and 1991.

URBAN WHITEWATER

Most *American Whitewater* readers are little interested in fishing, but the cost of federally-mandated anadromous fishery restoration has been the primary bar to reactivation of the hydro facilities knocked out by Hurricane Camille. **The elements that make the James attractive to hydro developers—flow and gradient—also create a haven for whitewater boating.** Indeed, here is found the nation's best urban whitewater. Although a modest commercial rafting operation has been in existence since the late 1970's, the James has not achieved the level of recognition it has deserved, and is generally underutilized.

The James River's major urban whitewater rival would have to be Washington D.C.'s Potomac. The Class VI Great Falls run on the Potomac is suitable for only a minority of boaters. Mather Gorge, downstream from Great Falls, and the Potomac's Little Falls are, together, rather less interesting than the Lower Section of the James in Richmond. The Potomac is not as clean as the James, and is degraded by incessant low-level jet traffic operating out of Washington's National Airport. The climb into Mather Gorge is arduous and dangerous, and the walk out below Little Falls is fairly long. And the Washington traffic en route to the putin . . .

In Richmond, on the other hand, shuttle driving at the busiest time of day is a matter of no more than five or ten minutes. There is no need to carry a boat more than 100 feet under most circumstances. Parking shuttle vehicles can be a problem, but is usually not a major difficulty.

YOUR FRIENDLY GUIDE TO THE FALLS OF THE JAMES

There are three recognized sections of the James River within the City of Richmond. The western-most, Huguenot Woods to Pony Pasture Park, has the four-foot-per-mile gradient characteristic of the James throughout most of its extent. If the parking lot at the popular Pony Pasture access point is full, boaters can use the Huguenot Woods access to this uppermost river section of 1 1/2 miles in length. Although the Huguenot Woods section is flatwater, at least 17 people have drowned on it in recent years, most at the deceptively innocuous-looking Williams Dam (aka "Z-Dam"). A fish passageway notch has now been cut into the dam by the City and the Virginia Department of Game and Inland Fisheries. **The fish passage may be run at some river levels, but terminates in a "keeper" hydraulic at others.** If you are not in the company of someone who knows this hazard well, portage on the river right side of Williams Island.

Charles Ware in the Pipeline Rapids.

The Upper Section of the James, Pony Pasture to Reedy Creek, is three miles of Class I-II rapids, and a mile of flatwater, within a wooded and scenic corridor through the inner suburban neighborhoods of the City. The Pony Pasture access area was exactly that—a private pasture for a few ponies and horses—before land for the James River Park System was purchased in the 1960's with money obtained through the National Park Service's Land & Water Conservation Program. **When one is a few yards out in the river, the scene is one of tranquility.** Osprey have been nesting in the area recently, and Bald Eagles are frequent visitors. Watch what you leave behind in your car, though, and don't forget that you are inside a major city.

The Upper Section is a scenic trip extension for expert and advanced paddlers, or an alternative to the more difficult Lower Section of the river for less competent paddlers. On the non-infrequent occasions in winter and in spring when the James is running bank-full, or higher, the Upper Section can provide exciting Class III, big-water paddling. The James is about a half-mile wide throughout the city, so paddlers who get into trouble may find themselves far from help. City police check for the required high-water permits when the James is higher than nine feet on the Westham Gauge. If the City is called to rescue folks without the High Water Permits, those fished out are billed by the hour. One unlucky fellow who slipped from the bank into a flood stage river was billed more than $2,000 for the Coast Guard helicopter dispatched from Norfolk.

Three bridges cross the Upper Section of the James. Their names have been stenciled in yellow lettering, which is also intended to mark the normal route for paddlers. (It is generally necessary to follow the suggested route in low-water conditions.) There are some great play waves below the arched railroad bridge at river levels above six feet.

After one passes beneath the Boulevard Bridge, a solitary high-rise brick apartment building will be visible on river right. This should alert paddlers that they are approaching the Upper Section takeout, also on river right, at Reedy Creek. **Miss this at high water, and the consequences could be grave.** The on-river signs for the takeout were destroyed by flooding this year, so those unfamiliar with the James could easily overlook the small side channel into which Reedy Creek (a small tributary stream) flows.

There is the James River Park Visitor's Center at the Reedy Creek river access, but is often closed because of the small number of park employees. While they are in the vicinity of this river access, paddlers should avoid doing some of the things which have strained relations with the park neighbors, such as changing clothes on the street and blocking driveways.

The Lower Section commences below the river-wide Hollywood Dam, at the western tip of Belle Isle. The James drops about 70 feet over the next two miles. The Grand Canyon of the Colorado has an average gradient of about 15 feet per mile, and **high-water flows in the James easily exceed those in the Grand Canyon.** The south channel of the river is dry until the James exceeds six feet on the Westham Gauge, and if you see water flowing past the south side of Belle Isle, you should carefully weigh your paddling options.

First Break Rapids.

The Hollywood Dam, which fed a hydro plant on Belle Isle, has been eroding away steadily since the first breach formed in 1969. This "First Break" into the north channel once formed a Class IV rapid, as most of the river flowed through a 12-foot gap in the dam, and a concrete section of the dam which had fallen forward. This gap is more than 100 feet today, and there is another large breakout a few yards to the north ("Variation" Rapids). A modern concern is the river's erosion of the extreme tip of Belle Isle, and the possibility that the river may break through the old hydro channel and dewater the Hollywood Rapids in the north channel. Virginia paddlers have been debating the appropriateness of riprapping the tip of the island to slow erosion. The old hydro dam was anchored on portions of Belle Isle built up of iron mill slag dating from the industrial age.

Hollywood Rapids. James River Corporation across the river.

The normal route through Hollywood Rapids is described in the Roger Corbett and Ed Grove Virginia whitewater guidebooks. Hollywood is a generally forgiving Class IV, since the hard Petersburg Granite forming these rapids does not tend to undercut. There is a horseshoe-shaped ledge creating hydraulics which become grabby at six feet (Westham Gauge), and pretty serious at levels much above that. The main six-foot drop is just below this set of hydraulics (called "Corner," "Upper" and "Lower" by area paddlers).

The name Hollywood is taken from the north bank cemetery which is the "Valhalla of the South." Buried here are Jefferson Davis, J.E.B. Stuart, George Pickett, and 30,000+ Confederate soldiers, some 12,000 of whom rest under one granite pyramid. Belle Isle, opposite the cemetery, was the temporary home of some 15,000 federal troops captured at Chancellorsville. This notorious POW camp site is to be marked by low earthen berms. The Tredegar Iron Works structures across the river include the gun foundry, which cast many of the cannon used by the Confederate States, and the plate used on CSS Virginia I and II.

As paddlers approach the eastern end of Belle Isle, they will see on the horizon scaffolding which once supported the tainter gates of the Brown's Island Dam. **High water creates an inescapable, lethal hydraulic below the right half of this dam (aka "Vepco Levee").** The dilemma facing high-water paddlers is that the easiest route through the dam hydraulic, the cutout created to provide fish passage, leads directly into Pipeline Rapids. Pipeline is Class VI when the James is over nine feet (21,000 cfs), and is pretty unforgiving above eight feet (16,000 cfs), as the river pushes hard under the pylons supporting a train trestle. The City of Richmond has removed a section of the walkway atop the scaffolding, so you won't be able to scout the Vepco Levee from atop the dam (people kept falling through the metal grating which forms the walkway). If the river's high, look for a faint "x" marked near the center of the dam, run immediately left of that, and then paddle strongly for the "Second Break" slot in the downstream Manchester Dam. This is the preferred route at low and moderate flow levels as well, but you may be more relaxed.

"Second Break Rapid" is a breakout in the Manchester Dam, located towards river right and downstream of the massive arched piers supporting the Ninth Street Bridge (or Manchester Bridge). **Paddlers who have been away from the James in recent years may be astonished by the aesthetic impact of the new city Floodwall,** which also creates a weird visual perspective obscuring the entrance into Second Break. If you miss the breakout in high water, you probably won't come out of the dam hydraulic for awhile.

Pipeline Rapids.

There are three interesting rapids downstream, but paddlers will have to select one per trip. Few paddlers have run "Triple Drop," which is entered immediately right of the mid-river electric power pylon. "Southside Rapids," appropriately located on the south side of the river, is the tamest selection, and the sensible high-water alternative. Watch out for those railroad bridge abutments in high water, though! **"Pipeline," over near the other (north) shore, is comprised of four drops, the third of which is a kicker.** This general area, just west of Mayo's Island, contains innumerable small islets which shelter birds and wildlife. I've recently seen more than 50 Blue Heron here at one time, in the shadow of central business district skyscrapers.

The river guidebooks published to date all describe the "Reynolds Metals Takeout" adjacent to Pipeline Rapids. Construction has temporarily closed this takeout from 1996 to 1998, but temporary alternatives exist at either end of the 14th Street Bridge, just downstream. Other alternatives include the public boat ramp (part of the James River Park System) called Ancarrow's Landing, and the private parking area operated by Richmond Raft Company at 4400 East Main Street (ask permission). These two takeouts are about a mile below Mayo's Island, and that mile is all flatwater. If you don't mind carrying your boat across a narrow canal lock gate, the Great Shiplock Park (Pear and Dock Streets) is another possible takeout.

STUFF YOU NEED TO KNOW

The City of Richmond has a river permit system incorporating some fairly sensible regulations. PFDs are required to be worn when the river reaches five feet at Westham. When the river reaches nine feet, paddlers must wear helmets, paddle in a group, carry a rescue rope, and must have purchased a permit. If you're planning a high-water run, Richmond Raft Company is a good source of information—(804) 222-RAFT.

RIVER LEVELS

Levels on all sections are measured in feet on the Westham USGS Gauge. A recording providing current readings and a forecast may be obtained by calling the National Weather Service at (800) 697-3373 (menu item #6, then listen for Westham level). The Westham Gauge readings for the previous day are printed daily on the weather page of the *Richmond Times-Dispatch.*

Recreational Minimum Flow Level:
  3.9 feet, Lower Section (1,900 cfs)
  4.2 feet, Upper Section (2,620 cfs)
But You'll Want This Much if You're Driving from Out of Town:
  at least 5 feet (4,620 cfs)
The Lower Section Gets Too Pushy for Intermediate Paddlers at:
  roughly 7 feet (11,340 cfs)
Pipeline Rapid Should Be Avoided at:
  roughly 8 feet (15,930)
Permit Required at:
  9 feet (20,960)
Flood Stage:
  12 feet (40,100 cfs)

Richmond Raft Company

Located just below the Annabel Lee, Richmond Raft Company holds the concession for commercial raft trips on the urban James. They use city-owned lands and roads for accessing the river, and for launching and taking out inflatable rafts. They float over 4,000 customers each year on the stretch of the James from the Huguenot Bridge to the Annabel Lee. Marc Kalman is the General Manager, and he shared his advice and expertise for this article.

For persons purchasing their own rafts, Marc recommends commercial-grade rafts such as Hyside or Riken brands. Small commercial rafts start at $1,800, but will last a private owner a lifetime. Undergoing almost daily use during the season with Richmond Raft Company, commercial rafts last approximately six years. There are three basic rules for maintaining a raft: keep it inflated, keep it clean, and keep it out of the weather.

Most of Richmond Raft Company's customers are people who are healthy and who can paddle. You should not participate if you are afraid of water, have knee or back or lung or heart problems, are too big for a life vest, or are under age 12.

But the Company does host special trips for special groups such as Richmond Athletes with Disabilities and patients from the Veteran's Hospital.

You WILL get wet during the raft rides. The Hollywood Rapids and Pipeline Rapids are Class IV rapids and they guarantee to produce sprays and splashes. And an average of one in 20 persons falls out of the raft in

James River Garden Club in 1993.

these rapids. Most of the rafts hold six persons plus a river guide.

The "Falls of the James" float goes from Pony Pasture to the Annabel Lee and lasts 5 1/2 hours and includes lunch. "The Lower Section" float goes from the Boulevard Bridge to the Annabel Lee and lasts 3 1/2 hours. There is now an "Upper Section" trip—a milder rafting experience which welcomes children under 12 as well as all other ages. Trips are available from March to November as long as the air temperature is in the 50's or higher. Wet suits and jackets are provided as needed. The company also provides specialized trips on an individual basis. There are also plans for future float fishing trips.

Richmond Raft Company, 4400 East Main Street, Richmond, VA 23231, (800) 540-7238.

April 19, 1985

A hundred years ago canal boats floated here. These days my aluminum boat is the only boat that ever touches these waters. Today is the first day of spring and I'm casting for bass in a disregarded, disrespected stretch of water in urban Richmond.

I've lifted my boat over the guard rail of the historic Kanawha Canal, just above the Great Shiplock. The canal goes a mile upstream before it disappears among the concrete bowels of the city. This little stretch of canal still hasn't been conquered by streets or buildings or sewers or railroads. It's modest and gentle, only 30 feet across, 13 feet deep, and thoroughly and thickly bordered by trees and shrubs and vines. There are a few open spots along the banks, but the only way to really fish it is by boat. But in my four Richmond years, I've never known of another boat here.

There are fish here: bass and bluegill, crappie and catfish, gars and carp. The canal receives its life from the James River, still quite cold this early in the season. My first casts with a slow plastic worm have been vacant. I switch to a brown jig with a chunk of black porkrind. It moves more slowly than the worm, and its weedless hook moves aggressively through the sunken trees along the banks. Still no bites.

I'm only 50 yards from the James—the tidal James just downstream from its first rapids. The few fishers who have parked their cars alongside mine at the Great Shiplock Park have all lugged their equipment over to the banks of the James and are casting cut bait and worms for stripers and white perch. Everyone ignores this canal.

The Professional Float Trip

It's October 12, 65 degrees, sunny, and the urban James is moving right along at three feet higher than normal. The peak season is past and ours is the only group going out from Richmond Raft Company: two rafts each carrying six customers and one guide. One raft will "lead" and the other will "sweep."

We all climb into wet suits, paddle jackets and life vests, deposit our car keys, and board a 16-passenger van for the drive to the launch area.

As we cross the Lee Bridge we all look down in anticipation. We can see that the river's up and stained. But the Hollywood Rapids way down below don't look like much of a challenge from up here.

I remove the jig and tie on a big willowleaf spinnerbait. It moves slowly and brightly and may quicken the appetite of a monster bass. I cast it up under the shoreline's overhanging branches and among its dangling vines.

Last year I fished this canal only twice. The second trip was when I discovered its bass. They're snuggled close to the vertical shorelines, thick among sunken wood, tight to the cover that's everywhere. I caught a few on a tiny shad crankbait—one that floated and dived.

I tie it on today but it swims without a look. Warm weather is still not here, and the foliage is only now beginning to bud. Some trees still sport their brown leaves of winter.

I throw every lure in my tackle box, and fish both banks for the entire length of the canal. At one point a car pauses on the canal-side street and tells me where to catch some canal crappie. I try a pink grub, but nothing bites.

There are big bass in here; I know it because I saw a 10-pounder lounging near a log last summer. It appears that last night's cold front and today's high skies and bright sun have made these fish unhungry.

I'll return in a month and won't recognize this place. Bluegills will be fat near the surface. Huge gars will mimic logs. **Trees thick with leaves will shield this corridor from the city. And snakes and bugs and wasps will twist among the shoreline shrubs and vines.**

We drive into the Main Entrance of James River Park and take the service road which parallels the river going upstream. We stop at a clearing just below the Boulevard Bridge. The river has gentle riffles here and it's the color of coffee and moving fast.

We board the rafts in pairs: two in front (the wettest spots, we're told), two in the middle and two in back. The river guide sits in the rear. We don't sit IN the raft, we sit ON its inflated edges. We are not tied or buckled onto anything. We are instructed to sort of wedge one foot under the inflated sides of the raft.

We shove off and practice some paddle commands as we drift towards the first rapids: paddle forward, back left, back right, back, and kick it!

All of a sudden we enter a Class II rapid which frightens me and wets me. I am amazed that we don't tip over and that I don't fall out. Our raft is leading and the other raft is sweeping. That means we get to go first through every set of rapids. And since I'm in the front of the raft, I get the first look.

We are told that one in 20 persons falls out of these rafts, and we are instructed what to do. If you fall in, float with your feet up and pointed downstream. Grab the rope if it's tossed to you (the guide throws a practice rope so we can see it), and be ready for someone to lift you back into the raft.

The person in the raft nearest the overboard person has the responsibility of pulling him back in. This is accomplished by grasping the two shoulder areas of the life jacket and then just leaning backwards into the raft. **Don't try to lift, just lean backwards. They say this method will work.** I hope we don't have to find out.

More Class II rapids arrive and after a few of them my fear is exchanged for exhilaration.

During the trip we see Cormorants, Mallards, Canada Geese, Great Blue Herons, and even one Bald Eagle. There are damsel flies flying and hatching and occasionally one lands on the raft. This trip usually takes three hours. Because of the high water, it will take only two today.

The trip moves quickly. There are no other rafts on the river today although we do see a few kayakers. Our guide—I'll call her Mary—points out natural and manmade sights along the way. She also sprinkles the conversation with hints of what's coming: the Hollywood Rapids.

In our pre-trip meeting at Richmond Raft Company's headquarters Mary told us that nobody has ever died or been seriously injured on any of the Company's trips, but we should all be aware that both are possible. We had to sign waivers.

Prior to the Hollywood Rapids I am frightened twice more during what Mary calls Class III rapids. Both times I am certain that I will depart the raft.

All of the other passengers in this raft are younger than I. Mary is 25. Next to me is Donna, 28; behind her are Carolyn and Jean, both 30; and in the back row is 16-year-old Richard and 35-year-old Melissa. Donna, next to me, and Richard are the only two passengers that don't appear to be frightened. Donna and I were the only ones willing to ride in front.

We hear the Hollywood Rapids before we see them. Class IV. I am very apprehensive. VERY. But why should I be? Tens of thousands of people have done this on these very rafts, so it must be safe.

I see it, but can't believe what's ahead of us and coming fast: a raging river which crashes and drops and curves among whitewater boulders. We'll never make it. I wedge my foot as tightly as I can.

We approach the first big drop and plunge over it. The bow goes headfirst, water splashes everywhere, and Donna disappears. **When the bow lifts, Donna is gone.** She's in the water a few feet away and she and our raft are crashing through the Hollywood Rapids. Carolyn—nearest to Donna—puts her paddle aside and leans out and grabs the shoulders of Donna's life jacket and lifts.

Don't LIFT! Lean backwards! The rest of us are paddling furiously to Mary's shouted commands. Carolyn struggles to LIFT Donna without success. Calm water has not yet arrived. The Class IV rapids continue.

I miraculously keep my balance as I make a fast decision and cross over to Carolyn's side of the raft. She lets go and I reach over and grab the shoulders of Donna's life jacket and lean backwards. This better work!

It does, easily, and a drenched Donna slides belly-first back into the raft. More paddling, more shouted instructions, and at last we reach the eddy at the bottom of the rapids.

The sweep raft comes through without incident, and then both rafts pull up onto flat rocks for a lemonade break. Donna is okay and smiling. Her wet suit has kept her from getting too chilled in the cold October water. She assures us that she has no cuts, scrapes nor bruises.

Mary tells us that Richmond is the only big city in the nation that has Class IV rapids. She tells us that the most difficult rapids are yet to come: the Pipeline Rapids. They're also Class IV, but they're narrower, have sharp turns, require more maneuvering, and are unforgiving. I decide that this will be my first and last trip through these rapids.

After a half-hour of drinking lemonade and stretching our legs we climb back into the rafts and start downstream. The Lee Bridge and the Footbridge look different from down here as we float below them.

Mary practices paddle commands again; she says we will have to respond quickly when we reach the Class IV Pipeline. "Forward" means what it says. "Back right" means the people on the right side paddle backwards and the people on the left paddle forwards. "Kick it" means to give it everything you have—to paddle forward strongly and quickly. We practice all of them.

Also we're reminded that it's vital to keep paddling while in the rapids. The most common mistake of most rafters is to lift the paddles and quit paddling while in rapids. We assure Mary that we won't.

We go through some Class II and one Class III rapid before reaching the Pipeline. My heart quickens as we near it. There is a narrow, snaking shoot with water erupting everywhere. I look down beside me as Donna wedges her foot.

"Kick it!!" is Mary's sudden command as the water drops ahead of us. I stab the water and pull hard. "Kick it!! Kick it!!"

The bow of the raft drops over the edge of Niagara Falls. We don't capsize and we don't lose anyone. We brace for the next one. "Back right!! Back right, and kick it!!"

I paddle backwards at first and then remember I'm sitting on the LEFT side. "BACK RIGHT!! BACK RIGHT!!"

We narrowly miss the boulder on the right and we hit the chute perfectly. "WEEEE!!" Mary shouts.

More commands come fast and furious, and apparently we do okay because we make it all the way through the Pipeline Rapids with no mishaps.

We get to slap our paddles on the water and hear the echoes as we float under Mayo's Bridge into the tidal James. Soon a Jon boat with a 15-horse engine arrives and tows us downriver to Richmond Raft Company's headquarters where we left our cars and keys.

We're 45 minutes early. The high water moved us through the route much more quickly than normal. It was a fast and dangerous ride, and I feel as if I have been initiated into a special club of daredevils. Until I remember that this club includes tens of thousands of people of all ages and all abilities.

I remove the wet suit, change into dry clothes, get into my car and drive home. Soon after I leave the parking lot I pass through Richmond's skyline—its business district—skyscrapers almost on the edge of the Pipeline Rapids. An amazing juxtaposition.

Coastal Canoeists

Charles V. Ware is Conservation Chairman of the Coastal Canoeists—a whitewater paddling club which is not limited by either of the words in its name. Mr. Ware provided the following information in an interview for this publication:

The Coastal Canoeists, founded in 1965 by Tidewater paddlers as one of the first regional whitewater clubs (that's the coastal part), now has approximately 800 members statewide. An affiliate of the American Canoe Association (ACA) and the American Whitewater Affiliation (AWA), the club's members may paddle canoes or kayaks (and occasionally something else). There are two requirements for membership in Coastal Canoeists: $15 annual dues, and a commitment to observe AWA Safety Code standards.

The club does not lead trips, but does coordinate paddling trips for its members. The organization's quarterly newsletter, CaNews, includes a trip schedule listing trips each week, which vary from flatwater to Class IV. Before going on trips, members should have appropriate skill levels. The Coastals offer river rescue and safety clinics to members and non-members, and can refer paddlers to certified paddling methods instructors.

The urban James River can cause real trouble even for advanced paddlers because of its size and power, and because of an abundance of manmade structures. Of particular concern are dam hydraulics, which may be avoided if you know the right routes—and have the skill and equipment to stay on the correct line! All who paddle the James must respect the fact that paddling difficulty varies

May 26, 1983 ≋

Just below the falls at Richmond the James River reminds me of the Manhattan Hudson. My years at 116th Street were filled with magic Hudson sunsets watching fish spatter the multi-glided currents, catching a few smaller ones, hooking some rare big ones.

Immediately below Richmond the James abandons its rocky rapids and sandy shallows. It abruptly changes from a sparkling clean smallmouth stream to a littered, tidal, downtown river.

Ocean fish travel all the way up to Richmond where they are stopped by the falls. There are stripers, white perch, herring and shad. Their spawning runs occur in the spring.

Today I spent an hour-long dusk on the shore of the tidal James. I watched fish splash across the surface in uncertain patterns. I saw weathered fishers sitting next to buckets of tiny bream and white perch they had caught on worms. Two of them each had a small striper about a pound.

Last year I saw a television film of a man catching 5-pound stripers in this portion of the James. He used a giant white grub with a plastic tail. Last Thursday's newspaper reported more big stripers.

Today I threw a big white grub nearly a hundred yards into the current. I reeled it as fast as I could, darting it through the depths. In 10 minutes my right arm ached from reeling the big lure so rapidly. But I continued. I wasn't after the smaller fish, the ones that were splashing. For them I would have used tiny spinners and spoons on light line.

My 7-foot rod is like a broomstick and it didn't bend much, even under the weight of the one-ounce grub. The grub picked up constant debris as my lures used to do in the Hudson. Today I caught various papers and plastics and occasional woody matter.

Today was my first encounter with the lower James, and even

as does the river level—which, because of the free-flowing nature of the James, and its large drainage, may range from trickle to torrent.

Conservation is an emphasis of the Coastals, and the organization has been active in various conservation issues in Virginia. Hydropower has been a major river conservation concern in Richmond, where dams and diversions once removed nearly all instream flow at several locations within the city.

Water withdrawal for other uses also has the potential for a significant cumulative impact on the river. ⟶

before I was in sight of it, I could smell it. It's a good smell, an unsalty ocean smell, the same smell that used to deliver bluefish and stripers from the Hudson.

I threw the big grub unnoticed—cast after cast. Occasionally it would hit a rock or a stump, never a fish. With only a quarter-hour before dark I switched to a sinking, diving plug—a Threadfin Shad. Perhaps it would look more like the baitfish in the river.

After a dozen casts a small boat motored past me, probably trolling for stripers. As the boaters moved their eyes away from me a sudden jerk shook the end of my rod. I reeled several yards of line, feeling the steady throb at the end. It was a good fish, at least a couple of pounds, perhaps much more.

But the line went suddenly tight and it wouldn't budge. The fish had gone behind a stump or a rock. I pulled as hard as I dared, taking the line close to its limit. Next I stripped off yards and yards of slack and let the swift current take it downstream. After 30 seconds I reeled it all back in. It was still hung.

I felt the line with my hand and could no longer detect a fish. The fish had come loose after depositing my lure behind a rock.

I let out more slack and put the rod on the ground and waited. After 5 minutes I tried again. This time it budged.

I felt the steady pull at the end of the line and it was no longer hung.

My fantasy ended quickly when the fish turned out to be a 20-inch piece of cloth, brown and ragged. I unhooked it and went home. Darkness arrived.

I didn't get an honest bite from the lower James. Like the Hudson, it is stingy with its bounty. **But its uniquely fishy smell, brewed over the centuries, and its teeming baitfish, allow me to conjure future memories.**

"Conservation pricing" for water in Richmond would likely lessen the amount of water consumption. This means you would be charged increasingly more for water once you passed a normal level of consumption. Currently in Richmond the reverse is the case: the more water you use, the less you pay per gallon. Conservation pricing would offer an alternative to mandated regulation of water use.

The Coastal Canoeists have also been actively involved in river cleanup projects, assisting the James River Park System staff and other conservation groups during "Clean the Bay Days" and other trash removal efforts. Tires and large bits of man-made debris are frequently deposited along the river by floods and freshets, but most trash finds its way into the river from storm sewers and combined sewer overflows after rainstorms. Most often found are plastic, metal, and glass drink containers discarded along streets and swept into sewer inlets, thence into the river.

Coastal Canoeists convenes quarterly meetings which include professional programs such as presentations by noted whitewater authors and experts. **The club welcomes and encourages new members.**

Contact: The Coastal Canoeists, Inc., P.O. Box 566, Richmond, VA 23218-0566

Paddling Tips

[*This information was prepared in 1982 by the Virginia Commission of Outdoor Recreation.*]

- Tell someone at home where you are going and when you will be back, so that if you are long overdue on your return, someone will know where to look for you.

- Be able to recognize the signs of a river in flood stage and do not attempt to paddle a flooded river.

- Make sure everyone has a personal flotation device.

- If your boat capsizes in whitewater, get away from it and attempt to stay on its upstream side. Once you have gotten clear of the boat, float through the rapids on your back with your feet up and pointed downstream to fend off rocks and other obstructions. If you swamp in flat water, hang on.

- Be prepared for emergencies. Carry a first aid kit, spare paddle, a proper and readily available rescue line, dry clothing, repair kit, bailer and a garbage bag.

- Respect the right of private property owners. Always obtain permission before crossing or otherwise using privately owned property.

- Respect the rights of fishers and non-paddlers taking part in other forms of river oriented recreation.

- Never attempt to run low-water bridges or dams. Both can be extremely dangerous.

- Never paddle alone. Plan your trip for at least two people and preferably two or more boats.

RAPIDS: DIFFICULTY RATING

Class I: Occasional small rapids with low, regular waves not over one foot high. Course easily determined. Rescue spots all along. Shallow.

Class II: More frequent rapids. Eddies and whirlpools offer no trouble. Ledges not over three feet high with a direct uncomplicated chute. Course easily determined. Waves up to three feet high but avoidable. Water more than three feet deep.

Class III: Long rapids, maneuvering required. Course not easily recognizable. Waves up to five feet high, mostly regular, avoidable; strong cross currents; a good rescue spot after each rapid.

Class IV: Long rapids, intricate maneuvering. Course hard to determine, waves high (up to five feet), irregular, avoidable; or medium (up to three feet) and unavoidable; strong cross currents, eddies.

Class V: Long continuous rapids, tortuous; requires frequent scouting. Extremely complex course. Waves large, irregular, unavoidable. Large scale eddies and cross currents. Rescue spots few and far off.

Class VI: Long continuous rapids without let-up. Very tortuous, always scout. Waves high (about five feet), irregular unavoidable; powerful cross currents. Special equipment, limit of canoeability, involves risk of life.

November 27, 1996

by Ralph White

Winter is a refreshing time to visit the woods and walkways in the James River Park. Vistas are open, free from the clinging confines of leaves and vines and briars and branches. There's a clarity to the air too that only cold weather can bring. Cold air holds less moisture to fog the horizon and slows plant metabolism so there isn't any pollen—or even mold spores—to blur the view. Stronger, northern winds dissipate any wood smoke from neighborhood fireplaces. It's a time to walk, watch and wait.

If spring is the time of wildlife courtship and baby care then winter is the time to observe animal feeding. In front of the Visitor's Center, where the variable Reedy Creek dumps its mineral-rich effluent from Midlothian Turnpike and the backyards around German School Road, a tiny Pie-billed Grebe appears for the winter every year in the week before Thanksgiving. This is a perky and comical little fish eater. **Toy-sized and jerky in movement it looks to me like a waterlogged softball with a lollipop stuck on one side for a head.** Floating on the surface it jerks and bobs in a funny mechanical way appropriate for a child's Christmas or Channuka gift. Of course it spends a lot of its time out of sight scouring the shallow bottom for small fish and the occasional invertebrate—in turn attracted by the possibility of intriguing new foods washed in by civilization. I make mental bets with myself on where it will reappear. Fortunately I make no cash commitments for I am almost invariably wrong. Thirty or forty feet off is not uncommon.

You can usually find a Pie-billed Grebe or two on the lakes at Byrd Park or the rocks at the Pony Pasture. (They will often be mixed with small flocks of Mallard and Black Ducks or even among the large gathering of Canada Geese so increasingly common in

Richmond during the winter.) But the elevated deck at the Visitor's Center offers an especially good vantage point. An extra treat there is the sight of the single Belted Kingfisher that arrives just before Christmas. This Blue Jay-sized bird sits prominently on the highest branches of the flood debris pile in the river directly opposite the building. It dives as if for tourist dollars fairly regularly during the civilized hours of the mid-afternoon. Listen for its distinctive rattle-like call when it flies. Usually that means, "That's all for today folks!"

There is a host of wildlife that becomes visible in winter. In the forests of the Wetlands look for feeding flocks of small birds. Stand still and they may approach like a swirl of fallen leaves in some unsensed gusty wind. The flock is a mix of several different small species like Juncos, Titmice, Chickadees and the like; none is large or aggressive. The birds work together to find and share caches of seeds and dried berries among the understory branches, or insect eggs and larva stuck in the crevices of tree bark.

One easy observation: the bird working its way up a tree trunk from the ground will be a Brown Creeper; it moves in loose spirals. The one coming down is a Nuthatch. It's the only bird that faces down. Downy Woodpeckers work a haphazard route on limbs, tree crotches and trunks, and they will tap away at a bark crevice they can't quite get into. Each species gets a very separate view of hidden food treasures and therefore doesn't compete. Move and you may hear a thin, high-pitched whistle before the birds all fly off. One of the many eyes has spotted you and the owner alerted the others. This, unless you've already been spotted by a flock of boisterous Blue Jays. In this case you will have been already betrayed by a chorus of raucous bird screams. For these reasons you'll have better viewing if you don't take a dog with you.

A riverside thought: keep a lookout for the occasional Great Blue Heron. Unlike the concentrated gatherings at rich fish migration spots in spring and early summer these winter birds are dispersed and therefore less common. Shorter hours, fewer fish and colder temperatures make this a hard time for fishers of many types—avian and human alike. **For seasonal drama there is nothing like the view of a solitary Heron in the snow—a dark Puritan minister with stovepipe legs and the stoic acceptance of inevitable winter privation.** Using a telephoto lens there are usually good views in the morning at the Pony Pasture police overlook (Don't stray long from your car as this is officially a No Parking area, but there is usually understandable leeway on early winter mornings), or at the Manchester Dam along the Floodwall Walk accessible from the Floodwall parking lots at 2nd and Hull Street, 7th and Semmes or from the climbers' lot under the Manchester Bridge.

A few thoughts for winter walks: luxuriant chickweed greens up the southern hillside of Belle Isle, animals' homes are revealed in trees (Pileated Woodpecker hole in the Sycamore by the Visitor's Center, raccoon dens in trees along Pleasant Creek near the bridge in Pony Pasture and along new RR trail; look for hairs in the bark). Food supplies are lavish on land in the Wetlands at this start of the "preserved food" season—ball-galls and mud dauber nests for Titmice and Chickadee raw bar excursions, overwintering queen wasps, flies, butterflies and beetles in the cracks of tree bark, while flocks of Grackles and Starlings turn over leaves searching out recently hatched acorn weevils and newly exposed earthworms in backyard lawns.

Paddling

Ralph Hambrick teaches and enjoys paddling on the urban James. He answered questions on a warm evening on the shores of the river.

Q: What advice do you have for beginners?

A: Take some lessons. Both Henrico and Chesterfield Counties provide paddling lessons for both canoes and kayaks. This is a good way to get started and learn some fundamentals. Also you can just get a boat and get on the river. There are several sections which are quite forgiving to the beginner. But the river is also demanding, so if you know some basics you'll be a lot more comfortable.

Q: What if you are an experienced paddler, but are unfamiliar with the urban James?

A: If you are interested just in paddling, first go to Huguenot Woods and paddle around. You can paddle for about an hour upstream to Bosher's Dam. The area has some current and rocks, but not much whitewater. If you go the other direction, it's all flatwater backed up by Williams Dam. And you can go on both sides of Williams Island and play around in terms of whitewater paddling. This is a good area to explore. The stretch from Huguenot Woods to Reedy Creek has some whitewater—mostly Class II water that is not especially demanding if you already have a little skill.

Flatwater above Huguenot Bridge.

Q: Does Williams Dam present any problems for paddlers?

A: The question is whether or not to run the notch—the fish passage. The hydraulic looks more menacing than it is. But the book is still out on whether people should do it. There is enough hydraulic to be cautious.

Q: Talk about the Classes.

A: There are six classes. Class VI is the limit of navigability. Even a raft would be challenged. Class V is tough. There are no Class V rapids in the urban James. Maybe under some conditions Hollywood Rapids would be Class V, but not most of the time. Class IV in a canoe is pretty challenging. In a kayak it's a little more manageable. Class III begins to get challenging in terms of needing to maneuver. Class II is non-threatening rapids. There is some whitewater, but if you turn over there is not any great danger. Class I is mild ripples and strong moving water.

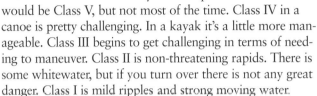

The slot in Williams Dam.

Q: How difficult are the Hollywood and Pipeline Rapids?

A: They're both Class IV. A good, experienced paddler could go through them without difficulty, but the first time you should accompany someone who knows the routes.

Q: What is Coastal Canoeists?

A: That's an organization—statewide—which coordinates weekly trips which are great opportunities to experience paddling on various waters. The trips range from beginner to expert. There are a few trips each year on the urban James—typically from Pony Pasture to Reedy Creek, which is about two hours on average.

Q: Can you paddle on the urban James during low water?

A: The James is interesting and quite paddleable at all levels. It holds up well at even the lowest levels—in contrast with many other rivers.

Q: What canoe should you purchase?

A. ABS material is the accepted standard for recreational paddling. It takes rocks well. Aluminum tends to grab rocks. ABS tends to slide, plus it's malleable and tough.

Q: Are there any particular cautions on the urban James?

A: Dams and historic structures beneath the surface can present problems. But this is only a possibility, not a probability. Williams is the only dam that doesn't have a break in it. Dams themselves on the urban James are only a mild problem.

Q: Can you paddle in the urban James in the winter?

A: The rule of thumb is that you should never go ON the water unless you're prepared to go IN the water. In the winter you should at least wear a wet suit, and preferably a dry suit. I know one experienced paddler who had a freak accident in the winter and turned over near Bosher's Dam. His son was in the canoe with him. By the time they got back to their car at Huguenot Woods they were close to hypothermia.

Q: Has anyone on the river ever caused you any trouble?

A: No, and I have seen all types of people in all areas of the river.

Q: What are the main differences between kayaks and canoes?

A: There is an open canoe and a closed canoe which looks like a kayak but you kneel and use a canoe paddle. An open canoe's big problem is that it lets water in and you lose mobility. A kayak can handle larger water. But the two are getting closer. Canoes are getting smaller and are adding flotation. They are more mobile, more buoyant. Now there is much more variety in shape and design. Tipability and maneuverability are better. Now there's a sit-on-top kayak. You can strap in and roll but are not inside the kayak. There are also inflatable canoes and kayaks of all qualities. The transition from canoe paddle to kayak paddle isn't that hard. The main thing to learn in whitewater is how the water works.

Q: What are mistakes people make in rapids?

A: People often tend to quit paddling when starting a rapid. They lift the paddle out. You should keep the paddle in the water or you'll lose stability. Another mistake is not staying straight. If you get sideways you can catch a rock and flip over.

Q: What should you do if you catch a rock and flip over?

A: Don't get between the canoe and the rock. Stay upstream from the boat, let it go ahead. Lie on your back with your feet up and downstream. You can see where you're going and use your feet to push off rocks. Get away from the boat and try to relax. Don't make the mistake of trying so hard to save the boat that you get yourself in trouble. Equipment is replaceable, but arms and legs aren't.

Q: Why do you enjoy paddling?
A: I enjoy paddling on both ends of the spectrum. On one end is the relaxation, getting away. **You can paddle through the city of Richmond and feel like you're a million miles away.** On the other end I like it because of the adrenalin rush when you're doing whitewater. Sometimes I talk about paddling being my "therapy."

The Float Trip

Mark Twain said you can learn something by carrying a cat by the tail which you can learn no other way.
The following first-person account demonstrates the potential dangers you can encounter on the James River if you are unprepared, uneducated, and irresponsible—as I surely was.

It's Sunday, August 25, and it's 4:00 p.m. as Hank and Thomas and I launch our blow-up rafts at Pony Pasture. We'll float downstream to the Valentine Riverside area where I've left the car. We've never done this before.
In another week Hank and Thomas will both be in middle school. They've never done that before. And for the first time they'll be in separate schools; Hank's family has moved to Charlottesville. You're on your own in middle school: seven different classes every day, no parental signatures on homework, and multi-week projects.
I've waded a lot of this stretch of the river, and I've seen for myself that the only dangerous part is the Hollywood Rapids alongside the northern edge of Belle Isle. We'll avoid that part. Piece of cake.
A friend who canoes this stretch has told me that it takes three hours at a leisurely pace. We'll do a continuous float with no stops and will likely make it in much less than three hours and be off the river a good hour and a half before dark.
We have three rafts. Mine and Thomas' are those two-person rafts that you get at toy stores that cost $20 and have instructions that say they are not to be used in open water. But we've used ours in lakes and ponds and at the beach for three years without the first leak, so we know they're worthy of this low-water James. Hank's is a heavy-duty rubberized raft with outer and inner air chambers. A

friend gave it to him used, and Hank's dad helped him patch its handful of small holes.

At 2:00 this afternoon Thomas and I went to St. John's Church up on old Richmond Hill and saw the reenactment of Patrick Henry's "Liberty or Death" speech. The simple word reenactment doesn't describe what we experienced. Eight actors in period dress sat among us in the pews and presented a half-hour's worth of fine theatre. **We were there at that secret meeting two hundred years ago. We listened to two convincing sides of the history-changing argument of whether to form a militia.** My own chemistry would have likely caused me to vote against Patrick Henry's resolution.

My raft starts leaking immediately. Water, not air. The raft's floor has a hole the size of a silver dollar and two inches of water wash over my feet. But that's all. I sit on the edge of the donut part of the raft which is a separate chamber. It's high enough above the river's surface that only so much water can inundate the floor area. It'll be fine. No problem. Hank's and Thomas' rafts are dry and tight and floating proudly.

The weather is perfect: high seventies, no wind, no clouds. Just drifting along on the most beautiful urban river in America.

Hank has a paddle and a bag of snacks in his raft. He wears a life jacket which he doesn't need. The river here almost never gets deeper than his height.

Thomas has a pole rather than a paddle. He says he'll be able to maneuver better with the pole—poking rocks and pushing the bottom.

I have a small cooler, my fishing rod, a pouch full of lures, a paddle, a pump, and a life jacket for Thomas just in case we come to a spot where he might need it.

Bill Gordon was magnificent in the role of Patrick Henry. He's one of three regulars who play that role. He puts his heart and soul into it in a manner that makes you believe.

That church—Richmond's first—was established when Christopher Newport encountered the upstream challenges of this river. There, at what is now Mayo's Bridge at 14th Street, he encountered the Fall Line—the rapids. The church was built atop the nearby hill and everyone was required to attend on Sundays—a **$10 fine if you didn't. No religious freedom back then.**

"Which way?" Hank asks as the river broadens among a spread of boulders. There are a dozen choices. Looking down from any of the bridges you can see obvious float routes. But floating along at water level you have no overall perspective. Just the boulders immediately ahead. Nothing beyond.

Any pathway I choose could funnel into a six-inch squeeze or drop into a tricky whitewater or roll over any of the ancient ironworks that liberally litter the river's floor.

"This way," I guess. "Just follow me, I'll go first." I maneuver my raft through a little chute between two boulders and come out clean amid open water on the other side. Hank follows. Thomas doesn't.

Thomas is caught above the chute, poling his raft in circles. His anticipated maneuvering skills with the pole have not materialized. I'll save my I-told-you-so for another day. He's shouting for me to help.

"I can't help!" I shout back. "The water's too fast for me to paddle back up there!"

"But Dad!?" he shouts.

"Just push on through that fast area!" I yell.

"I can't!"

I paddle hard and then climb into the water and wade upstream around the small rapids pulling my raft by its rope. When I reach Thomas I push him on through the chute as I climb back into my raft and follow.

When we reach Hank on the other side Thomas is laughing.

I see more small rapids up ahead—maybe 60 seconds away—and I make a decision. "Thomas, I'm going to tie our rafts together so I can paddle and maneuver us both. Hank, you tie on to the back of Thomas' raft."

In a minute we're a three-raft train entering a snaking chute of fast water. I realize immediately that tying the rafts together was a big mistake.

Another big mistake were the go-carts at the beach two weeks ago. Kelly and Thomas and I had never driven them before, so we paid our money and got into the cars on the "easy" track—the "slick" track. On the second lap Thomas spun out and crashed into the wall hard. You apparently can't damage a go-cart, but you can damage a driver. Thomas didn't break anything but he did get a headache. Kelly hit the wall two laps later and bruised her arm and cut her knee. That was one of the rare times Kelly has ever cried from pain.

Hank's raft quickly lodges against a boulder as our other two rafts pull against it in the current. Fortunately Hank is able to untie quickly. Thomas' raft floats onto the top of a boulder as mine dangles below filling with more water. Thomas and I both have to get out to untie and untangle and dislodge.

The railroad bridge approaches and I devise another plan. I swap pole for paddle with Thomas, and I give him the life jacket in case we encounter any more precarious situations. But surely we won't. We've learned our lesson now.

"I'll tell you what," I announce. "Let's all three get out of our rafts and sort of swim them through the bridge area. That'll be easier and safer, and we won't risk falling out of the rafts."

In a jiffy we're in the water hanging onto the sides of our rafts and sort of kicking along.

"Mr. Bryan?" Hank asks.

"What's up, Hank?"

"I think I'm losing air, but that couldn't be right because my dad and I patched all the holes last week."

Hank's raft is indeed becoming a bit limp and we climb up on a big flat rock to do some pumping. The leak is tiny and in five minutes we've firmed the raft to where it'll go for another half-hour. We'll just stop and re-pump every so often—no problem. Maybe add another 15 minutes to our trip, no more.

"Oh, this is a tale of castaways . . . ." I start singing the Gilligan's Island song. Hank and Thomas don't join in.

We're back in the water swimming our rafts beneath the railroad bridge. "This way," I lead.

And then I see what we're all of a sudden entering—the Choo Choo Rapids. Class III rapids. **"Thomas!" I shout back. "Put on your life jacket!" But too late.**

At the Outer Banks last year Thomas loved crashing in the Red Flag surf. The other kids were afraid to go in, but Thomas dove in and rolled over and came out laughing each time. I got it on videotape—a seemingly 100-foot-tall tidal wave pounding him each time. A monster compared to the James River's puny waves.

Thomas screams as he lets go of his raft and begins a wild un-life-jacketed tumble through Choo Choo Rapids. The Outer Banks didn't have boulders and logs and ancient submerged ironworks. I feel my legs hit and scrape underwater rocks. One rock feels as if it rips a gash the length of my thigh. It hurts bad.

Hank lifts himself onto his raft in time to avoid the worst of it.

Thomas tumbles a backwards somersault and goes under and then comes back up. Gasping, I keep my head above water. Hank is already through the rapids and has reached the shallow area below. His raft has lost air already.

At last we're all safely in the shallows and we are no longer smiling. I make Thomas put his life jacket on. I didn't bring one for myself. I check my leg and what feels like a gash is only a long red mark which will turn purple tomorrow and disappear in a week. Thomas has marks all over him, but no cuts and no breaks. A miracle.

After we pump Hank's raft again we climb into our rafts and I announce another plan. "Let's stay in our rafts from now on. Swimming through the rapids was a bad idea."

We make it through several more small rapids and then enter a long flat stretch

Next week at work I'll get my first new boss in 15 years. I enjoyed working for my former boss, and I realize that your boss can be the main factor in whether you enjoy going into work, whether your job is exciting, whether you like the challenges, whether you're proud of what you do. The new guy comes to us from the other side of the United States and we don't know him. We of course met him during the interviews, but what can you really tell from an interview?

Today I am learning that even though I have years of experience in this river while wading and hopping rocks, and even though I've floated an aluminum Jon boat through other wild rivers, I don't know much of anything about floating in an inflatable raft on the urban James.

In this flat stretch the three of us don't talk much. We each drink a soda and I cast a bit with a smallmouth lure. We see Canada Geese, a couple of Cormorants, a Piper of some sort, and several Mallards. I check my cell phone. It's still dry in the zippered bag.

There are no road signs on the river. Somehow I had thought it would just come naturally as to which routes to take. But that's wrong.

We see a dozen other floaters on this flat stretch. All seem to know what they're doing. There are kayakers too, gliding gracefully. I know the Hollywood Rapids are way up ahead on the right, so I start guiding us to the left.

We see a lone Bald Eagle flying at the treeline. It disappears after a few flaps. We see only one Great Blue Heron.

It sits and waits along the distant shoreline. And we now attract biting flies—those housefly-looking flies that land on you and then bite. We all spend ten minutes swatting at perhaps four of them.

I haven't told Thomas what I saw at the base of the Choo Choo Rapids near where he took his tumble. There were three iron spikes embedded in the floor of the river sticking straight up. Each was about three feet tall. Nobody should ever swim those rapids.

The flies leave and we talk about Winston Cup racing. Hank's favorite driver is Ricky Rudd although he also likes Rusty Wallace. His dad's favorite is Mark Martin. Mine's Terry Labonte because he won the one race I've attended—not a Winston Cup race but a NASCAR race nevertheless—one of the Supertruck events. Those guys speed around the tracks at 200 miles an hour and I'm now frightened from a little float down the river. Go figure.

This calm water is lasting much longer than it looked. My watch is moving, and now I know we'll definitely be home later than planned. And I guess there's a one in a million chance we won't actually arrive back home until almost dark.

"We're fine, but we'll be back a tad late," I tell Janet and Hank's parents on the cell phone.

Finally another group of boulders and swifter water arrives. Now we'll start making some time again.

I have no idea which route to take through here so I just head for the fastest, deepest water. Hank and Thomas follow. This is an exhilarating stretch and we're actually enjoying it until we hit some underwater pointed rocks.

Hank and Thomas will start middle school in another week. Hank's already visited his school over near Charlottesville and likes it. Thomas will go to Binford where Kelly has already been for two years. Thomas has gotten his notebooks and is already planning on how to arrange his locker. Lockers are big deals. You don't have lockers in elementary school. Kids love doing new and exciting things.

"Dad, my raft is leaking fast!" Thomas shouts from mid-rapid. The raft looks fine to me.

"Okay Thomas, we'll keep an eye on it," I respond as we float on through and enter a flat stretch.

"Dad, I think it needs pumping," he continues.

And then I hear it. I can hear the hiss from 10 feet away. We pull our rafts up onto another flat rock and take a look. Hank's raft has lost more air and we pump it again.

Thomas' has holes in the side and the bottom. Big holes. The raft can't be repaired. It loses all of its air and we fold it and place it inside my raft. Thomas will use my raft and I'll swim and wade. Still almost halfway to go.

My watch has advanced. The sun is nearing the horizon. **One thing is for certain: we don't want to get caught on this river after dark.** I should have investigated the timing of this stretch more thoroughly.

We continue on and I announce another plan: "We've gotta go as quickly as possible, because it'll be dark soon and we can't be on the river after dark. Both of you paddle and I'll wade and swim."

I see Belle Isle in the distance on the right. We proceed along the left bank. In a little while some shoreline fishers hail us: "Where you headed?"

"Down past the Lee Bridge," I reply.

"You plan on going this way?"

"Yeah, we want to avoid the Hollywood Rapids."

"You can't go on this side; that dam up ahead will tear you to pieces. You gotta cross over in a hurry."

Dam?

Then I realize that a four-foot dam is indeed up ahead—the largest diversion dam on this stretch of the river. Water gushes violently over it just up ahead. Our only choice is the other side. I'll have to get us across the river and make it to the upstream tip of Belle Isle where we'll have to take out and walk the rest of the way. Hank's raft has lost more air. The water is deeper now and I'm swimming more than wading.

I swim and guide the two rafts across the river to a very shallow, bouldered area. We all have to get out and wade and pull the rafts with the ropes. The sun is sinking.

On television yesterday I saw an interview with an 89-year-old man who had just climbed a mountain in Antarctica. "I dared to fail," he said.

I didn't intentionally dare to fail on this float trip. It was stupidity, not courage, that got us into this fix.

We have now climbed down onto the bottom side of the other end of the dam a hundred yards from the upstream tip of Belle Isle. We have abandoned the damaged raft. I see that after we cross more shallows the only way to reach Belle Isle is for me to wade African-Queen-style, pulling the two rafts behind me, across the swift, deep water which precedes the Hollywood Rapids—the swift water just below the First Break Rapids. Who knows if we'll make it?

"Okay guys," I announce a final plan. "I'm going to try to pull us across this final stretch, but it's deep and swift and we might not make it. If I lose my footing and we begin to float downstream, bail out of your rafts immediately and swim to those shallows over there. **Just let the rafts go on through the Hollywood Rapids. But don't worry, you'll easily be able to swim to the shallows,**" I lie.

I grab the ropes and wade into the final stretch between us and Belle Isle. I plant my feet and lean upstream. The rafts pull at me from downstream. Thomas and Hank sit in the rafts wide-eyed. Their life jackets are on.

The water rises to my waist and higher. The rafts bounce and the ropes throb tautly in the swift water. The water inches towards my chest. It can't get any deeper. I'm almost at mid-stream. If it gets one inch deeper I'll lose it. I lean forward. My feet lift one in front of the other as they feel their way along the bottom.

The water moves another inch—but shallower, not deeper. Then another inch and another inch and another inch until we're out of danger.

As we finally pull the rafts onto the flat rock at the tip of Belle Isle the sun pulls its last rays below the horizon. In the twilight we carry the rafts and our belongings the entire length of Belle Isle, across the Footbridge, and back along the street to our car which we left hours ago. When we drop Hank off at his house it's well past dark.

I learned some things.

Don't float anywhere unless you're familiar with the route or are with someone who is familiar with it.

Don't use cheap rafts to float through the rapids on the James.

Never even remotely risk floating down the river after dark.

Wear life jackets in rapids.

Don't assume anything about a float trip.

When we get home Janet greets us with a busy smile and a "Hi! Did you have fun? I want to go next time." Thomas and I never tell her.

Chapter Four:
Fishing

There are catchable fish in the James River within sight of Richmond's downtown skyline all 365 days of the year. Developing methods for catching fish requires you to first think about the James as being two different rivers in which the fish behave differently. Those two rivers are separated by Mayo's (14th Street) Bridge.

Look beneath the bridge. The downstream side is the final reach of the Atlantic Ocean's tide. The downstream side is flat and slow and deep and dingy and full of all sorts of fish—even an occasional flounder or spot or croaker just like you'd catch at the Outer Banks.

Fishing on Belle Isle.

On the upstream side of Mayo's Bridge begins the Falls of the James—the rocky cascade which stretches several miles through Greater Richmond. This side of the river is shallow and swift and clear and home to only a few species of regularly catchable fish in Richmond: bass, catfish and sunfish.

We'll call these two sections the Tidal James and the Upper James.

The Upper James

Because of the boulders and rapids and islands and general clarity, this is the section of the James which appears on the postcards. This is the section in which you can easily wade or float and easily catch fish in the summertime. But in the colder months you can't wade and boating is risky, and therefore fishing in this section is confined mostly to the shorelines, and the fish are extremely difficult to catch.

WARM MONTHS ON THE UPPER JAMES

These months are defined as those in which the water is warm enough to wade without insulated waders—generally very late April through very late October.

During these months there are some reliable patterns which will catch fish.

Redbreast Sunfish

These hand-size and smaller fish live under boulders and logs and can be found almost anywhere there is water—even in backwater areas which seem to receive no fresh current flow. The key to catching them on artificials is to use thin line (4# or 6#) and long casts.

Richard Edwards, a maker of bass lures.

They will bite most small artificial baits: grubs, spinners, tiny divers, and spoons. **One all-around favorite is the smallest size Beetle Spin in the darker colors such as purple, black and green.** Usually the best success comes from fishing the lures slowly—just fast enough to keep them off the bottom. Be certain to make liberal use of a hook hone. The sunfish can often bite and spit out a lure faster than you can react. An ultra-sharp hook is an important aid in catching a sunfish.

They will also bite live bait such as worms, crickets and grasshoppers. Fish these about 18 inches beneath a small float. Use small hooks (#10) and only a very tiny splitshot (or none at all). You can toss this rig in calm pools or drift it through gentle glides. Strike as soon as the float moves.

Smallmouth Bass

Although this is the glamour fish of the James River, smallmouths larger than 12 inches are no longer as easy to catch as they were 20 years ago.

The standard formula for catching smallmouths is no longer a secret: just drift a live minnow a couple of feet below a float—or deeper if you know the water is deeper. Use a #4 hook and a small splitshot. Don't waste your time in calm waters; keep the minnow moving. Let it drift downstream, reel it in, cast it back upstream, and let it drift again.

You should try a lot of areas. There is a rule of thumb: the deeper the water, the bigger the fish. The bigger fish also tend to live beneath logjams which are in or adjacent to swift water.

Use heavier line (10# to 14#) when drifting minnows for smallmouths. When you hook one, your line will rub against underwater rocks and limbs as the smallmouth fights. Regularly check the last six or eight feet of line for abrasions, and break off and retie as often as necessary.

You can also use other live baits such as crawfish and hellgrammites fished in a similar manner. Smallmouths will also sometimes bite grasshoppers, crickets and nightcrawlers. Nightcrawlers should be hooked in a manner that allows them to move freely in the water.

Artificial lures are not generally as productive for smallmouths as is live bait. However there are a few lures and patterns that produce regular results.

In recent years big three- and four-inch grubs have become popular—specifically the Yamamoto brand in the natural brown colors. These are fished with eighth-ounce or quarter-ounce jig heads, and are successful with three different styles of retrieve, depending on the moods of the fish.

One retrieve is swimming the jig through the water with a slow, steady movement. You can cast upstream, across the current, or downstream. **The goal is to keep the grub swimming through the water without touching the bottom and without breaking the surface.**

Another method is the stop-and-go retrieve. The idea is to move the grub as a crawfish would move. Let it fall to the bottom and sit a few seconds and then lift it and swim it a few feet before letting it rest again. The swimming movements sometimes work best when they're quick and rapid. The downside to using this method is that you will continually hang the grub in rocks.

The third method is the natural drift. The idea is to use the rod tip to gently flutter or vibrate the grub as it drifts naturally with the current. You'll find that the best way to effect this natural drift is to cast at a 45-degree angle upstream and drift the lure until it is directly downstream.

Topwater plugs can catch smallmouths. The standard lure for many years on the James River has been the Heddon Tiny Torpedo, but during the past couple of years its effectiveness has decreased. You'll want to try a variety of the other topwater plugs which are now on the market. Use the smaller sizes—not longer than three or four inches. The best way to try new lures is to take two or three with you and leave everything else at home. That way you'll be forced to fish an adequate amount of time with them without being tempted to replace them if the fish don't bite immediately.

Although some smallmouths bite all day long, fish larger than 12 inches bite best at dawn and dusk. This rule is especially true for topwater lures.

Smallmouths will hit four-inch plastic worms when fished in either of two very opposite ways. One way is to drift the worm naturally, gently shaking it during the drift. The other is to reel it quickly across the surface of the water with the rod tip held high. For both methods use a #4 or #6 wire hook rigged "Texas style" with a bb-size splitshot attached immediately above the hook. The surface worm works especially well during the very hottest days of the summer.

Smallmouths love diving plugs—the type generically termed "alphabet plugs." Bagley, Norman, Rebel and other manufacturers make a wide variety that will work. Use small, plastic-lipped plugs about the size of a pecan. The fish like natural color patterns as well as white, chartreuse and "firetiger."

The plug should dive deeply and rapidly so that it bounces off the bottom as it moves along. Use a stop-and-go retrieve.

Smallmouths will also hit jerkbaits—the slender Rapala-type minnow imitators—especially jerkbaits with lips that allow them to dive more than a couple of inches. Use the smaller sizes in both the silver and gold colors.

The Upper James has so many rocks that there is good habitat for smallmouths almost everywhere. Therefore you should try as much water as possible; keep moving until you locate fish. **Generally, the farther you are from the "easy" water—water easily reached by other fishers—the more fish you'll catch.**

Catfish

The Upper James now has three species of catfish, and the methods for catching them are different. Until recent years the channel catfish was what you'd catch. Channel catfish are identified by the specks—or sprinkling of black dots—on their sides. They average a pound or two, and large ones in the urban Upper James sometimes reach 15 pounds.

It's easy to catch channel cats. Just toss out weighted-and-baited hooks and wait. Use a #4 hook, 14-20# line, and a quarter-ounce sinker. Don't use a float; just let the bait rest on the bottom.

Channel cats readily hit chicken livers, frozen shrimp, live worms, dead minnows, and various store-bought catfish concoctions.

Channel catfish live everywhere in the Upper James, and you should try a lot of areas until you locate them. Let your bait rest on the bottom no longer than 10 minutes, and then cast it somewhere else. Eventually you'll find channel catfish.

Flathead catfish have become numerous in recent years. They get bigger than channel catfish—up to and larger than 25 ponds. Flatheads like live swimming bait: big minnows, small fish, eels, frogs, whatever will swim around with a hook in it.

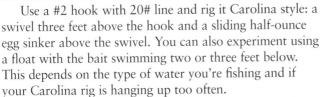

Catfish from the Huguenot Woods area.

Use a #2 hook with 20# line and rig it Carolina style: a swivel three feet above the hook and a sliding half-ounce egg sinker above the swivel. You can also experiment using a float with the bait swimming two or three feet below. This depends on the type of water you're fishing and if your Carolina rig is hanging up too often.

The best concentrations of flatheads are found in the tailwaters of dams and below rapids.

The Upper James also has blue catfish. These are true giants and can get up to 30 or 40 or 50 pounds. It's almost impossible to land a huge blue cat in the Upper James unless you're prepared with very heavy line.

Although conventional wisdom assumes that the blue catfish concentrate in the deepest holes, that has not proven to be the case all of the time. In fact, the blue catfish have thus far been unpredictable from year to year as to where they live in the Upper James.

What has stayed constant is what baits are best: live fish, live eels, fresh cut shad (or herring), and fresh cut eels. If you want to catch big blue catfish, be prepared to spend a lot of hours trying a lot of locations. Most likely you'll hook into one as most fishers do—when they're fishing for something else with lightweight tackle.

COLD MONTHS ON THE UPPER JAMES

Three words: slow, deep, minnows.

Only a very few fishers bother with the Upper James from November through March, but those who do can catch some truly huge fish. To catch fish in the winter you have to use live minnows in deep holes and be prepared to wait forever. Most winter fishers locate the deep holes by wading during low water periods in the summer, and then reach them by boat in the winter. Your best advice is to find a spot which looks good and try it a lot in a variety of situations: when it's sunny, when it's cloudy, in the morning, and in the afternoon.

Fishing near the Annabel Lee.

The Tidal James

This part of the river begins beneath Mayo's Bridge and goes downstream. Although you can't see most of them, there are plenty of rocks and boulders in the Tidal James.

SPRING ON THE TIDAL JAMES

The months of April and May are the bonanza months on the Tidal James in Richmond. Three varieties of migratory fish fill the river: stripers (rockfish), white perch, and the herring/shad/menhaden/alewife family.

Stripers

These fish were rare in the James—and the Chesapeake Bay—15 years ago. But in 1997 they are abundant, especially in April and May. In Richmond they average one to three pounds, but stripers up to six or seven pounds are not uncommon, and an occasional 10- or 15-pounder is caught.

The most effective way to catch springtime stripers is with bait fished on the bottom with a Carolina rig. The best bait is fresh herring cut into finger-size strips. Most other types of freshly cut fish work well too. Also effective are live minnows or small fish. There's no real rule to where you'll find the stripers. Sometimes they seem to be everywhere, and sometimes the only places you can find them are deep holes.

Use #2/0 hooks and at least 14# line. You'll need an egg sinker weighing at least a half-ounce, and larger in the faster currents. Cast the rig downstream and let it stay on the bottom for 10 minutes or so and then cast again.

Artificial lures are also effective on springtime stripers. The most common and most popular is the white bucktail jig in the 3-to-4-inch size weighing 1/2 to 1 ounce. Just cast these as far as you can and reel them in fast enough to keep them out of the rocks. **A few fishers use lighter bucktail grubs and let them drift naturally with the current.** But that method assures continual breakoffs in the rocks. Although white is the standard color, yellow and chartreuse also work well.

Another lure which is effective is the Rat-L-Trap in either the quarter-ounce or half-ounce size and in one of the chrome colors. Chartreuse works well when the water is stained. Rat-L-Traps cast a long distance and they have the best action when they're reeled rapidly.

Topwater poppers will also catch stripers—especially early and late in the day. The key to catching stripers on top is to select a lure which creates a lot of noise and a lot of splash. Move the lure in a rapid, jerking motion.

Many of the standard diving plugs—especially in the bone and chartreuse colors—will consistently catch stripers. But use the larger sizes or the white perch will get to the lures first.

White Perch

These hand-size fish sometimes get as large as a pound and are highly respected table fare. In the spring they're everywhere and it's not unusual to catch several dozen in an outing.

White perch will hit bloodworms or earthworms fished either on the bottom or beneath a float. They'll also hit a wide variety of small artificial lures—most anything that swims or flashes or undulates through the water. But the lure's color does often seem to matter.

One effective way of determining a proper color is to tie on two sixteenth-ounce grubs of different colors a foot apart. If you don't get bites quickly, switch to two other colors. Keep switching until you catch fish. The grubs are best when fished in a natural drift—wiggling them slight-

Bob Edwards with a white perch caught near Ancarrow's Landing.

ly—just above the bottom. Use 8# line and #8 hooks when fishing for white perch.

Herring

These are the silvery, shiny, slimy fish which arrive in huge schools in April. They will rarely hit lures or bait, but they commonly bite bare gold hooks. Some fishers tie three gold hooks—size #8—on their lines at the same time. The members of the herring family average about a half-pound, but the hickory shad and American shad get larger. American shad sometimes reach four or five pounds. The shad will not usually hit the bare hooks but will bite tiny grubs. Tackle stores sell appropriate grubs known generically as shad darts. White and chartreuse seem to be the best colors.

Herring from Mayo's Bridge.

The bigger shad are most often found in or beside deeper water—often on the edge of a dropoff next to an area with swift current. American shad are still uncommon in the James, but due to stocking procedures they're coming back.

SUMMER ON THE TIDAL JAMES

On a given sunny May Saturday Mayo's Bridge will likely have 50 fishers on it. On a sunny July Saturday there will likely be fewer than five. When June arrives the last of the migratory fish depart, and the Tidal James seems relatively empty. But it still contains good populations of some fish: catfish, holdover stripers, crappie, and largemouth bass. Two of these can be caught with regularity: catfish and crappie.

Crappie

This one's easy: live minnows beneath floats around cover. Use small minnows on #6 hooks and lower them among fallen trees, alongside pilings and walls, and in shaded areas. Use a float to vary the depth. Crappie suspend at various depths—sometimes for no apparent reason. Generally, the brighter the day, the deeper they'll be. Watch the float for a gentle bite, then lift quickly. Tidal

James crappie average a half-pound, but one-pounders are common.

Catfish

This is the bread-and-butter fish of the Tidal James. Just toss out almost any sort of cut bait—from chicken livers to shrimp to herring—and you'll more than likely get a catfish bite before long. Use #2 or larger hooks, 20# line, and a large enough weight to keep your bait on the bottom. Don't be concerned about high or muddy water; catfish feed by smell and will bite in the worst of conditions. **Be prepared for a giant blue catfish to grab your hook when you're using fresh cut fish.** Blues weighing 40 pounds and more inhabit the Tidal James in Richmond.

Catfishing in the Tidal James. Mayo's Bridge in background.

WINTER ON THE TIDAL JAMES

Catfish continue to bite all winter. Use the same methods as in summer, but fish in the deeper areas, and wait longer for bites.

Crappie also continue to bite all winter—even on the coldest, starkest days. You'll find the crappie huddled in areas which don't get much current.

Other Fish

You will of course catch some fish other than the ones discussed here. You'll catch an occasional largemouth in the Upper James and an occasional smallmouth in the Tidal James. You'll have a day every now and then when you'll catch several largemouths on the Tidal James in the Richmond area. You'll see large carp and large gars in both the Upper and Tidal James. You'll catch a striper every now and then in the Upper James, and if you're very lucky you might catch a walleye anywhere in the James.

Bluegills are fairly common in the Tidal James, and warmouths are common in some isolated locations in the Upper James. Every few years someone even catches a trout in the Upper James. And a couple of sturgeon were even documented near the I-95 Bridge in 1991. Although these "other" fish inhabit the urban stretch of the James River, you'll probably want to concentrate your efforts on the patterns and methods described earlier.

A Dozen Fishing Tips for the Urban James

Each of the following tips does work well. The author has experienced each first-hand.

1. Use fingernail polish to paint red eyes on grubs you use for smallmouths.
2. Tie a two-inch white grub 18 inches behind your Rat-L-Trap when fishing for stripers.
3. Use live minnows for crappie at the lock gates in Great Shiplock Park—especially in the winter when there are spots of ice on the water.
4. When fishing for smallmouths in the Upper James try a #2 silver Mepps Aglia with a white hair tail, but use scissors to trim the hair flush with the curve of the treble hooks.
5. Fish where you see Great Blue Herons.
6. Squirt Fish Formula on your grubs when fishing for white perch.
7. Use white six-inch worms on quarter-ounce jig heads when fishing for springtime stripers.
8. Pinch splitshots on the line above diving plugs to give them neutral buoyancy when fishing the Tidal James for stripers.
9. Jig a silver spoon in deep water when the Tidal James stripers won't seem to bite anything else.
10. Throw topwater poppers into the very midst of the rapids just above Mayo's Bridge when fishing for springtime stripers.
11. Throw four-inch purple worms along the grasslines in the upper James when fishing for smallmouths.
12. Use tiny grubs in the early spring to catch a variety of fish from the canals at Pumphouse Park.

August 23, 1983

On some days the urban James yields a bounty other than fish.

We filter ourselves into the wilted waters on a record-high Sunday. 103 degrees. Cookie-baking weather. With a little grease the river's rocks could fry a henhouse.

The river has exhaled and deflated and become an emaciated corpse with a protruding bouldered skeleton. Its lifeblood—a green-clear fluid from distant highlands—has slowed to a puny cadence. Its fish sulk in solemn pools, and are exposed to dangerous shallows and fearsome flats.

Rob tosses a spinning rod, I a fly rod. We leap stones, hopscotch across hundreds of yards, wade to our knees in brisk passages, and swelter in the late summer heat.

I cast a Whitlock Eelworm—a weighted streamer with a brown hackle tail. When stripped through the water it looks like an undulating worm. Last week I caught a fine smallmouth on it. Today I will catch nothing.

I pull it through lone pools, among rapid rocks, below undercut boulders and across wicked weeds. The fly is hard to cast. It is so heavy that I must wait an extra count on the backcast and then use firm forearm force to sling it properly. It crashes in a panic, certainly seeming an unknown bomb to unsuspecting fish.

Dave Whitlock himself tied the fly. It found its way into my box many years ago in New York. But the Eelworm, even though it bears the Whitlock touch, doesn't receive today's fishy respect.

Rob and I submit to the grinning sun and we put our rods aside to join the river. In a yard-deep rapid—a buffered low-water rapid—we sit on the pebbled bottom and relax as the river sponges the perspiration from us. Only our heads protrude from the river's surface, and they bob occasionally under.

We sit for the proverbial eternity, eyes dripping and melting into our cheeks, mouths askew and bubbling forth cerebral passages about the world's problems. We solve many of them there as our fingers dig into the graveled riverbed. We escape the horrid heat of the day, the tiny torments of life, the daily decision of which grocery line to stand in.

Eventually we rise and once again scramble across the fried-egg-splattered boulders and back into life's fold. The fish weren't biting anyway.

Fly Fishing

There is fly fishing and there is fishing with a fly rod. Fly fishing is using a fly rod to cast and fish lures (not bait) that are MEANT for a fly rod. Fishing with a fly rod is using a fly rod as a vehicle for all sorts of lures and bait. This essay refers to fly fishing.

First a few words about the fundamental plusses and minuses of fly fishing on the urban James.

If you think you will catch more fish with a fly rod you are wrong. If you think there are even isolated occasions when a fly rod will outfish all other methods on the urban James, you are still wrong. So, **if your primary goal is to catch as many fish as possible on the urban James, you shouldn't fly fish.**

There are two things people seem to enjoy most about fly fishing: its physical beauty, and the depth and richness of its context. Compared to other rods, a fly rod is long and willowy and slow and graceful. Its bend—whether during the cast or while retrieving a fish—can be pleasing to watch and feel. The fly rod's line is highly visible, and you can actually SEE it in the air as it makes its loop during the cast. There is indeed an aesthetic pride in watching a long, tight loop glide parallel to the water. Other lines are meant to be invisible, and  other rods don't bend much compared to a fly rod. So the physical beauty of the rod and the line are unrivaled.

Fly fishing's rich context includes a historic tradition dating back more than 300 years, fine literature written by a long line of poetic writers, hand-made rods and flies and reels whose makers receive Stradivarian respect, an infectious interest in the lives of the insects which inspire the artificial "flies," and finally a gigantic gaggle of gadgets and gizmos designed to hang from the fly fisher's vest.

Beauty and context are the reasons to fly fish.

There is another reason fly fishers sometimes offer: The fish are too easy to catch with other methods; I fly fish because it offers a greater challenge. This is not only wrong, but it is also unfair in that it implies that other types of fishers are less skilled and less interested in the challenge. There is a well-known story in fishing literature about a man who dies and awakens alongside a gorgeous trout stream in the afterlife. On his first cast with his fly rod he catches a three-pound trout. On his second cast he catches another big trout and he decides he must be in Heaven. He catches a large trout on his third, fourth and fifth casts, and on all the others too. Soon he realizes that he is not in Heaven. Fishers soon tire if there is no challenge.

Another author writes about the three ascending phases for fishers. In the first phase the fisher's goal is to catch the most fish. In the second phase the fisher's goal is to catch the largest fish. In the third phase the fisher's goal is to catch the most difficult fish. These three phases are available to all sorts of fishers—not just fly fishers. **Fly fishers as well as other fishers make their own challenges, and the difficulty levels of those challenges are equal among the various rod types.** Certainly it is much more difficult to catch a five-pound striper in the urban James on a dry fly than on a Rat-L-Trap, but certainly it is much more difficult to catch a rainbow trout in the Madison River on a Rat-L-Trap than on a dry fly. To put it simply and honestly and fairly: it all depends.

Good advice for beginning fly fishers on the James is to use an 8 1/2-foot rod, an 8-weight tapered ("weight-forward") line, an 8-foot 8-pound leader, and a handful of basic flies: a tiny topwater popper, a muddler-type fly, a white or silvery streamer, and a big nymph. Ask advice on specific flies from other fly fishers or from the salespeople at retail shops which specialize in fly fishing equipment.

The Upper James in Richmond is a fly fisher's dream water. It's shallow enough to wade, it has enough boulders to hop long distances, and it is so wide that you can always find room for the longest backcasts. And the scenery is gorgeous: clear water, colorful trees, abundant waterfowl, gentle rapids, and the absence of shoreline houses and docks. There are many areas of the river where your line of sight encompasses only nature and is absent of manmade structures.

Wade in anywhere on the Upper James with a fly rod and a small popper and you'll likely catch fish.

One caveat: you'll never get a bite fly fishing in the Upper James in the colder months.

September 26, 1995

by Ralph White

In the tallest trees huge flocks of Grackles and Blackbirds have begun their autumn rooting rituals. On the lawn around the James River Park Visitor's Center small flocks of Robins pick at the newly softened earth. Goldenrod and several kinds of sunflowers splash the meadows with the first broad brush strokes of fall color. After all the heat and bugs of summer, this is the time to get back out into nature!

In the daytime, look for migrating monarch butterflies. Try the Floodwall Walk on a bright and sunny day with a little wind. On an overcast day, look for preying mantises and their styrofoam-like egg cases on low bushes along the meadow trails. If there hasn't been rain for awhile, check out the drifts of flat spider webs on the low evergreens and tall grasses near the Visitor's Center. Each has a silken funnel at one edge and a gaudily striped grass spider inside. (You might coax one out with a gentle touch of a grass stem to the web!)

Mr. Williams

It's Mayday, 1996, and I head out into a suppertime group of 14th Street Bridge fishers. A dozen or so are scattered across the bridge, hanging their lines downstream into the James. I intend to get an interview and some photographs.

The first man is tall and about my age. He has dark skin and wears a black windbreaker. He is friendly until I say I want to photograph him. "No way."

The next fisher is an older man—small, skinny, tanned and weathered, with no visible teeth. His eyes are narrow and set. He moves his rod with a gentle pump, maneuvering a lure of some sort. He knows what he's doing. But his response to my request for an interview is to ask how much money I'm offering. Then he tells me, "Talk to the fat boy down there." I see another man fifty feet away. "He don't know nothing about fishing, but he'll talk to you."

The "fat boy" isn't fat. But he's young—maybe 25. He too refuses my request. He says it's because he's wearing a company shirt—a white work shirt with the company name above the pocket—and it's against company rules to have a photo taken in the company shirt. He says it as if I should have known about this rule.

The fourth person I ask says yes.

James Williams grew up in Richmond and has fished from this bridge for 15 or 20 years. "The spring is the best time—around the 15th of March until the 15th of May," he reveals with a calm smile.

James Williams on Mayo's Bridge.

Mr. Williams is older than I, but not much. He agreed to my interview out of politeness. He is glad to help.

"After that there's just nothing much in here," he continues. "They go back to the salt water."

It's 6:30 in the evening and although rush hour is an hour behind us, traffic still whizzes across this bridge. The little sidewalk on which the fishers stand isn't wide. Cars speed by an arm's length away. Mr. Williams doesn't seem to notice.

"You got mostly anything this time of year: rocks, largemouth bass, smallmouth bass, herring, perch, catfish, mullet."

"Which kind do you like catching most?" I ask him.

"Mostly herring and perch."

I ask about the stripers, rockfish. "Well, you can't get them up," he pauses, looks at the river, "unless you're using about 50- or 75-pound test line. Some people try to use nets to get them up."

As we talk Mr. Williams calmly untangles a glob of line at the tip of one of his spinning rods. I see that there are three hooks in the tangle. He looks up at me to answer my questions.

"Well, you have to catch the tides. High tides, incoming tides, or outgoing tides."

"What about dead low tide?" "Never!" he responds immediately. "You might catch a little small perch or something like that."

There is plenty of action on this bridge. Not only are there 12 fishers and continual cars, but gulls scream constantly. The fishers reel up a steady stream of perch. I watch one lady lift two up on the same line. I've left my own rod is in the car. The only way I can conduct an interview is to leave my rod behind. Otherwise I'd be fishing.

"Now when they're really biting good," Mr. Williams replies to another question, "you catch them every five or ten minutes. **You just catch them as fast as you can put in there when they're really biting.** I usually fish about two or three hours and then I leave."

There are white buckets scattered along the bridge near the fishers. I assume they contain fish. There is one near Mr. Williams and in a minute I'll look into it.

"I eat mostly everything I catch off here."

"You ever catch any crappie here?"

"Crappie? Oh yeah. They're mostly around the edges." He means the rocks that line the south shoreline here. Two days ago I caught a little crappie on a chartreuse jig along the rocks.

"Do you ever see any big fish swimming along when the water's clear?"

"Oh yeah." Mr. Williams' eyes widen. "You see a lot of large ones—what do they call them? Garfish!"

"You ever hook one?"

"Yeah, but there's nothing you can do with them. They tear your stuff all to pieces. You can catch carp too, but you can't get them up either."

Downstream there are three or four boats in the water. I have often wondered what the accepted etiquette is regarding boats fishing below this bridge.

"Oh yeah, the boats come up here." Mr. Williams glances at the boats downstream beneath the I-95 bridge. "Actually they don't worry about you. Sometimes they get right under—just where you're casting." He peers over the concrete railing. "They can catch the same fish down there around those other bridges," he nods towards I-95, "but instead of fishing over there they come over here."

I ask about bait.

"**Bloodworms, earthworms, and gold hooks. Gold hooks for the herring and for the perch too.**"

Mr. Williams always puts at least two hooks on his line. Sometimes he uses three. He ties a big weight at the bottom, and the hooks are tied on with leaders up above, about a foot apart. I examine his hooks and see that they are gold snelled hooks, about size #4.

"They bite both hooks about equal. But it all depends. Sometimes they'll run deep. I just cast out, watch the line, and reel it in a little."

I don't see any tacklebox full of lures.

"Artificials? Not from up here. You can't handle them."

I ask about his knowledge about other fishing locations on the urban James.

"I have fished down by the Annabel Lee. It was right nice, but it's not too good. Some people go down there, but I don't bother anymore since they started doing that work on things." There is some revamping going on and there is now a fence that limits the fishing space.

"Does this bridge ever get crowded?"

"Oh sure. In the spring of the year mostly when the season first begins a lot of people come out here. **Sometimes on Sundays you can't hardly get a space to stand.**"

In his bucket are 15 or 20 white perch. Some are large—a half-pound and heavier. He has two spinning rods, one with a two-hook rig and one with three hooks. Mr. Williams wears brown pants, a beige jacket and an olive green hat.

"Sometimes my wife will come down here. But mostly she likes saltwater fishing."

"What's your line of work?"

"I'm retired," he responds with a sense of pride. "I retired in 1989. Next January 4 I'll be 70 years old." He looks 20 years younger.

Mr. Williams tells me he used to fish this stretch years ago in his brother's boat. He tells me that although some people fish here at night, that doesn't interest him. He goes on in when it gets dark. We talk 15 minutes or so, and he untangles the three-hook rig the whole time. As our interview ends, he completes the untangling. He looks this way and that as I instruct him for photographs. We shake hands as I thank him for his time. As I walk back along the bridge to my car, he baits his hooks.

I pass other fishers, one of them lifting a perch as I go by. My steps quicken and I hurry for my rod to get in a possible hour of fishing before I have to leave.

January 31, 1982

From the top of the tower I can see through the bare trees to the river. The white January snow simplifies the terrain, and **far up- and downstream the thick riverbank forest is composed of thin, ash-gray trunks and branches which seem to harbor no life.** How different was the lush, green tangle which prohibited my view of the August James.

I wear chest-high waders, and their rubber soles are slick on the layers of ice which cover the concrete steps leading down into James River Park. Once down the tower, I walk briskly across the snow, and quickly reach the bouldered shoreline of the urban James.

Upstream to my left I watch cars cautiously creep across the Boulevard Bridge. The drivers are too busy avoiding ice patches to gaze downstream at a solitary fisher. Nevertheless I return their unoffered glances and consider my summertime goal of catching a fish from the tall bridge's pedestrian walkway.

The James flows swiftly in front of me. **It is high, swollen not with darkened mud from upstream farmlands, but with dazzling clear fluids from a month of snow and ice.** The river spreads onto my normally dry stepping rocks, and I leap precariously as I approach my fishing hole.

I wade knee-deep to cross a flattened boulder which is more accustomed to beach towels and oily bodies than to icy snow waters.

I reach my fishing spot and tie a tiny Beetle Spin to the thin line. Perhaps a hungry smallmouth will budge from his dormant hideout to inhale a flashing minnow. In October I put numbered tags on three of the fish in this modest glide. The one I pulled from behind the mid-current boulder was almost fifteen inches. Maybe he'll be the one to make this day a success.

I throw the Beetle Spin to vacant waters. I heave it all the way to the white cascade which feeds my spot. I retrieve it slowly, deeply, pulsatingly among the currents and crosscurrents. **I let it flutter into the eddies, bounce on the bottom, dive and dart within hidden crevices.** But the fish, if there are indeed any, are not willing.

I see two hawks circling high, a quarter of a mile apart, on the north shoreline. They are the first birds of any sort I have seen today. They are too far for me to identify. Three gulls fly westward, upstream, a hundred feet above the middle of the river. They are white and have gray wings with darkened tips. I must refer to my field guide when I return home. I see one other bird, much later, a lone duck of some sort. It flies low against the tree line, and I see only the silhouette.

The fishing is good but the catching is awful, and I turn to make my way back to the shore. I leap from boulder to boulder, and wade within the swift currents only when I must. From afar the bank looks quite different than it ever before has. **This is my first snow-covered venture onto the James.**

As I near dry land I see that my return route has obviously been somewhat different. I am confronted with a narrow band of deep water which I must cross. On the other side is a magnificently beautiful ice-crusted boulder. The ice has formed a tin-soldier row of icicles which overhang on my side of the boulder. Beneath the icicles is another row, and beneath that, another. They form three elegant tiers of an ice cathedral. I assume that each layer has resulted from an isolated day of above-freezing temperatures.

I realize that I must jump across and onto that ice cathedral in order to reach the shore. The water looks too deep to wade. And I see no other route.

I toss my fishing rod gently across. I plant my feet within secure holds, bend my knees, and spring forward. My feet land, as planned, on top of the icicled overhang. But, as the weight of my body crashes down, a crack slices through the ice in front of me. It widens and rumbles and I grab for the deep snow on top of the boulder. **I pull myself up as hundreds of pounds of sparkling ice crash into the river.** I erase a mental note to return later with my camera to photograph the ice cathedral. It floats downstream towards the Lee Bridge.

The January James is not generous with its living offerings. Not even the Bitternut Hickory tree which stands at the base of the entrance tower displays any leavings.

Fred Murray

Fred Murray is one of a very few urban James fishing gurus. He knows the fish of this section of the James as well as anyone. He is willing to share general knowledge, but unwilling to share the precise details of his fishing strategies. He is aware of what all of us who fish know: once you share a true fish-catching secret, it will quickly become widespread knowledge and too many fish will be caught and not released.

Fred recalls as recently as the mid-1970s that he would see no more than a half-dozen other fishers on the urban James all summer. Back then he could catch quality smallmouths almost at will, and four-pounders were not uncommon. Fred believes the decline of quality smallmouths is due specifically to fishing pressure and fishing knowledge. He believes that once people learned that a live minnow drifted through a smallmouth lair would cause the fish to bite, the decline in large fish was inevitable.

Nevertheless Fred was willing to share some general knowledge for this publication.

Flathead Catfish There is no big secret to catching flatheads. Drift live bait through rocky areas, or use a Carolina rig and tightline it downstream. Flatheads are now numerous in the James.

Blue Catfish The blues are hard to figure out from year to year. One year they'll adopt a certain pattern in certain areas, and the next year they'll have abandoned them. There is debate on why there are huge (40+ pounds) blues above 14th Street. Blues that big need a lot of food to survive, and there is much more food available in the tidal James (below 14th Street) than in the shallow, upper James. One thought is that the blues run upstream at times of high water and they go back down when the water is lower. But huge blues have been caught upstream during very low water. **The blues are highly predatory and they like live bait.** But you can't predict where they'll be: sometimes they'll be in water only a couple of feet deep, and at other times they'll be in the deep holes.

Smallmouths Fred doesn't fish for smallmouths nearly as much as he did 20 years ago. He says it's different now that so many people are fishing for them. He enjoyed the days when they were a shared secret by only a few fishers. Two ways to catch them now are by drifting a properly presented live minnow, and drifting a Yamamoto grub by letting it move with the current just like a live minnow would.

Walleyes Fred has caught several walleyes, but mostly when fishing for something else. Through the years he has tried several times to catch walleye but has never discovered a successful pattern.

Crappie There are plenty of crappie below 14th Street, and the pattern is simple: live minnows or tiny grubs fished in brushpiles and alongside other cover. The first time Fred ever fished off the 14th Street Bridge he reeled in several huge crappie from alongside the pilings.

Stripers These are Fred's favorites in the urban James. About eight years ago he put his boat in at Ancarrow's

Typical Tidal James crappie.

Landing one spring morning and proceeded to catch 200 stripers up to 12 pounds. That day they were everywhere. When they're that numerous they'll hit virtually anything. He recommends bucktail jigs, Zara Spooks, and poppers. When he fishes bucktail jigs he lets them sort of drift with the current—like a trout fisher fishes a nymph. When the stripers are not actively feeding he locates them on his fishfinder and vertically jigs a metal spoon.

Spring Fish

Bob and I hit a perfect river on April 22, 1996. We fished eight hours on the stretch of the tidal James below 14th Street.

The ramp at Ancarrow's was not muddy and not crowded. The river's clarity was just what you want: not that middle-of-the-summer crystal clarity, but not that spring-rain dinginess. Somewhere in between, leaning towards the clear side. The day was sunny, reaching the 80's. The wind was from the south. And Bob's boat and trolling motor ran well even though they'd been idle since our New Year's outing.

Bob Edwards with a Tidal James largemouth caught near Ancarrow's Landing.

And finally, we were fortunate enough to be blessed with an auspicious beginning. Those are usually good luck for me. Just as I had set one foot on the bow of the boat to push us away from the concrete walkway at Ancarrow's my pocket rang. I pulled out the cell phone and answered.

"What are you up to today?" A colleague from work.

"I'm just this second launching a boat for a day of fishing," I answered. I pushed the bow, stepped aboard, and we drifted out into the current. I gave Bob the just-a-minute signal.

"That's great," my colleague responded. "I'm glad you're going to get in some fishing today. You're going to get some good weather."

"I hope so," I responded quickly, trying to put some let-me-off-this-phone body language into my tone of voice. Bob had the key in the ignition, ready to crank the motor. I gave him the just-a-minute signal again. I looked at my watch.

My colleague kept me on the line 10 minutes. Precious fishing minutes as our boat drifted downstream with the current. Precious minutes of doing what I'd waited to do since January. Precious minutes of Bob waiting to do what he'd wanted to do since he'd had his hip replaced in February. He'd circled this date on his calendar for the target date to be out on the water again, and he was here now ready to go with a brand new hip and itchy fishing fingers ready to fling a Rat-L-Trap or a Power Worm.

"Well, you have a good day and I'll talk with you tomorrow," he finally concluded. I don't know what he said in between. I was too busy scanning the river's surface, looking at all that ripe water waiting for me and Bob. But the phone call provided good luck. We caught a lot of fish. And we saw interesting things.

The fish: **we caught largemouth bass, stripers, white perch, American shad, bluegill, and catfish—all on artificials, most within sight of downtown Richmond.**

The interesting things: we saw a Bald Eagle, a man rowing, a crew rowing, an Osprey with a fish, a Turkey, and two jerks in a Jon boat.

The largemouth were few and far between. We spent the first few hours attempting to find a pattern, but we couldn't. Bob caught the first one: a one-pounder near a shoreline fence which hit a blue-fleck Power Worm. I caught the largest: a two-and-a-half-pounder from behind a rock which hit a big chartreuse crankbait into which I'd drilled holes and added more weight to make it neutrally buoyant. Surprisingly we didn't catch even one bass on a Rat-L-Trap.

A natural color Shad-Rap—the smaller size—produced a variety of fish during one little stretch of shoreline: a bass, a bluegill, and a two-pound channel cat. The little Shad-Rap looks just like a minnow and it dives about five feet on thin line. Later Bob caught a couple of white perch on a large orangeish Shad-Rap near the I-95 Bridge. Nothing would hit my natural color lure up there.

The Turkey was the first Turkey I'd ever seen in the wild. I heard him as we threw our lures against a downriver shoreline. I thought it was a squirrel, but then he came into view. On the other side of the river a man rowed by in a long, thin shell. Simultaneously a Bald Eagle soared a few circles above the treeline. I kept hoping he'd fly directly above us, but he didn't. Must be nesting over there somewhere.

It was Bob who cracked the code on the white perch. Up in that swift and shallow water near the I-95 Bridge I knew there were schools and schools of white perch. This was the time of year. Usually they'll hit little grubs, and I tried several colors: black, white, pink, smoke. I also tried a spoon, a small Rat-L-Trap, the Shad-Rap, even a Super Duper. But no white perch.

Bob tied on a tiny chartreuse grub and after he'd caught his third white perch I put one on too. We ended up catching between 50 and 100 fish on those little lures. Mostly white perch, but a couple of bonuses. Bob caught a tiny striper on one of the grubs and also a small shad. I caught two large American shad on the chartreuse grub; they must have gone almost two pounds each. And I hooked and lost another. Near the end of the day a very large fish bit Bob's grub, and it bent his rod for five minutes before it finally got off. We never saw it.

The author with an April shad caught near the Annabel Lee.

There was one spot where we caught a lot of fish. It was just downstream from that group of rocks that sticks up in the middle of the river just upstream from the Annabel Lee. Mostly we stayed 50 yards downstream from the rocks. The water is 15 feet deep there with shallows on both sides. On the depth finder I could see white perch hovering near the bottom.

We fished the grubs deep there, but we also threw Rat-L-Traps and crankbaits up towards the rocks. The bigger bass hit my chartreuse crankbait there on my first cast. I also caught a striper there on a Rat-L-Trap. That striper as well as the one I caught later up under the I-95 Bridge on the chartreuse crankbait were both about two pounds. They looked 10 pounds as I reeled them to the surface, but my digital scale confirmed their true weights.

It was behind the rocks that we saw the two jerks in a Jon boat. This was a Monday and there were very few boats on the river. That is, there was plenty of room to find a good fishing spot. At any rate, we were there catching fish about 50 feet from the pile of midriver rocks and two guys in a Jon boat pulled in in front of us, not 20 feet away. They didn't say anything, just proceeded pull in front of us and fish the spot where we were casting. These days you see that happen from time to time on weekends. It always makes you angry. Bob and I just cranked the engine and went on upriver to another area.

I'm still trying to figure out the perfect thing to say or

do in that situation. I try to stay away from confrontations about unimportant things, and it's never been my nature to say anything to inconsiderate fishers. Still, it bothers me that I can't think of something to say to shame them into not doing it again.

Once when Kelly and Thomas were little, the three of us were in a boat catching stripers while anchored near a jetty on the James. We'd cast to the jetty and reel back in. This was on a weekday and I had not seen even one other boat on the river. A boat appeared and the guy proceeded to pull into the spot between our boat and the jetty—right in the middle of our casting path. But of course I didn't say anything. We just left the area. **According to my own philosophy concerning life's mysteries, fishing spots are not among the things worth fighting for.** But still . . .

Later downriver we saw a rowing crew going upstream. And I saw an Osprey circling as if to land. At first I thought there was a muskrat in its mouth, but when it glided close by I could see it was a herring. It's hard to do a James River outing without seeing Ospreys.

The trolling motor blew a fuse about 7:30 p.m. while we were still catching fish and we decided to call it a day even though there was still another half hour of daylight left.

That day we learned what people learn every year on the urban James: **if you're fortunate enough to schedule a day of fishing on a non-muddy mid-April day, you have the opportunity to catch a lot of fish.** April is the month of abundance in the tidal James. The spring runs of white perch, stripers, shad and herring are in full force. The bass have emerged from their winter patterns. The shoreline fish are beginning to awaken. And the flora and fauna are blooming and mating and feeding and showing themselves.

JOHN BRYAN

Belle Isle Quarry Pond

Located near the western tip of Belle Isle, this gorgeous little pond is bordered by the main path on one side and by a rocky bluff on the other. It also has a dock which is accessible by wheelchair. The pond is 19 feet deep, is usually quite clear, and has been stocked by the Virginia Department of Game and Inland Fisheries. Largemouth bass and bluegill are its most catchable fish. Although you'll be tempted, do not try to walk around the bluff side of the pond. Footing is treacherous and tricky, and it is an easy matter to experience a dangerous fall.

August 8, 1983

My fly rod sampled the James River for the first time on a steaming August Saturday. My long rod, lean and limber, lofted lengths of grease-laden line.

The James was created with the fly rod in mind. Its very name, James, connotes the degree of royalty one traditionally attributes to the long rod—certainly much more so than those unfortunate waters named Ohoopee, Muddy and Turkey.

Its rushing white waters, swirling eddies and frothy boulders harbor seasoned fish which wait cautiously for drifting insects and nymphs. The fish respond to willowy, wetted, feathered foolers and to buoyant, corky, rubber-legged floaters. They know their summertime treats, and they feed on the river valley's healthy hatches and on the mimicry of artificial flies.

The James is also known for its silent viridian glides, stretching and oozing upstream and down, layering themselves in drunken courses, caressing golden sands, tickling grassy flats and massaging round-shouldered boulders. Dry flies alight gently and float proudly and majestically on these princely waters.

My own flies took the place of Meppses and Beetle Spins last Saturday at dusk. How frustrating it was for me at first—unable to shoot a quick line beneath an overhanging branch or drop a lure deeply among an undercut boulder. But how pleasantly satisfying it became as the floating popper began to be slurped into hungry jaws.

My rod is an 8 1/2-foot stick of gorgeous graphite, a gift from a distant friend, and it throws a high and graceful loop of tapered line. That loop melted into Saturday's thick dusk, and it transported my bright yellow popper to dozens of frisky redbreasts and smallmouths.

Every fish brought out the true beauty of the fly rod: the wonderfully dazzling arch. One 14-inch smallmouth sculpted the rod into a bend beneath which you could have erected a French Gothic cathedral. A hand-size redbreast curved the rod into a gentle John Hancock curlicue.

The evening was a fine one—one which will settle into my memory and carve an ever growing niche which will ripen with the years.

"Yes I remember the James," I'll tell my grandchildren. "Many an evening I'd drop a tiny Cahill on the end of a 6X tippet onto that sparkling river and pull out dozens of bass and redbreasts. Those fish would leap and somersault and do a thousand tricks among that river's quick currents. What I'd give for just one more hour in a 1980s dusk."

October 8, 1984

The leaves are changing. **Oranges and yellows and reds festoon the shores of this Sunday morning October James River.** Fall freshets have begun to fatten it for frosty days, and it has inhaled a bellyful of cool autumn rain.

I step into it, without waders, and my jeans soak it into my surprised legs. My plastic thermometer measures a swift current: 62 degrees. Another five degrees and it'll be bracing.

My lure and line are small: a yellow Garland jig on 4-pound Stren. They travel far and fine and search the rising pools.

This river is full of life now. It's fall, and the few river walleye are moving. The big creek chub minnows are finning in schools upstream. Two weeks ago I caught two dozen chubs. Each was a floppy, flipping cigar; some were 12 inches. One giant weighs a pound now in my memory. There are a few small shad planing the boulders in half-dozen schools, flashing silver into fishers' eyes.

The unshaded shores are wildflowered, sprinkled with Aster and Tickseed Sunflower. The skies are ducky, and I spy an Osprey winging strong with a taloned meal.

The first fish on my line is a smallmouth. It's like the dozen that will follow in these two hours: small. The largest I'll see this morning won't reach 12 inches.

Next there's a redbreast, and another. Twenty will grab the yellow grub on this morning. They are strong fish. **At the end of the line they fight sideways, they gallop beneath rocks, they charge into swift rapids.**

I catch only one of the creek chubs today. Its mouth is small, and is beneath the head. Its head is speckled with knotty bumps. It's a fish modest of beauty.

Beneath a huge rocky shelf my line dangles and is snapped off by an unseen fish—perhaps a walleye or a catfish. I feel only the first yank.

The river is sad today. Next week, or perhaps the next, its greening glides will be graced with leafy flotsams of Sycamore and Poplar, Beech and Oak. Its cooling waters will calm the fishes. Its shores will undress, and its big boulders will be absent of sunners, swimmers, singers and seekers.

A month from now I'll drive home across the afterwork Nickel Bridge and see a naked winter water.

The First Striper

Somebody has to catch the first striper from the urban James each spring. I mean, something has to precede those warm April afternoons when the stripers are gulping topwater poppers and slurping underwater bucktails and gobbling bottom-digging crankbaits. Before mid-April is early April, and before that is late March, and before that is mid-March, and before that is early March. And that's when somebody has to catch the first striper.

I try it on a thirties Sunday afternoon in early March on the south side of Mayo's Bridge—down along the rocks at the base of the Floodwall. There is still snow on the rocks, and teen and twenty nighttimes have left frozen puddles between the rocks. I wear gloves and a stocking cap.

A sunny Sunday, an hour before sunset, and I am the only fisher. The only one. Nobody lobbing big sinkers from the bridge above. Nobody anchored out in the eddies of the pilings. Nobody jumping these shoreline rocks. Nobody on the island.

I start with a white plastic eel. A wonderful lure of my own creation—just a large Sluggo-type strip in pearl white with a right-angle jig head embedded at the head. The eye of the hook is pushed through the plastic so the eel can't slide on the hook no matter how hard it is cast. The supersharp jig hook is hidden just along the surface of the belly of the eel—deep enough to avoid tangles, shallow enough to pierce the jaw of a hungry striper.

In the water my eel looks terrific. It can dart erratically or it can swim smoothly—depending on what I do with the rod tip. And it sinks just enough for the swift current of this area of the urban James—fast enough to get down into the thick of things, slowly enough to avoid the bottom. Surely this will be the lure to attract the first striper.

The river looks void of life. No shoreline minnows, no gulls above, not even a Great Blue Heron in the shallows. The gulls are all downstream; I can see them drifting below the I-95 bridge. Drift down and fly back up. Drift down and fly back up. Why always below that particular bridge? My bridge, Mayo's Bridge—aka 14th Street Bridge—has me for its only sign of life.

The river is just the right level, just the right clarity. Clear enough to see a foot and a half below the surface—not that crystal clear low-water state that makes the fish wary. High enough to gently cover all the good rapids, but not so high to make it unfishable. If you had to rate the river's clarity and depth fishability on a scale today, everyone who knows anything would rate it a 10.

A dozen casts with the eel produce nothing. **I fantasize a huge striper following it to the shore, and with each retrieve I look hard into the water through my polarized glasses.** These are the expensive ones Janet gave me four years ago—the first pair I've been able to hold on to. The first pair I haven't sat on or dropped into the lake or lost. I did sort of lose them last fall—left them in a rental car in Nashville—but Dollar Car Rental sent them back to me in a bubble-packed tube good as new. When Woolworth's went out of business I bought 15 pairs of plastic polarized glasses that had originally sold for $14 but were marked at $1, and I still have that bagful for when I start losing them again. All fishers have to have their polarized glasses.

A Great Blue Heron lands a hundred yards upstream. Great! They always know where the fish are. I break off the eel and put on a topwater popper. The Heron stands erect in the shallows, his long neck at attention.

The popper is one of those weighted kinds that actually sink unless you keep it moving. **Quick flicks of my wrist make the popper scatter in short bursts across the surface.** You'd think something was chasing a frantic shad. I toss it into the eddies of every rapid I can reach with this long-line spinning rod. The lure's commotion is an announcement that food has arrived. Surely the year's first striper will grab it.

The Heron is now joined by another—50 feet upstream from the first. Great! Two Herons. They must mean business. My watch says five-thirty. I have to be home by six. Sunset is at about six-fifteen. I can be late if they really start biting. I can even call on my little cell phone. (Worth the investment if only to extend one's fishing time past the designated deadline: "I know I'm supposed to be home right now, but I'm in the middle of a once-in-a-lifetime blitz, and I'm going to have to stay another half hour. Listen, did you hear that?" and you splash water with your foot while pointing the phone at it, "That's another big striper. Look, I gotta go. I just wanted to tell you I'm okay and I'll see you in thirty minutes.")

A dozen more casts with the popper go unnoticed. I throw it another dozen times—upstream along the shoreline rocks, downstream along the shoreline rocks, way out in the middle where the current seems to swirl both directions, up against that boulder to the left, down across the flat area to the right. Nothing.

Then I notice a third Great Blue Heron—this one all the way across next to the island. It appears to be standing right in the rapids; it must be on a rock or a slackwater shallow. **Three Herons on a very cold day. They must be here for a reason. There must be baitfish in the water. And stripers must be feeding.**

A big Rat-L-Trap will likely do the trick. I pick a silver one from my thin plastic box. A half-ouncer. The quarter-ouncers are good on the smaller fish; but I'm after the big early fish. Everyone knows the biggest stripers come first. They come often unnoticed and quickly depart for the downstream ocean. I saw a film where they shocked February 20-pounders on the James. Here in Richmond in April you'll see some seven- and even 10-pounders, but the really big ones will have already departed. A big Rat-L-Trap for the big first striper.

The Rat-L-Trap feels perfect. It throbs that tight vibration that all Rat-L-Trap fishers love. And this one doesn't swim to the right or to the left, just straight ahead. Sometimes they'll favor one direction or another, and sometimes, no matter how much you try to adjust the eyelet they'll still not swim straight. But this one does. Perfect. And it casts a mile. Not only is it heavy, but there's something about its aerodynamics that allows it to slice right through the air. A great lure for windy days. My six-foot spinning rod and 16-pound line toss it way out into the

James' currents. I retrieve it almost as fast as I can turn the reel's handle. You can't swim a Rat-L-Trap too fast. I scatter 10 casts which cover a lot of water, but no bites.

A fourth Blue Heron. It's across the way with the third. He looks taller, must be on a higher rock. A while ago there were no Herons here; now there are four. I know from experience that on cold days the hour before dark is when the fish often feed most aggressively. The Herons are hopefully heralding their arrival at the dinner table. Now a fifth one has arrived on my side of the river. We make a line with the afternoon sun: me, Heron, Heron, Heron, sun.

Something hits the Rat-L-Trap just 10 feet out at the end of a long retrieve. I set the hook, lean into the bent rod, and the fish at first comes towards me and then thrusts back into the current. Then towards me again and I see that it is not a fish—just a wad of old fishing line that's caught on a root. Leaning out on an edge-of-the-current rock I'm able to jiggle the Rat-L-Trap loose. Most often such tangles are unforgiving; they steal lures and grow with their greed. At low water you can sometimes find tangles of several lures. When they drained the big lake at Byrd Park I stepped out across the lake's floor and lifted three of my Rat-L-Traps from a wad of line on the backside of what was formerly an underwater stump.

I steer several more casts clear of the root without a bite. Now back to the white eel. It takes me less than 60 seconds to remove my gloves, bite off the Rat-L-Trap, exchange it with the eel in the plastic box, tie on the eel with a looped Palomar knot, bite off the line tag, slip my hands back into my gloves, and be back in business. **When you're in the business of short-time fishing, you can't spend five minutes changing lures.** If they were to hold national time trials for changing lures, I'd pay an entry fee and take my chances. There could be a warm day division, a cold day division, a cold rainy day division, and a snowy windy day division. Those snowy windy days will take a bunch of seconds off your time. Numb fingertips and watery eyes don't help.

Two more Herons are here: another on my side and another on the far side. My eyes are on them as I throw the eel. The most upstream Heron on the far side dips suddenly and comes up with a fish. Bigger than most other Heron fish I've witnessed through the years. From here it appears to be 10 or 12 inches. The

Heron struggles with it, sort of flaps its wings, shakes its head, jumps over to the sandy shore of the island, and works on consuming its prize.

The other Herons stand erect. The downstream one sort of leans out over the water with a cocked head. I cast the eel and watch the Herons. **Any second now the year's first striper is going to hit my lure.** I look down from the Herons at the end of each cast to watch the final few feet of the retrieve—the part where I can actually see my eel swimming back to me, the part where I could see if a frantic striper were to bust it madly at my feet.

A five-pound bass did just that last week during a 10-minute before-dark outing at Byrd Park's Boat Lake. I pulled a giant willowleaf spinnerbait through the winter-dead lily pads, and watched it as it flashed through the stalks. On one cast a huge bass sort of rolled up from the bottom and engulfed the lure right at my feet—right there while I watched. Five pounds is a guess; I didn't have my scale, just a tape—20 inches.

He may have gone six pounds. That's probably what I'll tell people. I'll tell them sort of casually as if it's an everyday occurrence. And I'll wait for them to ask: "Hey John, it's almost spring—you getting' ready to do some fishing'?" "Hope so. I did catch a nice one the other day over at Byrd Park," and I'll wait for their response. "Oh yeah?" "Yep, a six-pounder," and I don't pause here, I just move right on in to the next phrase, "you know those big ones over there move into the pads to feed about this time of year," as if I haven't done anything special.

Now there are ten Herons—six on my side of the river, four on the other. The one that got the fish is now back at his station standing alert. I have five minutes left until I have to leave. Still no first striper. Ten Herons! All in this one general area. You don't see that very often at all, even in the summer. Ten Herons!

I cast faster now and with even greater anticipation. The sun is approaching the horizon, the Herons are poised for food, the river is at perfect depth and clarity, and I'm unencumbered by the crowds of fishers that will be here next month. A perfect setting for the first striper.

The white eel is so gorgeous. It darts wonderfully. I'll have to try it at Kerr for bass. I cast it with confidence each time. I throw it far into the currents and let it sink just the right amount before I start the retrieve. Every so often it'll hit a rock and I'll jerk it off—each time thinking an underwater striper will turn and attack the fleeing fakery. Please, please, please be a striper! Please, fish, come out of the winter quietude and burst into spring frenzy. It is I. I am here waiting. I'll throw you back. I want just one of you. Just one long striper. Just a nice bend in my rod.

My watch says it's time and I throw a final cast—without the first striper—and I wind in and head home.

I know for a fact that people who don't fish don't understand all this: how can you not catch a fish and still enjoy yourself? They think it has to do with being outdoors, being at the riverside, enjoying nature, some sort of spiritual release, communing with the deity. Naaah. Not even close. Not for me.

It's all in the anticipation. If the anticipation level is at a ten, then I'm going to have a great time even if I don't catch a fish. If the anticipation level is at a two or three, I won't have as good of time even if I do catch some fish.

The other ingredient is the difficulty of the game. If it's too easy to crack the code—to discover how to catch them—there's not much satisfaction. But if it's a tough code that you finally crack after two dozen lure changes and two dozen location changes and two dozen retrieve changes and two dozen mental analyses of the ways of the fish, then there is great satisfaction, great fulfillment, great confirmation of your skill at the game.

Gary Kasparov can score points in chess matches against third-graders all day and have a truly lousy time; but he can have a grand time in a two-week match against a multi-computered, seemingly unbeatable super-foe. Against the super-foe is the challenge of uncharted territory, the glorious anticipation of the remote possibility of victory, the joy of unleashing every synapse and electrode of analytical and poetic strategy. Even if he loses, he experiences a million-dollar anticipation and an exhilarating level of difficulty.

That hour-long try for the first striper was right up there at the top of what I enjoy about fishing.

"Did you have fun?" was Janet's greeting when I arrived at home.

"Sure did," I respond with a big smile.

"Did you catch a lot?"

"Didn't get a bite," I respond with a big smile.

Chapter Five:
History

Stand on Mayo's Bridge (14th Street) and look upstream. Those are the rocks and rapids which Christopher Newport and his group of 21 men saw on May 24, 1607. Unable to proceed up the river any farther, this first group of English explorers stopped and planted a wooden cross beneath where you are standing.

Now look downstream. Those are tidal waters which are pushed and pulled by the moon all the way to the Atlantic Ocean. **Great numbers of fish arrive at this bridge every spring and then crowd up through the shallow rapids to reach upriver spawning grounds.**

"The most important factor in the history of Richmond—the reason it was settled both by Indians and by English settlers—is the falls," confirms Dr. Charles F. Bryan, Jr., Director of the Virginia Historical Society. "The area was an important source of sustenance for the Indians, and it was a critical site along the major transportation route used by the settlers."

The James River in Richmond is replete with visible remnants of its history. You'll see them as you enjoy fishing and floating and hiking and biking along the river.

Mayo's Bridge in 1996—the area where Christopher Newport stopped in 1607.

This chapter provides merely an introduction to the river's history. But you'll want to learn more.

Why? **Why do we need to know anything about what happened beneath Mayo's Bridge 390 years ago?** "It is each person's responsibility to have a sense of the history of his community," continues Dr. Bryan. "It's important in both the process of governing and being a neighbor. History provides the essential building blocks for the decisions we make for the present and future."

Now look upstream again and then back downstream and then back upstream again. If it's warm today you're likely to see people enjoying the river in dozens of ways. You'll see clean water, and you'll see plenty of areas accessible to the public. The reason we can enjoy our river is

131

because today's and yesterday's decision-makers for the urban James have had an appreciation of the river and its history.

Just two rules:
1. Continue to increase your knowledge of the history of the urban James River.
2. Don't disturb historic artifacts—no matter how large or small.

Timeline of Richmond's James River
[*This was written by Ralph White and initially published by the James River Park System.*]

1600's and before—Powhatan Indians harvested eight- and nine-foot sturgeon from the river.

1607–1700's—Early colonists sent sailing ships up the James as far as the falls at Mayo's Bridge.

1607—Captain John Smith purchased the land of the falls from Chief Powhatan.

1700's—The river was lined with floating fish traps.

1730's—Earliest industry on the James begun by William Byrd.

1742—William Byrd operated two flour mills in Manchester.

1772—Bateaux shoot the rapids.

1771—The Great Flood crest around 40 feet.

1785—James River Company incorporated to build canal system.

1800—Hollywood Paper Mill established along north bank, serviced by canal in 1887 and became a hydroelectric plant from 1940-1972.

1801—Flour mill established at Tredegar Iron Works site, became an armory in 1802 and Tredegar Iron Works in 1837.

1804—Manchester Mill Canal formed.

1834—Gallego Mills established on the north bank.

1865—14th Street Bridge destroyed by retreating Confederate soldiers after setting fire to Richmond.

1865—Stone and brick sewers installed by the city.

1958—Primary treatment of waste water entering the river begins.

1969—Hurricane Camille, crest 28.6 feet.

1972—Hurricane Agnes, crest 36.5 feet.

1973—Secondary treatment of waste water begins.

1985—Tropical Storm Juan, crest 30.76 feet.

1990's—Fish passage at Williams Dam. Floodwall protects 750 acres of the city. New CSO plan to carry combined sewer overflow closer to sewage plant and out of the James River Park.
Bosher's Dam fishway, migrating fish passage through Richmond.
Renovation of the Kanawha and Haxall Canals.

Thomas Bryan stands in front of the Floodwall beneath markers designating crests of past floods (before the Floodwall's construction).

A Brief History of Canals on the James

During the 19th Century Richmond's main commerce to the western part of the state was via the river and Kanawha Canal. The primary goods that traveled on the canal were lumber, coal, tobacco, corn, wheat, stone and iron ore. But by the turn of the century railroads had taken over.

As America was being settled, rivers provided the easiest access west. Gradually the idea of building canals to connect rivers on both sides of mountains became dominant. This idea was of course dependent on first making the rivers navigable. This included making sluices (channels through shallow areas of the river), diversion dams (to direct water in a certain direction), and riverside canals to bypass difficult areas of the river.

200-year-old canal in Pumphouse Park.

It was in 1765 that the Virginia General Assembly first authorized the building of a canal to bypass the Falls of the James—approximately seven miles from Westham to Richmond. For the next 100 years the Kanawha Canal was an ongoing project along much of the length of the James.

The seven-mile Falls section of the Kanawha Canal was completed in 1795. Virtually all of the work was done by hand. They used hand tools, wagons, and dangerous black powder. Blasting holes were drilled by hand into the rocks.

Always a concern was to build the canal such that it would stay full of water. Feeder dams and feeder channels often had to be built.

Also the canal had to have enough bank to separate it from the river's floods. Plus it had to have a parallel ditch to carry rainwater and a parallel towpath for the livestock which towed the boats.

Finally, **there was the formidable challenge of making the canal hold water.** Even lining the canal with clay often didn't stop leaks. Animals were also sources of holes for leaks.

A lot of the work on the early sections of the canal—especially around the Falls of the James—was done by rented slaves. Because of the difficult conditions and modest wages, white workers could be sources of complaints.

By 1808 the James River Company—which had financed the canal with much risk, many hardships, and much more expense than had been anticipated—was making a good profit. The James River Company had "cleared" the river all the way to Buchanan, and goods could be floated—precariously—all the way to Richmond. Politics, troubles, and complaints eventually resulted in the James River Company's transfer to state ownership in 1820.

The transfer did not result in much improvement, and in 1832 a new private company was authorized: the James River and Kanawha Company. In spite of expenses, floods, continual problems, and the growing reliability of railroads, sections of the Kanawha Canal were built and improved all along the river from Richmond to Buchanan—with the visionary goal of connecting to the Ohio River. As the Civil War approached, the James River and Kanawha Company had reached its most active and prosperous time.

The War not only left the canal without maintenance, but it was also intentionally damaged along much of its length. By 1870 most sources of private and federal funds for the canal were gone.

The earliest boats used by both Indians and settlers were dugout canoes. They were followed by the bateaux which could hold much more. The canoes were approximately 50 feet long, and a bateau was slightly shorter but more than twice as wide. The bateaux were poled both downstream and back upstream, and were the largest boats able to navigate the rapids.

Next, with completion of more sections of the canal, came freight barges: approximately 90 feet long and 14 feet wide. They were pulled by mules.

For about 15 years there were also a few packet boats—80 feet long and 11 feet wide—which were designed to carry people. The packet boat's limited space was continually convertible and had sections designated as dressing areas, dining areas, sleeping areas, kitchen, and bar. Travel on a packet boat could be a charming, slow, social experience. But everyone agreed that the cramped quarters made sleeping on a packet boat very unpleasant.

In 1880 all property of the James River and Kanawha Company was transferred to the Richmond and Allegheny Railroad, and tracks were soon laid along the towpath, thus ending all practical use of the canal.

Reynolds Metals Company preserved the stone locks at 12th and Byrd Streets, and published a brochure about

Painting of packet boat on the Floodwall at 17th and Dock Streets.

135

The James River and Kanawha Canal. The brochure concludes with a section entitled, "The Canal Today."

"The Tidewater Connection locks of the James River and Kanawha Canal have been preserved by the Reynolds Metals Company as part of the design of its Reynolds Wrap Distribution Center located at 12th and Byrd Streets in Richmond, Virginia.

"The double locks, Nos. 4 and 5 of the Tidewater Connection, are magnificent examples of the stonemason's art. Each lock is 100 feet long by 15 feet wide. The lock gates, constructed of wood, rotted through toward the end of the 19th century.

"The 13th Street bridge, with its two arches, was built in 1860 by Richard B. Haxall and Lewis D. Crenshaw, proprietors of the nearby Haxall-Crenshaw Flour Mill. Their initials and the date of completion can be clearly seen inscribed on the key stone of the bridge, spanning the canal.

"Many other works of the James River and Kanawha Canal are still present in Richmond today; including the Canal from Bosher's Dam west of the city to Gamble's Hill below 5th Street; the locks at the Pump House at Byrd Park, the Richmond Dock east of 17th Street and the Great Ship Lock at Dock and 26th Streets. These works are inscribed on the prestigious National Register of Historic Places and in the Virginia Landmarks Register.

Ruins on Chappel Island in Great Shiplock Park.

"The Canal in Richmond is today a priceless treasure of not only the City of Richmond and Virginia's heritage but the heritage of this nation."

March, 1996 ≈

by Ralph White

It was about the end of the second snow, the second week of February, that the first birds began to sing. Not the Bald Eagles along the river opposite Pony Pasture that chuckle to one another occasionally throughout the year, and not the owls that have been 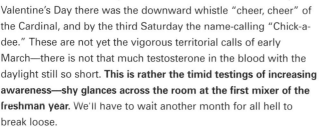 hooting clear courtship calls since December, but the musical trills of perching songbirds. The "peter, peter, peter" of the inquisitive Tufted Titmouse was first. By Valentine's Day there was the downward whistle "cheer, cheer" of the Cardinal, and by the third Saturday the name-calling "Chick-a-dee." These are not yet the vigorous territorial calls of early March—there is not that much testosterone in the blood with the daylight still so short. **This is rather the timid testings of increasing awareness—shy glances across the room at the first mixer of the freshman year.** We'll have to wait another month for all hell to break loose.

The sap is rising and the earliest trees are pulsing with new life. At the Visitor's Center the Slippery Elm overhanging the deck has buds about to burst like the tiny trinkets typically thrown during Mardi Gras further south. The Red Maples at the railroad crossing have created a mist of soft purplish red—their flower buds about to open. The yellow threads of Spicebush flowers will soon be hanging from slender branched shrubs all along the riverside trails.

For a step back in time be sure to catch the Devonian experience at the Wetlands. In early evenings from March through May (and especially during light rains) the frog community comes out to frolic. A flashlight, boots and a rainsuit will set you up. Look for the expanding throats (like tiny white balloons) of the singing males by holding the light to the side or top of your head. Females don't sing, but do make a dramatic appearance: they are the ones that move about searching for the best singer. And they are the 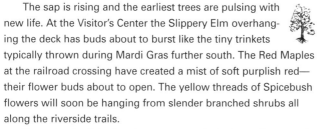 ones like movie starlets that garner all the public attention as males crowd and clamor to get close. A backpacker's headlamp is excellent to observe all this; the light doesn't seem to bother them. Movement and ground vibrations do. It will take a few minutes for the threatening effect of your walking to wear off, so patience is the name of the observation game. Personally, I like to take a light folding chair (clipped to a backpack for easy transport) as I enter this alien world—and a thermos of hot chocolate is great too!

History Surrounding The James River Corporation Headquarters

by Brenton S. Halsey
Summer, 1996

James River Corporation was founded in Richmond, Virginia and maintains its headquarters and a significant presence in that historic city. Richmond, founded in 1733 at the falls of the James River by William Byrd II, was the capital of the Confederacy and has been the capital of Virginia since 1780.

The Company was named for the James River, not only because of its origins on the banks of the river, but also because of the historic significance of the river to the nation, the state and to Richmond itself. **The first permanent English settlement in America at Jamestown in 1607 and the exploration of the James by Captains Christopher Newport and John Smith marked the beginnings of our nation.** The falls of the James at Richmond ended deepwater navigation from the Atlantic, creating a natural site for trade and development, first by the Indians and subsequently by the settlers. The James River played a significant role in both the Revolutionary War and the Civil War. Transportation in all forms developed in and alongside the river. Richmond's position today as a major transportation, industrial and cultural center owes its existence to the James River.

James River Corporation as seen from Belle Isle.

The riverfront location of the James River Corporation headquarters complex is within a literal stone's throw of six of the city's major historic sites: Belle Isle, Hollywood Cemetery, the James River & Kanawha Canal, the Tredegar Iron Works, the 1832 City Pump House and the Hollywood Paper Mill.

BELLE ISLE

Lying directly across the northern branch of the James River from the "Riverside" headquarters building is Belle Isle. The history of Belle Isle parallels the history of Richmond.

Before the arrival of the English, native Americans exploited the island's strategic location amid the rapids to provide food from the once great spring fish runs. Captains Newport and Smith, in their exploration of the James River in 1607, reached the falls of the James at a point just below Belle Isle. The first recorded owner of the island, dating from the late 1600's, was William Byrd I. His son and Richmond's founder, William Byrd II, inherited the island and referred to it as "the broad rock island." Thus it was known as Broadrock Island through much of the period prior to the Civil War.

William Byrd III inherited the island in 1744 and then, in desperate financial straits, sold it, along with his estate, Belvidere (the current site of Ethyl Corporation's headquarters) to a Lawrence Hylton. Bushrod Washington, George Washington's nephew and a justice of the U.S. Supreme Court, owned the property briefly in 1795 and for a short period it became known as Washington's Island. It was subsequently owned by another famous American and hero, "Light Horse Harry" Lee, one of Washington's Revolutionary War generals and Robert E. Lee's father.

Thomas Bryan on Belle Isle.

Benjamin Latrobe, the famous American architect whose works included the south wing of the U.S. Capitol and the White House, took an intense interest in Broadrock Island. He either owned it briefly or intended to own it. He sketched it and wrote about it in some detail. He called it a "beautiful, fertile, and romantic spot" where he hoped to "become independent, and shutting myself up in my island to devote my hours to literature, agriculture, and friendship and education of my children."

At the turn of the century, Broadrock Island was acquired by the Harvie family, whose interest was in the commercialization of the island's natural assets. The quarrying of granite commenced during this period and continued into the 20th Century. The family also brought horse breeding and racing to the island.

In 1815 the Belle Isle Rolling and Slitting Mill and Nail Factory was established. Thus the island became known as

Belle Isle, although another version has the island named after James Bell, a popular Scottish quarryman. The nail factory prospered and, having been renamed the Old Dominion Iron and Nail Works, became one of the largest nail manufacturers in the nation.

The Island's infamous period as a prison for Northern soldiers commenced in 1862. In the period 1862-63, the number of prisoners varied from none to 5,000 and conditions were tolerable. The camp was located on the flat southeast corner of the island and consisted of tents for the prisoners and a few buildings for the officers, guards and services.

Beginning in 1864, the population grew to as many as 15,000 and the shortages of food, medicine, textiles and other materials in Richmond resulted in minimal supplies to the prison camp. While the numbers indicate that the Belle Isle camp was less deadly than some other Southern camps such as Andersonville, the suffering from cold and hunger in the winter of 1864 has been described by prisoners as beyond human description. While exact numbers will never be known, estimates are that of the 30,000 Northern prisoners who passed through Belle Isle, perhaps 1,000 died from exposure, malnutrition and disease.

Following the war, the Old Dominion Iron and Nail Works thrived. Over 300 workers were employed on the island in the 1870 period. Virginia Power constructed a hydroelectric station on the southwest end of the island, which supplied power to Richmond for 60 years. A rail line connected to the south shore of the river and by the early 1900's an automobile bridge connected the island with Tredegar Street. **This bridge was washed out in Hurricane Camille in 1972.** Shortly thereafter the Old Dominion Iron Works ceased operations and the City of Richmond purchased Belle Isle and placed it in the James River Park System. In 1989 the Richmond Renaissance "James River Discovery Program" resulted in the clean-up of the island and Tredegar Street and provided for a pedestrian bridge slung underneath the new Lee Bridge. James River Corporation was the primary private contributor to the construction of this bridge along with the Commonwealth of Virginia Department of Transportation. A bridge on the south side of the island was restored for emergency vehicular access.

Thanks to this program, Belle Isle today is an extraordinary natural asset in the middle of the city. Its trails, views, wildlife habitat and its environmental education programs for the city schools make it a place that Benjamin Latrobe would continue to find to his liking.

HOLLYWOOD CEMETERY

Directly above the James River Corporation headquarters site is Hollywood Cemetery. Established in 1849, it is the most historic cemetery in the South. It is so named because of the prolific growth of Holly trees within its acreage. **It contains the remains of two U.S. Presidents, James Monroe and John Tyler; the President of the Confederacy, Jefferson Davis; J.E.B. Stuart and 21 other Confederate generals**; six Virginia governors; 18,000 Confederate soldiers; and many other distinguished Virginians. Among these notables are Matthew Fontaine Maury, oceanographer; James Branch Cabell, novelist; Edward Valentine, sculptor; Ellen Glasgow, novelist; and Douglas Southall Freeman, historian.

Overlooking the James River, the aesthetic design of the cemetery lent itself to use as a park and picnic ground as well as a burial ground. During the late 1800's and early 1900's it was a popular picnic and family gathering place. The hilly terrain and winding roads, panoramic views, and the lush wooded growth make Hollywood a place of truly remarkable beauty. It contains one of the finest collections of mortuary art, both stone and cast iron, to be found in America. Still an active burial ground for many Richmond families, the cemetery currently is the final resting place for over 60,000 individuals.

In 1866, the ladies of the Hollywood Memorial Association established an annual day of memory to honor the Confederate dead. This tradition spread throughout the South and then evolved into our present national Memorial Day holiday, honoring the dead of all of America's wars.

THE JAMES RIVER & KANAWHA CANAL

The huge granite walls that support the southern edge of the James River & Kanawha Canal adjoin the James River Corporation headquarters site. In 1784, the general assembly of Virginia, at the behest of George Washington, established the James River Company. Its purpose was to build a canal that would connect the navigable portion of the James River at Richmond with the Ohio River, providing an uninterrupted transportation system from the

Atlantic Ocean to the Mississippi River. Washington was elected as the Honorary President of the James River Company and Edmund Randolph its first active president. Construction commenced shortly and continued in spurts off and on for the next 60 years. By 1820, The James River Company was the largest corporation operating in Virginia and by 1830 passenger packets were in operation from Richmond to Lynchburg. In 1832, after a series of financial difficulties, the canal company was reestablished as the James River & Kanawha Company with Chief Justice John Marshall as its chairman. By 1851 the canal was open the entire 197 miles to Buchanan, Virginia. From there, cargo moved by cart to the Kanawha River and thence by boat to the Ohio. Although additional work was done on the portion between Buchanan and the Kanawha, this section was never completed.

During the peak traffic period in the 1860's, the Canal employed 75 deck boats, 66 open boats, 54 bateaux, 6 passenger packets, 425 horses and 900 men.

By the late 1870's, the economics of rail transportation had become overwhelming. In 1880 the canal company was sold to the predecessor railroad company of the C&O and CSX. The present James River Division of CSX was constructed on the canal tow path. Thus ended Washington's, Randolph's and Marshall's vision of a water connection to the mid-continent.

THE PUMP HOUSE

The westernmost and newest of the James River Corporation headquarters buildings was built upon the foundations of the 1832 pump house that supplied Richmond with its first central drinking water. The design of the eastern facade of this building is an historic interpretation of an addition to the original pump house. This addition was made to accommodate the 1911 conversion of the pump house to a hydroelectric power plant. Many elements of both the pump house and the Hollywood Electric Plant were incorporated into the design of the new headquarters building.

Before 1832, numerous wells provided Richmond with all of its drinking water. With an expanding population, 16,000 in 1830, the city leaders determined the need for a central water supply. Through a vote of the freeholders, the construction was authorized and the entire system completed at a total cost of $76,000.

A wooden dam was constructed at the location of the present concrete dam west of the site which fed the "headrace." The headrace was built as it is currently configured and the pump house was constructed between the headrace and the river. The pump was driven by an 18-foot-diameter water wheel. The water flowed from the headrace into a "forebay," thence to the water wheel in a "wheel race," and finally through a "tail race" into the river. The head was 10 feet. A double forcing reciprocating pump, driven by the wheel, pumped 400,000 gallons per day of river water through pipes that ran under the James River and Kanawha Canal. These pipes extended up the hill to a new reservoir located east of Hollywood Cemetery. After filtration, the water was carried by gravity to a point at Adams Street, and then through a multiple pipe system that extended to 23rd Street.

As the City expanded, additional wheels and pumps were added such that at its peak capacity in 1874 there were seven wheels and pumps. The building was extended both to the East and West. In 1876, the "new" Byrd Park pump house and reservoir were completed and gradually expanded to the point that the old pump house was shut down in 1908.

Thereafter, the building was reconstructed and equipped with four electric generators driven by the existing water wheels. The generators were placed in the old arches where the pumps had been located. Two new steam generators were also installed. The power plant commenced operations in 1913 and initially supplied power to the new pump house in Byrd Park. Additional hydro and steam generators were added in 1918 and 1930. The plant continued to operate in this final configuration, supplying power for street lights and public buildings, until the plant was closed in 1982.

The new office building, the "Pump House," constructed in 1991, rests precisely on the original 1832 pump house foundation and extends to the final pump house expansion of 1874. The present basement exercise rooms are essentially unchanged: Exercise room No. 2 was the original 1832 forebay and the water wheel was located opposite in the main exercise hall. The outline of the stone arch of the tail race can be seen on the wall next to the river. The pump room is now the No. 3 exercise room. Similarly, in the expanded pump house, the lady's locker room and the Nos. 1 and 4 exercise rooms were forebays and the men's locker room was a pump room. The stone arches of the newer tail races may also be seen on the south wall. The "A" frames and ceiling in the third floor executive office are original to the 1930 hydroelectric plant additions.

The Richmond architectural firm of Bond, Comet, Westmoreland and Galusha combined an important historic interpretation with a uniquely attractive and functional building design. **The river views are unsurpassed and, given the urban setting, the wildlife activity is extraordinary.**

THE TREDEGAR IRON WORKS

Adjoining to the east of the James River Corporation headquarters site lies the property of the Tredegar Iron Works. Tredegar's operations spanned 130 years of Richmond history and was one of the more important factors in Richmond's industrial progress. **It is noted particularly for its role in the Civil War, as it served as the most important source of armament for the Confederacy.**

Chartered in 1837 simultaneously with the adjacent Virginia Foundry Company, Tredegar promptly absorbed the Foundry and they operated as one thereafter. Pig iron was purchased from numerous blast furnace operations upriver from Tredegar that had come into existence as a result of coal deposits on the upper James that had been mined since colonial times. Rails and other products for the railroad industry were produced in a modern rolling mill. Joseph Reid Anderson, a West Point graduate, was employed as its commercial agent. Shortly thereafter, Anderson leased and then in 1848 acquired ownership of Tredegar. General Anderson and his name were synonymous with the Tredegar Iron Works until his death in 1892.

Prior to the Civil War, Tredegar became an important supplier of cannon to the Federal government and between 1844 and 1860 supplied 881 ordinance pieces to the United States. It also supplied boilers, machinery and iron plate to the Navy and was a major producer of locomotives. Anderson acquired the neighboring Armory Rolling Mill in 1859.

Although the outbreak of the Civil War almost bankrupted the Company due to defaults on orders from Southern railroads, Tredegar quickly became the major supplier of cannon to the Confederacy. Following a serious fire, a new gun foundry was constructed in 1861, now restored and highly visible on Tredegar Street. Tredegar is particularly noted for its innovation in developing the banded and rifled Brooke gun and for having provided the armor plating for the C.S.S. Virginia of Merrimac and Monitor fame. Tredegar also produced limited supplies of rifles and pistols, which have since become collectors' items.

Following the war, Anderson was pardoned and Tredegar became a significant factor in the rebuilding of the South's industrial base. Through periods of both financial stress and prosperity, Tredegar continued in business through two world wars, its product lines evolving as newer technologies outmoded Tredegar's older processes. Products included horseshoes, nails, artillery shells and freight car wheels.

Finally, the items caught up with Tredegar and, in 1957, all of the real estate was purchased by Albemarle Paper Manufacturing Co. The Tredegar Company moved and continued to operate for a few years on Route 1 before finally closing its doors. Albemarle, whose name subsequently changed to Ethyl Corp., used the property for its paper research and development headquarters and also for its initial cast coating manufacturing plant, subsequently acquired by James River Corporation and moved to Deepwater Terminal.

Ethyl also restored the 1861 Gun Foundry, converting it into a public facility for meetings and social events. In 1991, Ethyl leased a major portion of the property to the Valentine Riverside Museum, which restored many of the buildings and installed displays of original Tredegar operations as well as electronic displays of early Richmond. Valentine Riverside ran into severe financial difficulties, however, and was forced to close its doors in 1995. The property reverted back to Ethyl, which is currently exploring other opportunities for public purpose uses.

THE HOLLYWOOD PAPER MILL

The northern portion of the headquarters site is occupied by the Hollywood Paper Mill, constructed in 1887. **The mill has been in continuous operation since that date and today is a profitable operation of the Specialty Paperboard, Inc. group.**

Extraordinarily, the Hollywood mill has been the incubator for three independent Fortune 500 companies: Ethyl

Corporation, James River Corporation and SCI, Inc. and is currently a key unit of a fourth independent company, Specialty Paperboard, Inc.

Constructed by the Albemarle Paper Mfg. Co., it originally produced pulp from rags which was converted into blotting and other absorbent type papers. It became the world leader in the production of blotting paper and, as blotting paper demand declined, the filter saturating plant at the east end of Hollywood was constructed and the mill became a significant factor in the production of automotive filter paper. **The early success of the Hollywood mill led to the expansion of Albemarle into one of the nation's important paper manufacturers.**

In 1963, Albemarle purchased the Ethyl Corporation, changing its name to Ethyl. In 1968 it sold its major paper operations, remaining as a leading chemical producer.

At this time, 1969, a management group from Ethyl/Albemarle purchased the mill from Ethyl, thus founding the James River Corporation. A successful turnaround of the then unprofitable mill enabled James River Corporation to embark upon an acquisition program that resulted in James River Corporation becoming a paper industry leader. For a period in 1988-89, **James River Corporation was the world's largest paper manufacturer as measured by annual sales.**

In 1990, James River Corporation sold its specialty paper business to a newly formed company, SCI, Inc. The Hollywood Mill was a component of this business and James River Corporation leased the mill property to SCI. In 1993, SCI was purchased by the Bowaters Group of England, who promptly sold five of the smaller specialty operations, including the lease of the Hollywood Mill, to another start-up company, Custom Papers Group, Inc. In 1996, CPG merged with Specialty Paperboard, Inc. Thus, Hollywood is now leased to SPG, Inc. and is a profitable component of that successful group. The configuration of the mill is not substantially different from that in 1887, although a series of modernizations have been undertaken over the years and the last remaining component of the original paper machine was only recently replaced.

The spawning of three major corporations through the operation of a small 1887 paper mill is perhaps unique in the annals of American industry.

The early success of the Hollywood Mill resulted in excess demand such that Albemarle was able to construct the Riverside Mill in 1925. Riverside is the current James River Corporation headquarters building containing the reception area, the cafeteria and a number of corporate departments. In 1925 it contained one paper machine and related converting facilities. In 1953, after the paper machine had been removed, the first floor became a multi-wall shipping sack manufacturing plant for Albemarle. The second floor was converted into an asphalt laminating plant producing waterproof commercial wrapping paper.

When acquired by James River Corporation, the bag plant had ceased operations and had been removed. James River Corporation operated the asphalt plant until 1975, when it was moved to the new plant at Deepwater Terminal. The first conversion of the building to a corporate office occurred in 1978 when the third floor was reconstructed as the corporate office. This was followed by the renovation of the second floor in 1980, and completion of the fourth floor and the first floor cafeteria in 1986. A fifth and sixth floor were added in 1987 along with the east lobby and the east elevators. This completed the Riverside corporate office in its present configuration.

EPILOGUE

Today, the James River Corporation headquarters complex is one of the most beautiful and unique headquarters in corporate America. Its proximity to the river for which the corporation is named, the views of the rapids, rocks and falls together with the abundant wildlife, all within the downtown area of a major American city, is awe inspiring. The river-walk looking west has been described as one of the more beautiful scenes in America. The recreational opportunities for employees who choose to take advantage of them are extraordinary. **The history that surrounds the site parallels the history of America: exploration, industrialization, war and peace, life and death and entrepreneurship.** One can hope that such a place will continue to inspire achievement in the future.

November 14, 1995

by Ralph White

Shorter daylight and cooler temperatures have brought an end to most leaves on the deciduous trees and shrubs in Richmond. While the lush greens of summer and the crisp yellows of fall have disappeared from the forests, a new x-ray view of the woods has developed.

Bundles of brown leaves reveal squirrel homes, platforms of sticks can be hawk nests, small songbird nests abound in the lower branches of small trees and dense shrubs, and in the evening twilight it is not uncommon to see the silhouette of a Barred or Great Horned Owl. A walk through any park or forest will reveal these. The Pony Pasture, Wetlands or Main Area of the James River Park System are especially good places.

On the ground a time machine has evolved amongst the leaves and forest duff. Examine a leaf pile and it reads like a picture story book of what lived and ate, made homes on or burrowed in, what fell on or broke through the leaves and stems. The cellophane-like holes and worm-like trails are empty homes of leaf miners—the tiny larva of certain flies and gnats that lived in the succulent thin softness of the tender leaves in spring. Jagged holes that break through leaf veins are probably scars from hail or a falling stick. Holes between veins are usually places where caterpillars have fed. Tears are scars from the fights between leaf and wind. Swellings on stems and leaf veins are galls—nutrient-rich 'tumors' that provide both food and shelter for the larva of certain moths, flies and midges. Oak leaves have the widest variety of galls; Hackberry and Witch Hazel seem to have the greatest number.

Virginia Department of Historic Resources

H. Alexander Wise, Jr. is Director of the Department of Historic Resources for the Commonwealth of Virginia. In the fall of 1996 he discussed the urban James River:

"The duty of the Department of Historic Resources is to identify historic places, make information on them available to the public, and promote their productive use. We are vitally interested in the Richmond Riverfront Development Project—especially in regard to historic interpretation. We don't yet know the precise direction this will take, but there is agreement on some basic themes.

"First, the Project has to bring people to the river—for commercial, recreational, and historical purposes. Second, historic interpretation should include natural history. And third, the project will tell the story of the river in all of its layers. Richmond being Virginia's capital, we have the opportunity to tell the story of the entire James River Basin.

"Regarding tourism, there will have to be a focal point, an anchor. We know, for example, that there are tourists who go to Philadelphia specifically to see the Liberty Bell. An obvious focal point here could be the Civil War, and a redeveloped Tredegar Iron Works could be the tourists' first stop. They could park there, enjoy Tredegar, and then be dispersed by canal boats and trolleys and other means to enjoy the rest of the city including, of course, the James River.

"The James River is the raison d'etre of the city. You can't appreciate the history of Richmond without understanding the history of the river."

The Falls of the James Atlas

Get a copy of the following: *The Falls of the James Atlas*, prepared for the Virginia Canals & Navigation Society by W.E. Trout III, James Moore III, and George D. Rawls, Second Edition, December 1995. Call or write to William E. Trout III, 35 Towana Road, Richmond, VA 23226, (804) 288-1334. The cost at this writing is $8.

This is the most comprehensive, invaluable book there is on the historical artifacts in and alongside Richmond's urban James River. Although the book's primary purpose is to describe and and give information about the history of the river's structures, it is full of other information. Its map alone—an extremely detailed map of the river and its surroundings—should be owned by anyone who has anything to do with the urban James.

The *Falls of the James Atlas* contains information and regulations about the James River Park System, historic photographs with detailed captions, safety tips, diagrams of the river's rapids, information about parking and river access, a vision for Pump House Park being a future museum, a topographical map and diagram of Belle Isle, true stories such as "The Tragedy at Vauxall Island," a self-guided walking tour, a list of reference sources and maps, and dozens of charming bits of history. I was intrigued, for example, by page 24 which shows "masons marks on the old Belt Line Bridge." This page has a hand-drawn reproduction of hundreds and hundreds of stones which built the piers of the 1891 Belt Line Bridge—stones which contain marks inscribed by individual stone masons to identify the stones they shaped.

The book's authors continue their work, and they include the following paragraph on page two: "We have only begun to rediscover these historic sites, to put them back on the map, to figure out what they were, what they did, how they worked and what they meant to the people of Richmond. You will not find all the answers in this guide, because many are still scattered about in records and memories, if they exist at all. As you come across new sites and information for yourself, we would like to know about it!"

On June 3, 1996 I visited Pump House Park on "Batteau Day" and talked with members of The Virginia Canals and Navigations Society—the organization which publishes *The Falls of the James Atlas*. The Society is open to everyone. Its brochure states: "The Virginia Canals & Navigations Society was formed in 1977 to preserve and enhance Virginia's rich inland waterways heritage in all its fascinating aspects. **History, exploration, archaeology, modeling, local lore and legend, restoration, preservation, park and trail development**—these are some of the many areas of interest our members pursue, to their own great satisfaction and frequently to the lasting benefit of their communities and state. The society is increasingly active as a focus for waterways interest, and a collective voice of all those are concerned about the future of this priceless part of our past."

Ruth Harris, president of the Society, has been a member since 1992. I asked her about the enjoyment she receives from the Society: "I think it's discovering artifacts that have been overlooked by new construction and bringing them back so the public can be told about them and be aware."

I talked with Bill Trout and Jimmy Moore—primary authors of the Atlas; George Ramsey who lives in Suffolk and represents the Dismal Swamp district of the Society; Phil Eckman, the Society's archivist who moved to Colonial Heights from Michigan; and with others who were dressed in costume and showcased displays and models representing the way things used to be on the James. I watched George Ramsey wade into the almost-dry canal and retrieve a briefcase-size stone which bore the results of three splitting holes. He placed iron wedges and "feathers" into the holes to demonstrate how the stones were split.

The Society has done much good along the river, and I recommend membership—especially for anyone who has an interest in the river's history.

Found Objects ≋

In freshman art class you always have to make a project using a found object—something which has been cast aside, which has been long-forgotten and long-ignored, which has been long-retired from any practical application. You use the context of art to examine and study the object, to carefully look—really look—at the object, and finally to celebrate the object. The object becomes elevated, exalted, a cause for celebration and awe. Once a side-alley orphan, it now becomes a cherished only child.

The shores of the urban James River are rich with found objects. They are everywhere. You can't walk the length of a garage without passing several. But you don't see them. They have become, along with the flora and fauna and rocks and water, a blended part of the very fabric of the urban James. You don't notice the river's found objects; but if they were all of a sudden absent, you would notice.

JOHN BRYAN

Freshman art students sometimes stumble onto a wrong definition of the term. A found object is neither a lost object nor a hidden object. A found object is an object which when seen is ignored, which when touched elicits a "So what?", which when lifted by illusioned children commands a "Put that down!"

On the other hand, a lost or hidden object is an object over which we rejoice, which sparkles a "Hey, look at this!", and which you pick up and take home with you. A plastic-banded, rusted, digital wristwatch is a found object; a golden-chained pocket watch is a lost object. A two-liter plastic Sprite bottle is a found object; a 1956 glass six-ounce Coke bottle is these days a lost object. A copper penny face-down in a mall parking lot is now a found object; a folded-over 20-dollar bill in the same lot is a lost object. There is usually a distinct difference.

The urban James abounds with found objects awaiting celebration, awaiting notice, awaiting a glance, awaiting even a pick-up-and-throw-into-the-river.

March 9, 1996 was a very cold Saturday; the prior evening had dipped to 15—a new all-time record low for the March 8 urban James. I bundled up Thomas and his friend Hank into gloves and wool caps and took them with me for some urban James research. Our quest: Found Objects. Our site: just upstream from Pumphouse Park. As had been the case during the pick-up-trash Cub Scout service project at Kiptopeake, there would be a verbal congratulations for the best waterside discovery. Hank had won at Kiptopeake with a singularly awful pair of men's jockey underwear which he lifted from the sand with plastic gloves and a long stick. We made a photograph of him and the prize; it's in the mini-album on the page opposite the one of me holding my rod and a tiny Sea Bass. Hank's smile is even wider than mine.

We parked at Pumphouse Park, walked the upriver path to its end, crossed the railroad tracks—depositing a handful of coins to be hopefully flattened—and made our way upstream along the river. The little strip of land between the river and the tracks averages perhaps 50 feet across, and you have the delight of discovering castoffs from the trains as well as drift-offs from the river.

Our first find was not remarkable at first—a 20-ounce plastic Big Slam Mountain Dew bottle. But we made it remarkable. We discovered that it was dry inside and that its top was air-tight. These two qualities were important because they allowed us to prepare and insert a secret note before casting the bottle to the river's currents. It was a simple note asking the finder to call Thomas and report the find. Thomas and I have inserted such notes before, but not inside damp bottles and not inside bottles with unsecured caps.

Janet's father found one of his twin-brother's helium balloons 20 years ago with such a note. His twin brother had set sail 100 helium balloons filled from a tank he'd bought for nothing at a salvage store. He'd tied a self-addressed postcard to each balloon: "Drop this in the mailbox and I'll be able to see, from the postmark, how far my balloon went."

The next morning there were downed, limp balloons all over the neighborhood. Janet's father quietly removed the postcard from one of them, put it in an envelope, and sent it to a friend in Dallas asking him to drop the postcard in a mailbox. A few days later his twin brother proclaimed that one of his balloons had drifted all the way from Nashville to Dallas, and he had the postcard to prove it. The newspaper published an article and photograph about Janet's uncle and the long-distance balloon. Janet's father never did tell him.

Thomas and I always hope for such success with our bottles. One of our notes said, "There is a buried treasure 100 feet upstream beneath the fallen tree." That'll keep 'em busy.

After Thomas and Hank and I said goodbye to our Big Slam bottle we continued our search party upstream along the river's edge. An interesting find greeted me hanging from a River Birch tree: a lifejacket. Oddly, they are not all that rare along urban water-sides. This one was a "Cut n Jump" brand, bright red, Coast Guard Approved. The back panel had been ripped and the jacket was no longer any good. We looked and then discarded it.

Next was a Garcia Cardinal 782 spinning reel, peeking from the sand, which I dislodged with the toe of my very old Etonic sneaker which itself should have been discarded several holes ago. The reel was no good; all of the parts had been welded tight by exposure to sand and sun and water. We all handled it and briefly discussed taking it home. Its spool was filled with that bright yellow fluorescent line which is often used in saltwater. Hardly anyone uses it on the James.

I picked up a Lays Potato Chip bag. This one got my attention because it was still brightly colored. All connoisseurs of riverside trash know that discarded potato chip bags fade almost immediately. Why was this one still so bright? I looked at the expiration date: April 3—still weeks away. Obviously a recent discard. But how did the bag come to rest here on this relatively remote stretch of shoreline? Perhaps tossed by the conductor of a passing train.

I saw a glass bottle that was not familiar to me. The label was gone and I read the embossed glass: "Mistic Royal Drink." "Hey Thomas and Hank," I heralded, "you ever heard of a Mistic drink?"

"Sure," Hank laughed, "Get Mistic and Go Naked."

"That's a great drink," echoed Thomas.

I left the bottle and made a note to take a closer look at the Mistic display at the grocery.

My favorite finds are the railroad spikes. They're like Easter Eggs—hidden enough so that you delight in finding them, numerous enough that you can fill a generous basket. Thomas put the first three in his coat pocket, but when he realized there would be dozens more he settled on keeping only two, occasionally swapping for better ones. What makes a better railroad spike? Some of them are curved in interesting ways. Some are freer of rust than others. Some are more classically defined than others. It all depends on what you want. I kept two in my pocket with the idea of painting them gold and making paperweights for the office. They're heavy.

"Hey Dad!"

"Hey Mr. Bryan!"

Hank and Thomas were over at the river's edge, and I shuffled through the low trees to join them.

"A volleyball!" they announced.

Sure enough, a regulation volleyball in perfect shape except for the discoloration. **Formerly volleyball gray, it had become chartreuse. All riverside scavengers know this color; it's from exposure to algae. We of course kicked the ball before we abandoned it.**

There's a Dr. Seuss story about a pair of pants with nobody in them. The pants are frightening until the end when the narrator learns that the pants are just as much afraid of him as he is of them. They wind up being friends. The long blue pants I found hanging on a riverside bush were not frightening; they were pitiful. They had not been hung there; they had been deposited there by high water. The zipper and metal button were rusted, and there were rips in both legs. However, the pockets were intact and I felt them imagining a coin or a roll of bills or a pocket watch. Nothing. Washed up clothing is common along the urban James—mostly socks and sneakers. This pair of pants was not common.

"Hey Mr. Bryan," Hank alerted, "look, I found a bobber." He held up a red and white fishing float. "You want to keep it, or can I throw it into the river?"

The answer was of course easy. I told him to do what anyone would do: throw it. **When you find any sphere of any sort among the riverside flotsam, you always toss it out into the river.** You can't NOT toss it. Tennis balls, golf balls, rubber balls, whiffle balls, you find them all. And you toss them all. Somewhere way upstream there must be a generous and continuing source of balls. They surely don't come from downstream. They get their start somewhere up there.

We found a lot of beaver marks: chewed-around trees, many of them gnawed to a stump. We saw one huge tree, maybe eight feet in diameter, that had been long-ago chewed a foot deep all the way around. I guess the beavers gave up on that impossibility.

On the ground near each other were a Reeses candy wrapper, still bright with its orange coloring, and a Canco Party Ice bag with bright blue lettering. Non-faded containers get your attention along the urban James.

We reached the railroad bridge, and while Thomas and Hank explored the area beneath it, I continued to scrounge around along the river. That's when I found the find of the day: a Redskins t-shirt. This one was special. It was printed—in color—with a copy of the front page of the *Washington Post* sports section: "Redskins Steal the Show: 37-24." There was the headline, the printed story about the game, and a photograph—all in color. **The small print revealed that this was the shirt commemorating the 1992 Superbowl victory against the Buffalo Bills.** This had been a premiere t-shirt. Now it was river trash. Someone had once worn it with a proud swagger; now I was the only person in the world who even knew it existed. I stretched it out on the ground, face up, and weighted it with a rock on each corner. If anyone else passed by before the next bunch of high water, they might see it.

I found a container for a large order of McDonalds fries. I assume they span the globe these days. I also found a 7-Eleven Super Big Gulp cup. I assume they span most of the nation. And I found a small white plastic cup with Comfort Inn printed on it. Who knows where it originated.

My other finds—Hank and Thomas had lost interest in found objects and were content hiking and climbing and exploring—included a single white shoestring, a Budweiser can (a dime a dozen), a foot-wide square of green Styrofoam, and a deflated purple mylar balloon which read, "Let's Celebrate."

We walked back along the ribbon of land next to the railroad tracks. At one point I looked behind me and saw Thomas standing on the tracks leaning over looking at something. "Thomas, I don't want you on the tracks," I said firmly. "A train could come around that corner at any time." And of course a train arrived just 30 seconds after he left the tracks.

I found something along the tracks that made me think a lot: pieces of coal. The most recent two novels I'd read had passages about families whose children's daily chores were scavenging railroad tracks for coal. The pieces I was finding were mostly smaller than golfballs. In two hundred yards I found only one piece as large as my fist. Most pieces were tiny—the sizes of coins. My grandmother had a coal furnace when I was a child, and she would let me have a piece of coal to take outside and attempt to compress into a diamond as Superman did each week on television. Every piece of coal I saw as a child was a potential diamond.

The train flattened our coins, and we found six of them. They had scattered down among the rocks: four pennies, a dime, and a quarter. We each put two into our pockets.

Back at the car the flattened coins were the souvenirs we saved of our outing. Thomas soon forgot about his; I don't know about Hank.

Chapter Six:
Nature

Richmond's James River has an abundance of life in and around it. Cleaner water and protected lands are continuing to create huge changes in the river's flora and fauna.

There are deer, beaver, river otter, muskrats, and more than 100 species of birds. On Belle Isle there is a red fox family and grey foxes have been spotted.

Near the James River Park System Visitor's Center there is a butterfly trail—a meandering path with overnight and overwintering accommodations for butterflies. (See the Resources section of this book for the brochure on butterflies.)

Bald Eagles are now sighted regularly on the urban James, Cormorants are here by the hundreds, the river teams with striped bass (rockfish), and American shad will be reestablished as soon as a fish passage is created through Bosher's Dam.

The River Otter is one indication of the health of the urban James.

Wildflowers blossom most of the year (Newton Ancarrow compiled a list of 471 species published in David Ryan's 1975 *The Falls of the James*), and the river is bordered by a wonderful forest of Blackgum, Sweetgum, Sycamore, Beech, several Oaks, and many others. A bear cub even wound up on the urban James having followed the river corridor from his upstream nativity.

Perhaps the best way to learn about nature on our urban James is to visit the James River Park System's Visitor's Center, introduce yourself to the naturalist, Ralph White, and sign up for some of the many "classes" provided by the Park System.

157

January 23, 1983

375 years now separate me from Captain Christopher Newport's arrival at the rapids of Richmond's James River. I am drawn to those rapids today in the midst of a frigid winter weekend. I am pulled alone into the southside's James River Park. The picnickers of spring, swimmers of summer, and boaters of fall are all gone now. The woods and the rapids are vacant today as they were for Christopher Newport. Perhaps Indians await me as they did him.

I cross the railroad tracks on a span of towering concrete. A graveled trail leads me along a backwater stream. Hungry boulders ferry me across to Archer's Island, and I am whisked quickly into a century long past, far from civilization.

Dizzy Poplars and Beeches surround me and a Carolina Chickadee catches my eye as it darts among sky-high branches. The bird's dee-dee-dee-dee pierces the frosty stillness.

I walk, face up against the mid-morning sun, through the riverside forest. **The trees have banished their leaves except for a few scattered Oaks and Beeches, and against the blue sky are silhouetted open Poplar pods, Sycamore balls and lonely Hickory shells**—all clinging tightly to their final lofty weeks.

Brown ground birds disappear into a thicket before I can identify them. They have lowered my eyes, and I now examine the trail on which I walk. There are no beer cans nor candy wrappers. The trail is made of clean, pressed leaves, and vines and saplings reach boldly into its opening. Certainly it is no different from 375 winters ago.

Luscious green moss covers a patch of ground along the path. My gloved fingers sink deeply into it. From six inches it looks like a thick forest of tiny Pines.

A pair of giant Pines looms above, and the dead limbs beneath support myriad lichen colonies. One group looks like miniature shelled oysters, colored with pale grays, blues, greens and whites. Light brown rings mark the lichen-oysters' cavities. Another lichen cluster looks like raisins, rich and coffee-colored, plump and juicy.

Ragged River Birches announce the end of the woods and the start of the giant James. It stretches before me, just as it did back then, absent of bee-busy urbanites. Huge boulders checker and clutter the shallow river. These are the rocks which stopped upstream travel and forced the early 17th-century pioneers to settle Richmond.

Three gulls soar high above the rocks, too high to look for fish. Perhaps they too are gazing at the past.

Highwater puddles are all iced over. I am tempted to break the ice windows with boots and rocks, but I don't. I hop across monstrous stepping stones to the edge of the river's major current. Through my standing platform runs a crevice from which grow a dozen eight-inch saplings. I reach into the thin crack and pull out a black rock—the shape of a cube and the size of an acorn.

Before me the river glides silently and noisily by, its silver-blue strands caressing everything. **This is where Indians built rock weirs—dams of stones—among which they wedged cone-shaped baskets of reeds.** The baskets caught fish, as did hooks of bone and stone.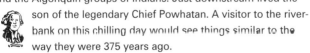

I leap over to a shoreline pile of rocks and pebbles. Perhaps one wintry day I'll sift through such a pile and find a bone hook or a piece of pottery. Today I find only rocks and shells and driftwood.

The shells are small freshwater bivalves—descendants of the mussels the Indians used to grate the hair from their heads and tweeze the hair from their bodies. These shells were also used for decoration and currency. Disk-shaped shell beads, called Roanoke, were their pennies, nickels, dimes and quarters.

I find two round stone balls and one egg-shaped stone. This river's ancient inhabitants used such stones for several games of skill.

Today is the coldest one yet of 1983, and my fingers and cheeks are numbing. I capture some of the river's treasures on film, and then begin the brief walk back to civilization.

As I near the concrete tower I notice, for the first time today, an 18-foot Sycamore, naked except for 15 balls at its top. Somehow it conveys a withered Christmas tree.

Back across the railroad tracks I walk over to look at the markings on this woods' largest Beech tree. "Js 75" "BK NK," "AL MAR 1971," are engraved around its 15-foot circumference. Other older markings are too scarred to read.

This James River Park is on the fringes of both the Monacan and the Algonquin groups of Indians. Just downstream lived the son of the legendary Chief Powhatan. A visitor to the riverbank on this chilling day would see things similar to the way they were 375 years ago.

The eloquent Mr. Virginius Dabney gives us a glimpse of those long-ago waters, "where year after year the murmuring waters splashed over the rocks, with none but the Indians, the wild birds, the deer, the leaping bass and the slithering water moccasins to keep them company."

Birding With Charlie Blem

It's early afternoon on an April Wednesday and I watch Charlie Blem watch birds from atop the lookout near Reedy Creek. The river is high and brown and noisy today. The sounds of the river's rushing currents mask bird sounds, so we rely totally on our eyes.

Charlie says you can see a variety from this lookout. Bald Eagles—nonexistent here 20 years ago—can now be seen often. **There's a Peregrine Falcon which dives through Virginia Commonwealth University's campus just a half-mile on the other side of the river**—a bird not one in a thousand persons ever notices.

There is a colony of maybe 100 Cormorants out there on the river rocks right now. Back in 1978 they began nesting south of here in Colonial Heights—the first place in Virginia—and since then they've spread.

In the ripple just above the little dam are a few Bufflehead. The males are strikingly colored in black and white; they get the name from a white patch on the head. The females are drab gray-brown with just one tiny little white mark. I watch one Bufflehead through my binoculars as he dives and surfaces and dives again like a porpoise.

"Do you see those birds flying high above the tree line?" I ask Charlie. I'm not a birder, and I need help even with the commons.

"Yeah, they're gulls," he replies without raising his binoculars. "Ring-billed Gulls."

"You can tell from here they're Ring-billed Gulls?"

"Oh yeah," he says matter-of-factly. "Well can you tell they're not?" he smiles. "Nine out of ten are Ring-billed Gulls; the remaining one is a Herring Gull," he pauses, "except when it isn't. We get some rare gulls here—like Iceland Gulls. We get about four or five other species."

"How do you tell a Ring-billed Gull from a Herring Gull?" I ask. We both have zeroed our binoculars on the flock.

"The Ring-billed Gull has yellow legs and a little black ring on its bill," he describes quickly. "The Herring Gull is about a third bigger and it has a big ole yellow bill with a red dot on the lower mandible. —Here he comes!" he interrupts himself. "Watch this guy coming right here now." He focuses down below to the right.

"What is it?"

"Mallard. This is breeding season. This stretch right

here is full of breeding Black Ducks and Mallards."

I spot another bird near the tree line. "What is that big bird flying near -"

"Crow," he answers before I can point.

"You know what that one is?" I point up above our heads.

Charlie laughs. "Yeah, that might be Whit Baldwin—you ever fly with him?" The helicopter speeds on across the sky and out of our view.

"What about that bunch up there?"

"Those are gulls. Crows coming across low, gulls circling high." He distinguishes what I thought was all one species. They're so far away, I'd likely have trouble even with the binoculars.

"We're at the low point though," he tells me. **"In the winter ten to fifteen thousand gulls use this area.** They go to the Henrico dumps and come in here and rest at night."

The gulls make me think of fish. "Did you know that the herring are in now?"

"Is that right?" He shows excitement. "I would have thought it was still a week or two early."

"No, they're thick down there below 14th Street," I nod downstream. "I saw a guy scooping them out with a hand net on Sunday.

"Now are they a real herring?" I ask the biologist to clear my confusion.

"There are five species of herring," he explains. "American shad at the top and then alewives, menhaden, bluebacks, herring and hickory shad."

"Which ones was the guy probably scooping with the net?"

"I haven't gotten the small ones—the bluebacks and alewives—I haven't got that all sorted out. The hickory shad and the American shad are the two big ones."

"The ones in now are about a half-pound," I tell him.

"Yeah, those are the bluebacks," he confirms. "Great catfish bait, boy. Good striper bait."

Two birds fly across 50 feet in front of us. I recognize them. "Are those Grackles?"

"Grackles, Common Grackles, that's right."

"Do they fly in male-female pairs?"

"Quite often."

"So that'd be a good guess on those two?"

"Well, the males have a big tail."

"Can you tell the difference between those two?" They have alighted in a nearby tree.

"Sure, the male is the one on the right," he replies without hesitation. "The male has a big keeled tail like this," he demonstrates with his hands, "and the female's is shorter. The bird itself is also a little smaller. The coloration is exactly the same."

"There goes another Crow," I point.

"**You know there are two Crows here: Fish Crows and American Crows,**" he says as his eyes follow my Crow. "The coloration is the same, and there's three inches difference in size. The voice is the diagnostic thing." He looks at me for a sign of recognition. "The Fish Crow is the one you hear going Ahhh, Ahhh."

"And the others go Caw Caw?"

"A real Caw, yeah.

"Did you see the pet Crow on the VCU campus this winter?" Charlie's eyes widen as he tells me. "Strangest thing. There was this Crow standing in Shafer Court—Crows don't do that; they're real wary—and a guy was there feeding it. I asked him if it was his pet, and he replied no, the Crow just sits there like that. Later the Crow found a coin on the ground and picked it up and swallowed it. Then we threw down a penny. He swallowed 12 cents; he'd bring them back up and swallow them back down." Charlie looked through the binoculars again at something off to the right. "It had to be somebody's pet.

"You know how many birds they see along here?" He looks back at the river. "It's way over 100. There's some rare things that pop through here."

A couple of strange—but certainly not rare—things approach our lookout spot: a man and a woman. She wears a nicely pressed flowery dress. She's clean and shiny and ready for a Sunday morning Easter service. But her hair—her thin blonde hair—has a do which I've never before seen. It's flattened vertically in front—as if a very flat pancake—as big as a plate—has been glued vertically to her forehead. The rest of her hair is normal.

The man with her is different. He's not clean. His clothes are drab and dirty and he wears old shoes that don't seem to fit. His hair is dark and shiny—unwashed, but combed. His face is deep red with burst blood vessels. The two of them don't look like a couple. But they are together.

Until they split. Fifty feet before they get to us she

speeds up and he slows down. She walks on by us and pauses a few steps down the lookout's stairway. He remains 10 feet from us in the other direction. One on one side of us, one on the other. They just stand there and wait, eying us with corner-eye glances. If this were a New York City midnight alley I'd start praying.

"**What's the rarest bird you've personally seen,**" I ask, pretending to ignore the couple.

"The rarest?" He thinks, not taking his eyes from the river. "Oh, something really odd—we had Black Terns here in July. I don't know what they were doing here." He continues to scan the rocks and rapids and islands that stretch down below us. "But the rarest bird I've seen here?" He looks perplexed. "Oh geez . . . ."

"Those two over there," I point, "is that a Mallard?"

"Black Ducks. The male and female look virtually the same."

"If you saw one without the other could you tell?"

"No."

"Where do they nest?"

"Little islands, little tucked away places. You'd be amazed. The base of a tree here someplace," he designates a little spot nearby. "These guys, genetically, if you get into the real fancy schmancy biology, are so similar to Mallards it's ridiculous. There's more genetic difference within races of Black Ducks than there is between Black Ducks and Mallards. And Black Ducks and Mallards are mating now. The Black Ducks are disappearing. They're going into Mallards."

"Do you see hybrids?"

"Oh yeah. In fact hunters talk about hybrids all the time."

The pancake-haired woman has walked on down the stairs into the wooded park. Her friend remains up here. He now seems harmless.

"Is that a Crow there, going right across -"

"The bird that just took off is a Cormorant." He corrects my error. "**I love to go over there on the Hollywood Cemetery side,**" he motions. "**You can see a lot from up there.**"

I ask Charlie about field guides. He tells me Peterson's Guide is the best. The Audubon Guide with the photographs? He, like other birders I've asked, hates it. He tells me it was originally planned to be a coffee table book, but they decided that field guides sell more copies.

163

"Have you ever seen the Master Guide?" I haven't.
"It's three volumes. Photographs. What I like about that one is it's got a lot of information in it. You'll actually read something in that one you won't find in Peterson.

"And the thing is," he continues, "birds change so much that no field guide you can buy has every bird you can possibly see in it. But most have 99%."

I spot some more birds: "Right above the tree line straight ahead there are a couple of birds."

"That one that looks kind of big—and it's brown—is an immature Herring Gull." He focuses his binoculars. **"They have different plumages for three years before they take on the adult features.** So that bird was born last spring."

His binoculars scan a vacant area of the sky. "There're some Swallows in right now. And that's kind of neat. We're right on the edge of that."

"Swallows?" I haven't seen one Swallow. And I think I know what they look like.

"Yeah. Barn Swallows and Ruff Wings and Tree Swallows all come real early."

"I haven't seen any."

"Oh, they're specs in the sky. I only saw them through the binoculars."

"What's that one there?"

"It's a Crow. The Crows are working on nests right now. They probably have eggs."

"Any Humming Birds at all within the city limits?"

"Yeah. It's going to be three weeks though before they show up," he precisely predicts. "Around April 19, 20, 25th, in there."

"Ever see them along the river?"

"Yeah. This is a better place to see them than anywhere else. Water seems to be important to them."

We switch to Great Blue Herons. We haven't yet seen any from our lookout. They may just be the most popular bird along the urban James.

"Herons are really smart birds!" Charlie turns and looks at me as if to confirm his statement.

"If fish were feeding would they pick up on it?"

"Like that!" And he tells a Heron story. "These guys were ice fishing in Ohio last winter and the Herons came down and started panhandling minnows from them. They couldn't find anything else to eat, but they knew to do that. The stories about GREEN Herons are just legend.

They do all kinds of weird things to get fish."

The man has left his spot near us and walked back towards the parking area. The woman doesn't return.

Our brief stint of birding reaches its end; I have appointments back at work. Charlie has excited me, has interested me, has amazed me at the wealth of stuff you can consider while watching just a few birds for a few minutes. I resolve to learn more about watching birds so I can add it to my enjoyment of the river.

Birds Along the Urban James

In his *A Field Guide to the Birds of Eastern and Central North America*, Roger Tory Peterson states, "Birds undeniably contribute to our pleasure and standard of living. But they also are sensitive indicators of the environment, a sort of 'ecological litmus paper,' and hence more meaningful than just Chickadees and Cardinals to brighten the suburban garden . . . or rare warblers and shorebirds to be ticked off the birder's checklist. The observation of birds leads inevitably to environmental awareness."

In 1997 birders know that Richmond is frequented by Cormorants, Bald Eagles, and even a Peregrine Falcon—birds which were rare here not too long ago. The river's water is healthier, the food chain is stronger, and there is no better evidence of the overall health of the urban James than the abundance of birds on and along its length.

Obviously plants and mammals and reptiles and fish are also indicators of the river's health, but with birds you get a more global picture. Many of the water birds which pass through Richmond spend time elsewhere in this hemi-

Canada Geese behind the James River Park System Visitor's Center.

sphere. Thus birds are significant indicators of the environment well beyond Richmond.

The following checklist includes most of the birds which are sighted on or alongside the James River in Richmond.

I have put together the list using three sources: the "Birds of the James River Park" brochure published by the Richmond Audubon Society; the checklist in David Ryan's book, *The Falls of the James*; and personal input from Dr. Charles Blem, Professor of Biology at Virginia Commonwealth University.

Loons:
  Common Loon
Grebes:
  Pied-billed Grebe
  Eared Grebe (rare)
  Horned Grebe
Cormorants:
  Double-crested Cormorant
Herons:
  American Bittern
  Great Blue Heron
  Great Egret
  Cattle Egret
  Green Heron
Ducks, Geese, Swans:
  Tundra Swan
  Canada Goose
  Wood Duck
  Green-winged Teal
  Black Duck
  American Mallard
  Blue-winged Teal
  Gadwall
  American Wigeon
  Redhead
  Ring-necked Duck
  Lesser Scaup
  Common Goldeneye
  Bufflehead
  Common Merganser
  Canvasback
  Ruddy Duck

  Red-breasted Merganser
  Hooded Merganser
  Surf Scooter (rare)
Hawks, Vultures, Falcons:
  Turkey Vulture
  Black Vulture
  Osprey
  Bald Eagle
  Cooper Hawk
  Sharp-shinned Hawk
  Red-shouldered Hawk
  Broad-winged Hawk
  Red-tailed Hawk
  American Kestrel
  Northern Harrier
  Peregrine Falcon
Quail:
  Northern Bobwhite
Rails, Gallinules, Coots:
  American Coot
  Sora
  Common Gallinule
Shorebirds:
  Killdeer
  Lesser Yellowlegs
  Greater Yellowlegs
  Solitary Sandpiper
  Spotted Sandpiper
  Common Snipe
  American Woodcock
Gulls, Terns:
  Laughing Gull
  Bonaparte's Gull

Ring-billed Gull
Herring Gull
Great Black-backed Gull
Caspian Tern
Common Tern
Black Tern
Semipalmated Plover
Pigeons, Doves:
Rock Dove
Mourning Dove
Cuckoos:
Yellow-billed Cuckoo
Black-billed Cuckoo
Owls:
Eastern Screech-Owl
Great Horned Owl
Barred Owl
Goatsuckers:
Whip-Poor-Will
Common Nighthawk
Swifts, Hummingbirds:
Chimney Swift
Ruby-throated Hummingbird
Kingfishers:
Belted Kingfisher
Woodpeckers:
Red-headed Woodpecker
Red-bellied Woodpecker
Yellow-bellied Sapsucker
Downey Woodpecker
Hairy Woodpecker
Northern Flicker
Common Flicker
Pileated Woodpecker
Flycatchers:
Eastern Wood-Pewee
Acadian Flycatcher
Eastern Phoebe
Least Flycatcher
Great Crested Flycatcher
Eastern Kingbird
Swallows:
Purple Martin
Tree Swallow

Northern Rough-winged Swallow
Bank Swallow
Barn Swallow
Cliff Swallow
Jays, Crows:
Blue Jay
American Crow
Fish Crow
Mimic Thrushes:
Gray Catbird
Northern Mockingbird
Brown Thrasher
Waxwings:
Cedar Waxwing
Shrikes:
Loggerhead Shrike (not seen in years)
Starlings:
European Starling
Vireos:
White-eyed Vireo
Solitary Vireo
Yellow-throated Vireo
Red-eyed Vireo
Warblers:
Blue-winged Warbler
Golden-winged Warbler
Tennessee Warbler
Nashville Warbler
Northern Parula
Yellow Warbler
Chestnut-sided Warbler
Magnolia Warbler
Cape May Warbler
Black-throated Blue Warbler
Yellow-rumped Warbler
Black-throated Green Warbler
Blackburnian Warbler
Yellow-throated Warbler
Pine Warbler
Prairie Warbler
Palm Warbler

Bay-breasted Warbler
Blackpoll Warbler
Cerulean Warbler
Black-and-white Warbler
American Redstart
Prothonotary Warbler
Worm-eating Warbler
Mourning Warbler
Ovenbird
Northern Waterthrush
Louisiana Waterthrush
Kentucky Warbler
Common Yellowthroat
Hooded Warbler
Wilson's Warbler
Canada Warbler
Yellow-breasted Chat
Tanagers:
Summer Tanager
Scarlet Tanager
Cardinal Grosbeaks, Sparrows:
Northern Cardinal
Rose-breasted Grosbeak
Blue Grosbeak
Indigo Bunting
Rufous-sided Towhee
Chipping Sparrow
Field Sparrow
Savannah Sparrow
Fox Sparrow
Song Sparrow
Swamp Sparrow
White-throated Sparrow
Tree Sparrow
White-crowned Sparrow
Dark-eyed Junco
Blackbirds, Orioles:
Bobolink
Red-winged Blackbird
Eastern Meadowlark
Rusty Blackbird
Common Grackle
Brown-headed Cowbird

Orchard Oriole
Baltimore Oriole
Finches:
Purple Finch
House Finch
Pine Siskin
American Goldfinch
Evening Grosbeak
Weaver Finches:
House Sparrow
Chickadees, Titmice:
Carolina Chickadee
Tufted Titmouse
Nuthatches:
Red-breasted Nuthatch
White-breasted Nuthatch
Creepers:
Brown Creeper
Wrens:
Carolina Wren
House Wren
Winter Wren
Marsh Wren
Kinglets, Gnatcatchers:
Golden-crowned Kinglet
Ruby-crowned Kinglet
Blue-gray Gnatcatcher
Thrushes:
Eastern Bluebird
Veery
Gray-cheeked Thrush
Swainson's Thrush
Hermit Thrush
Wood Thrush
American Robin

April, 1995

by Ralph White

By the middle of March wildflowers abruptly popped out in profusion. Check the islands for Bloodroot, Toothwort, Spring Beauties and Spice Bush. Check the damp cracks of boulders or cliff faces for Saxifrage and in along the trail edges for Chickweed and Violets.

Check out the Wetlands in the evening for the mating calls of Spring Peepers (a "peep" naturally), Chorus and Cricket frogs (a click) and American Toads (a trill).

February, 1996

by Ralph White

Within certain limits floods are a pretty good thing for a river. The rising waters reach onto the banks and remove fallen trees and brush that encroach on the river channel. Spreading waters carry rich nutrients onto the flat floodplain leaving them in a deposit of fine mud. The relatively calm waters formed in these areas create rich, temporary feeding areas for fish which also seek them as a refuge from the torrents. In the main stem of the river the raging waters carry logs and other debris along with nutrients further downstream, and out into the bay and or ocean creating new habitat structure for fish and food for aquatic plants and plankton. Yes, there is also destruction too, but the impact on natural ecosystems of small to moderate floods is generally beneficial, sort of Mother Nature's Sneeze.

Interpretative Guide to the Geology Walk

[Written by Ralph White and originally published by the James River Park System]

The walk along the Geology Trail provides a hands-on learning experience about how rocks were formed and how you can read their stories. The walk is ideal for family groups touring the park with children above age 10 and for small groups of students studying geology in high school. Begin your walk at the 22nd Street Parking Lot (near the Lee Bridge on Riverside Drive).

NOTE: Read the introduction first! It helps everything else make sense, and it will give you a winning vocabulary in Scrabble.

INTRODUCTION

When the planet Earth was formed about four billion years ago it resembled a ball of hot liquid and bubbling gases. As the surface cooled a crust developed, but the bubbling liquid rocks underneath (called magma) cracked the crust into huge chunks and moved them about. (You can see what it looked like by tossing crackers on top of boiling soup.) This is the essence of the Theory of Plate Tectonics.

North America and Africa were once a part of the same huge "cracker" or crustal plate. Columns of hot liquid rocks and gases rising out of the core of the Earth cracked this huge crustal plate and pushed the pieces apart about 600 million years ago. (Look on a world map. The two continents look like pieces of a puzzle that fit together.) As they slowly moved, mud and sand (sediments) washed off the land were deposited along the edge.

About 500 million years ago, the movement of the plates reversed and the continents began to come back together. The plate which had Africa also had most of the ocean over it. That made it more dense (hard and heavy) than the North American plate with mostly land. The dense African crust then plunged under North America. The intense pressure and heat that resulted from these crusts rubbing together caused the sediments to melt and change their makeup. Rock and sediments changed by heat and pressure are called metamorphic rock.

The crashing together of these crustal plates caused cracks and weak areas that also allowed liquid rock from inside the Earth to squeeze through in places. These rocks, formed from the liquid core of the Earth, are called igneous rocks. (Liquid rock is called magma, remember?) By 350 million years ago North America and Africa had fully collided. They have been slowly drifting apart ever since. (In perspective, if the history of the Earth is compared to a year, the history of man on Earth is about one second.)

When liquid or semi-liquid rock squeezes through soft spots in the crust, it forms huge blobs of rock called plutons. They are found in a variety of shapes and sizes, but are usually longer than they are wide. Some of the largest plutons are several hundred kilometers long. (A kilometer is a little longer than a half mile, about 6/10 of a mile.) Rock that has squeezed through and pushed aside existing rock is said to have "intruded" into the surrounding "country rock," as when strangers intrude upon a private party or a secret meeting. Bits and pieces of country rock that did not fully melt into the new intruded rock look like blobs and swirls of chocolate in a marble cake. They are called xenoliths.

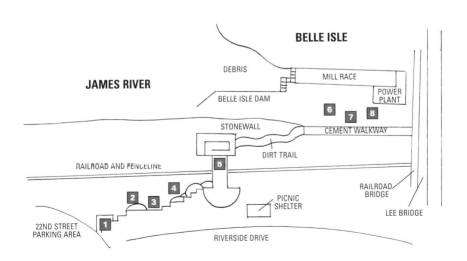

TO BEGIN YOUR TOUR
Begin the trail from the east end of the parking lot. Head towards the stairs and the stone wall. Stop at the wall made of cobblestones to the left of the steps.

Stop #1: Quarried Granite
These rocks were cut from slabs of granite quarried in the park. Can you notice that the black specks are more concentrated in some blocks than in others and that some grains and crystals are larger than others? **Rock that cools quickly is usually near the surface of the Earth and consists of a finer mix of parts, while rock that cools slowly is usually deeper underground and contains bigger crystals.** (It's like pancake batter: if it stands for a long while the parts will separate out, but if made into a solid pancake right away, the ingredients stay together.)

How fast did this granite cool? How many different colored minerals can you find? Try to find these four. Biotite (black mica) is shiny and black. Quartz is clear and shiny. Feldspar is white or yellow. Hornblende is brown, black or green.

Now walk up the stairs and about 10 steps beyond. Stop at the rock to your right with loose sandy material on top.

Stop #2: Effects of Acid Rain
"Faith will move mountains," it is said, but so will raindrops. Water falling through the air picks up carbon dioxide and makes a weak acid called carbonic acid.

This acid dissolves some of the minerals that act like glue, causing others to break away as individual grains of sand. (Note: Rocks are a collection of minerals. Sand and gravel are broken down rocks. Soil is sand and gravel mixed with organic matter like dead leaves, rotten wood and the remains of animals.) Do these grains resemble some of those in the granite blocks in the wall? (Please feel only a pinch on the ground or others will not be able to enjoy this investigation stop.)

Walk on about another 10 steps, as far as the Beech tree roots across the trail.

Stop #3: Root Force

Many forces in nature can shape rocks. Much faster than rain is the pushing and expanding power of roots. They wind their way down tiny cracks in search of water and a firm base to support the plant. As the plant grows, the roots get thicker and longer and the cracks are pushed apart.

Freezing water also widens these cracks. This was one way colonists quarried or cut out big chunks of rock. (If you don't think ice expands, look at the tops of ice cubes. Notice the raised edges where there was once only flat water.)

Walk another 20 or more steps to the next set of stairs.

Stop #4: Colors and Patterns

The rock ahead and on the right has a modern painting like mix of several colors: green, tan, black and light blue or gray. Some of the colors are the work of Mother Nature. Stop for a minute to take a closer look and admire its beauty.

Green plants come in all shapes and sizes. The trees around you are the largest plants visible. The shades of dark green along the base of the rock on the right are the smallest called algae.

The spattering of light gray or blue to the right is another tiny plant colony called a lichen (pronounced like-en). Lichens create a weak acid water product as they grow. What do you think this might do to the surface of the rock?

Feel the black colored places on the rock to the left. How do they feel? What might dissolve away some of the minerals and leave only these bumpy ones? From what you know about how the rate of cooling affects crystal size, did this cool slowly or quickly?

Walk onto the pedestrian bridge which crosses the railroad tracks. Stop at the lookout at the other end of the bridge.

Stop #5: A View of the River

Look at the river. Can you pick out the flat area on either side and the steep edges where hills overlook the river?

Look upstream. Over the centuries (eons) the river has cut its way down through the land. Floods swell the banks of the river every year. The flat land on either side gets covered with water regularly. It is therefore called a flood plain. It is flat due to layers of mud left after floods.

The many rocks exposed in the river give this area of the river its name, The Falls of the James. Rapids are formed because the hard granite does not wear down as fast as the rest of the river bed. Seven miles long, they begin at Bosher's Dam about six miles upstream and end at Mayo's Island a mile downstream. This probably marks two sides of the pluton of granite that is exposed here in the park and stretches all the way from New Jersey to Georgia! Underground it is much larger still and it may be a different shape too.

Look slightly downstream. The nearest island is Belle Isle. During the Civil War it served as a prison for captured Union soldiers. Before and after the war it housed a nail factory and a rock quarry. It also marks a major geographic change in land types. To the west (upstream) are the rolling hills of the Piedmont and to the east (downstream) is the flat land of the Coastal Plain. Which do you think used to be the bottom of a shallow sea? How far did that ancient sea come?

CAUTION: Do not attempt the following part of the tour if the river is flooding the area.

Walk down the stairs and at the bottom turn right toward the "Attention Rock Hoppers" sign. Behind the sign is a path. Follow the dirt path which becomes concrete until you reach a large block. Go around the block and continue on the path for 100 more steps. Turn left and walk out onto the rocks in the river.

Stop #6: The Rocks

Several forces which shape rocks, such as plant roots, freezing water and lichens, have already been mentioned. Another force that can shape rock is a fast moving river. The water in the river carries small particles of debris which become

Thomas Bryan and a James River pothole.

JOHN BRYAN

trapped in the natural fractures in the rock. The force of the running water causes these small particles to move around in the fracture, grinding away part of the rock like sandpaper. As the hole increases in size, larger debris becomes trapped and these also begin grinding. The result of this grinding away at the rock forms a pothole.

Gently reach into one of the potholes (be careful of glass) and pull out one of the stones. How does this stone differ from one you would find on the trail? Is it smooth or rough? What is its shape? Can you give an explanation for the shape? (Please put the rock back where you found it.)

Turn so that you are facing the river bank and path. Walk three fourths of the way to the path and a little towards the railroad bridge. Look for a place where the rounded rock surface changes to squared off edges and flat rock surfaces.

Stop #7: Signs of Quarrying

This is one of the many quarry sites where rock slabs were cut in the park. As the river washed away the soil and debris, which at one time covered this pluton of granite, the pressure on top of the granite was decreased. **The pressure underneath, pushing up on the granite, caused horizontal stress lines to develop.** These made the granite crack in layers. (It looks like the layers of an onion.) It is termed exfoliation. Can you find some examples?

The movement of the crustal plates, one plate pushing against another plate, is responsible for the parallel fracture lines found here. Look across the rocks towards the opposite bank. Do all the fracture lines run in the same direction?

The occurrence of both parallel fracture lines and horizontal stress lines make this an excellent site for a quarry since the rock was already cut on two or more sides. Curb stones found throughout the City of Richmond were quarried from these sites and similar ones along the James River. There are several sties between here and the old railroad bridge to Belle Isle. There is also a large quarry at the 42nd Street Parking Lot.

Get back on the cement path and continue walking toward the old railroad bridge. When you reach the bridge, and the end of the path, turn left and walk out on the rocks.

Stop #8: Xenoliths

As the liquid rock that formed this pluton squeezed through the crustal plate the country rock was melted and mixed with the new rock. In some instances the mixing was not complete and remnants of the country rock can be found in the granite. These remnants or xenoliths are the darker patches of rock that you see here and are responsible for the marble cake appearance of the rock. Locate one of the larger xenoliths. Can you determine the direction this liquid rock was flowing?

This concludes the geology walk. You have investigated, at various steps, from the formation of the Earth's crust to the use of granite for man's needs, but not necessarily in chronological order. As you walk back along the trail, think about what was pointed out at each of the stops and try to place the information in order as it occurred in time.

Answer Key for selected questions asked at each stop:

Stop #1: The speed of cooling is reflected by the size of the mineral crystals observed. Smaller crystals indicate that the rock cooled quickly, while larger crystals indicate that the rock cooled more slowly.

Stop #2: The grains of sand contain minerals that were once part of the granite. Feldspar is one of the first to weather and break away from the rock, and it forms clay.

Stop #4: Acids created by the lichens dissolve away the softer minerals that bind other minerals in the rock together. The dark colored places on top of the rock should feel bumpy. Softer minerals are dissolved by acids from lichens or by acid rain. Remember, rocks with small crystals cooled more quickly than rock with larger crystals.

Stop #5: The Coastal Plain was the bottom of the shallow sea, and the ancient sea came as far as the 14th Street Bridge where the Coastal Plain ends and the Fall Zone begins.

Stop #6: The stones in the potholes are usually smooth and round because the rocks are swirled around by the river water and rough edges are ground away.

Stop #7: Not all of the fracture lines run in the same direction. Most run northwest and southeast.

Stop #8: The direction the liquid was flowing can be determined by examining the pattern of dark bands in the rock.

February 10, 1996

We've had a ton of snow already this winter and the kids have missed a ton of school. But it's between snows now and it's a sunny Saturday. I take Thomas and his friend Hank on a hike alongside the river.

Last fall an employee of the James River Park System told me they're preparing a trail from the Maury Street Landing upriver to the I-95 Bridge. He told me the Park System now owns that land, and that's where we are today.

We park at Ancarrow's Landing near the ramp. The huge parking area has only one other car. A lone fisher stands on the elevated platform at the end. He hasn't caught anything. Last week the temperature got down to minus four; surely the river's cold enough to stymie the fishes' feeding routines. Even the catfish which normally cooperate to some degree all year.

Almost two feet of snow fell recently, and a lot of it has melted. The small field adjacent to the ramp is soggy. Our shoes squish into the ground and they are quickly soaked. The grasses are wet, and where there is no vegetation there is mud. The field borders the river and makes an abrupt 10-foot drop at the river's edge. It's deep here. I tell Thomas and Hank not to go near the edge. If they were to slip into the icy river I doubt that I could survive a rescue plunge. They do stay back. In the middle of the field is a multi-station bird house on a 20-foot pole. We see no birds in or on it.

Woods begin at the field's edge and we enter them. There is a brief trail, but it is too close to the river's edge to suit me. I guide us away from the trail into the woods. These woods are narrow. They are bordered on one side by the river and on the other by the railroad track—maybe 75 yards at the thickest point.

There are of course no leaves this time of year, so we can see deeply into the woods. Big, thick trees support big, thick vines everywhere. **There is still a carpet of snow everywhere that the sun has not burned away. We crunch through it.** Twenty feet from the river's edge—in the woods—is the high water line from the snowmelt flood of a couple of weeks ago. There is a thick trail of drift-twigs and all sorts of debris running parallel to the river. Two-liter soda bottles are everywhere. No telling how far upriver they floated from to come to rest here. There are also pieces of Styrofoam—most small, but some as big as sofa pillows.

Hank and Thomas climb aboard a long-fallen tree. They hold their arms out and balance as they walk thirty feet along its length. At its end they discover a hanging vine big enough to support them, and they take turns swinging. I reach down and dislodge a loose piece of bark from the tree and see a multilegged insect scurrying along. It's two inches long, deep burgundy in color. It's gone before Hank and Thomas can look.

This summer these woods will likely be impenetrable except for the trail. And they'll likely be full of life—both flora and fauna. Today I hear a Chickadee high above us somewhere, but don't spot him. Except for the gulls, I'll see only two other birds today—little reddish-brown bush birds which I can't identify.

The snow has made my feet wet and I suggest we walk along the railroad tracks for a bit. We exit the woods opposite the river and we step single-file onto one of the narrow tracks, balancing on it as we walk along. **A hundred feet ahead on the right is a rectangular piece of metal with a snake sunning on it.** He doesn't depart when we arrive. In fact, he lets Thomas and Hank lift him draped over their two sticks.

He's gray on top, pale yellow with gray checks on his belly. He's a long one—at least five feet. At home later Thomas will show me a king snake in his Audubon reptile guide book which seems to match what we saw. The snake is docile enough to let us touch him, but I don't allow the boys to hold the snake with their hands. It's not poisonous—I'm certain of that—but I've seen non-poisonous snakes bite people who have picked them up. The bites have not been damaging, but they have sometimes broken the skin, and I don't want any mothers angry with me today. We spend ten minutes with the snake and then proceed on towards the I-95 Bridge.

The tracks have interestingly colored rocks between them, and we stoop and pick up and examine one every now and then. Next fall there will be an abundance of wildflowers showing their colors alongside these tracks.

A surprise awaits us beneath the bridge: a field of driftlogs and other debris deposited by the flood. All three of us climb out on it. We can't resist. The drift is probably three or four feet deep, and when we step on weak wood we crash through onto the big rocks below. We have fun looking at everything that drifted here: all sorts of bottles and cans and jars and fishing floats and foam and planks and boards. Eventually after a couple of close calls we decide that stepping among this stuff could result in a broken leg, and we exit onto the riverside rocks that form the base of the Floodwall.

This is where the Floodwall ends/begins, and after a brief climb we are on the path at the top. This Floodwall walkway goes a long way upriver, and it is great for bikers. We will see several in the few minutes we walk on it.

The intriguing thing I see is the gulls. Perhaps hundreds. They float downstream from the pillars of the I-95 bridge. The river is high and muddy, and the gulls are white bobbers on its surface. They float downstream for a hundred yards and then they fly back up and alight again just below the I-95 bridge. There is a lot of river above the bridge, and they could just as well start their float way up there but they don't. They start just downstream from the bridge. Thomas presents the only explanation: "They don't want to hit the bridge pilings."

We each select, but don't take, a favorite piece of driftwood. Thomas finds and collects a twelve-foot cane pole like the ones my Dad and I used 30 years ago to catch crappie. I kick a two-liter Sprite bottle onto the tracks, and we take turns footballing it all the way to the car. The snake is gone, but Hank spies a lizard which is too fast for me and Thomas. Hank says it had some blue coloration.

At the car I tie the cane pole on the roof luggage rack with a long piece of yellow police tape Hank found among the driftwood. The lone fisher has left.

Snorkeling in the City: Underwater Exploration of the James River in Richmond

[*The following was written by Ralph White and first published by the James River Park System.*]

ANIMALS THAT ARE EASILY VISIBLE

Oriental Freshwater Clam

These clams are small (1/4 to 1 1/2 inches), round and often seen as piles of shells. Recently eaten ones may be found on top of rocks, put there by muskrats. Look for old ones distributed by water along the shoreline at the ends of islands and in the sand behind rocks.

These clams were first seen in the James River in the early 1970s, clogging up cooling pipes at an electric power plant near Hopewell. They were probably brought over in ballast water used to weigh down ships. No one knows what their impact on the environment will be, except that they filter the water in order to feed and have become very common. Small ones are eaten by Redbreast Sunfish and Bull Chubs.

Dig your hands into sand bars and fine gravel to find live ones. Watch them underwater as they dig back down by sticking their soft bodies out of their shells—sometimes they'll do this while you hold them between your fingers under water.

American Freshwater Mussel

The mussels are medium to large in size (one to five inches across) with a thin shell and have a slick, shiny lining. The flesh was once eaten by Native Americans, but is not safe to eat in city areas now because they concentrate pollutants in their bodies by filter feeding. Some mussels from the Mississippi River are shipped to Japan where tiny bits of flesh and shell are added to Japanese oysters to stimulate pearl growth!

Feel the smooth, lustrous inside called "Mother of Pearl." It is the substance that pearls are made of and was once used to make buttons. Look for live mussels sticking up like a wedge in gravel bars where the water is a foot or less deep and moving quickly.

Fish Nests

"Bowl-of-Sand Nests"

Look in calm water near the shore or behind boulders for these six-to-nine-inch-wide sunfish nests. Males guard the nests in June and July. With patient waiting you can see the male flair his fins and show his colors. This attracts nearby females and chases away any other fish that may try to eat the tiny eggs. Gently drop a tiny pebble or snail onto the nest and he'll quickly remove it by biting it and spitting it out away from the nest.

"Table-Top-of-Walnut-sized Rocks Nest"

Look in moving water for these two-to-three-feet-wide Bull Chub nests. The male guards the nests but not very well. Watch other fish come up to the nest to lay their eggs or to eat someone else's!

Snails

There are at least a half-dozen kinds of aquatic snails in Richmond. Each has its own special water conditions, but many can be found near one another, often on the upstream and downstream sides of the same rock!

Long Spiral-shelled Snails
1. "River Snails" are the most common kind and have many ridges around the shell.
2. A smooth-surfaced, thinner-shelled kind is a rare find.

Short Spiral-shelled Snails
3. "Pond Snails" are small and smooth with rounded edges.
4. Another small, smooth kind has one wide, flat ridge around the edge.
5. "Little Pond Snails" are tiny, thin, smooth and cone-shaped.
6. " Orb Snails" look like a coil of rope and are also rare.

ANIMALS TO LOOK FOR UNDER ROCKS

Aquatic Insects

These bottom dwellers hatch and live underwater for most of their lives—six months to two years. They come out of the water, shed their skins, and become winged adults that breathe air. These live only a few days or weeks—long enough to mate and lay eggs in the water. At night the small water-dwelling nymphs and larvae feed on algae (and on each other) on top of submerged rocks. During the day they hide from fish under rocks. (That's why fish feed best at dawn and dusk!)

Nymphs live underwater and include the Mayfly nymph (three tails, legs in close), Stonefly nymph (two tails, legs held out), Damselfly nymph (three tails, legs held out), Dragonfly nymph (plump body), Caddisfly larva (green), and Hellgrammites (sharp pinchers and many legs).

In the air are the adult Mayfly (body arched with three tails), adult Stonefly (wings folded on back), adult Damselfly (wings held up over back—eat mosquitoes, do not sting), adult Dragonfly (large, wings to sides, do not sting, eat mosquitoes), adult Caddisfly (long antennae, moth-like wings), and adult Dobsonfly (large mouth parts, wings flat on back).

Hold the Mayfly, Stonefly and Damselfly nymphs in your palm full of water. Watch them vibrate their "tails" and/or side flaps in the still water to get more oxygen. These are actually gills.

Cup some water in your hand with a Dragonfly nymph and watch it walk. Put one in a swim mask full of water and it can also move forward quickly by pumping water out through its rear end! These plump nymphs are voracious feeders and have a special way of catching their prey: their lower lip covers their entire face like a mask and extends out like a scoop! Their food includes other aquatic insects, tadpoles and tiny fish.

As you crawl over the rocks, some of the small, green, worm-like Caddisfly larvae may attach to you. (It feels like a little pin prick.) They live in tiny nets like bits of nylon stocking attached to rocks (sometimes by the millions) and strain the water for tiny bits of animal matter. Some kinds also live under rocks in tube-like cases of sand or twigs. See if you can find a surface without Caddisfly "nets" . . . they are everywhere . . . except in deep or still water.

Carefully lift plate-size rocks in shallow, fast-moving water to find the slow-moving predatory Hellgrammites. With your face under water, watch them walk through very fast current holding on with their many sharp legs. (They may crawl on your hand if you stay still but can pinch if you pick them up!) Hellgrammites eat other nymphs and are in turn a favorite food of bass.

Crayfish

Crayfish look like little lobsters and in Louisiana big ones are eaten. The two claws hold and tear dead creatures which are their food. While they normally walk forward, they will scoot away backwards when alarmed. The female carries her eggs and young under her tail. In the river they are small: one half inch in the first year and one inch or so in the second . . . and then they get eaten.

Place a crayfish in a face mask full of water to watch it move. Look for eggs. If left a few minutes with a worm, it will usually catch and eat it.

ANIMALS THAT MOVE QUICKLY & ARE HARDER TO SEE

Small Fish (one to four inches long)

Young Smallmouth Bass
   Look in pools and behind rocks. It has red eyes and a yellow dot on the tail.

Darter
   Look under rocks. It walks on its fins.

Satinfin Shiner
   Look in potholes. It resembles a guppy.

Bull Chub
   Look for fish forming schools. Underwater it has a dark line with a gold line along the side. This is the most common kind of fish in the river—and one of two that eats clams!

Medium Fish (five to 10 inches long)

Sunfishes
   Many kinds. Look for a dark dot on the gill cover.

Channel Catfish
   Look for smooth skin, forked tail and "whiskers" on face (barbels) used to taste the river mud; can be large.

Smallmouth Bass
   The most popular game fish. It has red eyes and dark stripe on the sides; can be large. Babies have a yellow tail.

Large Fish (one to two feet or longer)

American Eel
   Snake-like fish seems to "bite" water to breathe and may be found in rocky cracks and "caves."

Carp
   Silver or slightly yellow and heavy bodied with big scales and tiny whiskers on the mouth.

Longnose Gar
   Look for black dots on the sides of this long and slender fish. It usually stays still then moves away very fast near the surface.

Stand on your head under water and pull your face close up to rocky overhangs. (It's spooky, but you'll often come face to face with a large fish.) Swim up into a stand of Water Willows in one foot of water and wait quietly with half of your mask above water and half below. (Breathe with a snorkel.) Lie in a shallow rapid (six inches deep) with your arms out to either side and small fish will often use you as their new territory!

October 18, 1981

   Although the hundreds of acres of wooded slopes and lowlands near the urban James are filled with all sorts of birds and trees and wildflowers and shrubs, I had always confined my interests to the water. The woods had always been just something to walk through to get to the fish.
   But my interest in other forms of life was kindled by a friend, and finally I purchased a field guide.
   The *Audubon Society Field Guide to North American Trees* doesn't tell me a thing about nature's real beauties—the birds and the flowers—but it does give me a start. I bought it on my birthday.
   I guess I must have made leaf notebooks as a child, but as an adult, until a month ago, I didn't know a Birch from a Beech. My new field guide describes 360 trees of the eastern half of the country, and I've already identified two dozen of them. And they fascinate me.
   Now, when I have a spare hour, I shove the little Audubon book in my pocket and head for the James.

I've learned to identify a big-leaf member of the figwort family, the Royal Paulownia. It was named for Anna Paulowna (1795-1865) of Russia, princess of the Netherlands and ancestor of the present queen, Juliana. (The Audubon is filled with juicy information like that.)

I learned to identify Beeches (the ones with the permanent initials carved in them) and Birches (the ones with the layered bark). I learned that the nuts of the Beech tree don't taste like the chewing gum, but they do taste like tiny chestnuts. (An advantage to autumn treeing is that you can eat some of what you find.)

I learned that the River Birch is the one the Indians used for their canoes, and that if you remove a hunk of the bark for a souvenir, it'll make a permanent black scar.

The first trees I looked at were the ones in my own yard: American Holly, Southern Magnolia, Apple, and a couple of Oaks which I first thought were Scarlet Oaks, but that I now think are something different because the acorns are too short.

There are some trees growing in a crowded warehouse area near the James. In the middle of the big city I thought it was special to identify an Ailanthus tree right there next to where I've parked my car—until I read the Audubon guide: **"Tolerant of crowded, dusty cities and smoky factory districts, often even growing out of cracks in the concrete."**

I've been having trouble with Hickories—there are so many of them in the woods near the James—and I've spent a good bit of time trying to distinguish one from the other.

One particular tree last week had baffled me until I finally determined it to be a "Butternut" Hickory. And, appropriately, the ground beneath it was covered with delicious looking nuts. I grabbed one, crushed it with my foot, and popped the seed into my mouth and gobbled it down. It was like a mouthful of alum, the bitterest stuff I'd ever tasted. Like a green persimmon.

But I had of course misread my guide. I had indeed identified the tree, but I had misread the name: "Bitternut," not Butternut.

Later a couple of fishers passed me on their way back to their cars. "What kind of tree is that?" one of them asked as I studied a small trunk.

"It's a River Birch," I responded, glancing up from the field guide.

"Yeah, I thought it was a Birch," he smiled.

"Catch any fish?" I asked.

"No, not even a bite. We had hoped to get a mess for supper, but they're just not doing anything this evening," he reported. "Where'd you get that bag full of nuts?" he continued.

"At that Butternut Hickory tree a hundred yards on up the path," I grinned.

"Butternut?"

"Yeah, that's right. You can't miss it; it's right next to the gate and there are nuts all over the place."

"Thanks," he waved, and walked on up the path.

I took a pocketful of Beech nuts home to Janet. She enjoyed them, but I couldn't get her to try the Hickories. She got suspicious when I wouldn't eat one first.

The Audubon guide says people used to eat them as a cure for rheumatism. I'll save them for future agues.

Christmas Morning, 1994

"Daddy, what's the fall line?"

"It's where you live, hamster-brain!" Thomas is generous with his reply to his 18-month-older sister.

"Daddy, what's the fall line?" Kelly repeats.

"THUH fall line, or THEE Fall Line?" I enunciate.

"I don't know," Kelly responds, "just the fall line."

"**It's Richmond,**" **Thomas declares. "Richmond is ON the Fall Line. Your BRAIN is on a fall line.**"

"But what is it?"

"The Fall Line is where the ocean's tide stops," I explain. "It's the last point where the tide goes up and down every day. Thomas is right. Richmond is on the Fall Line. Below the 14th Street Bridge the James is tidal. Above it it's not. And usually there is a waterfall or a series of waterfalls at a Fall Line. That's why they call it the Fall Line."

"But why do they call your brain a fall line?" Thomas makes a face at Kelly. Brains are popular points of ridicule in the fourth grade.

"Do we have a waterfall here?" Kelly continues. Ability to ignore one's brother is an uncommon quality of maturity for a sixth-grader.

"Not like Niagara Falls, just a bunch of small waterfalls. They call them rapids." Then I remember, "But the whole area is called the Falls of the James."

"The falls of her brains!" Thomas points at Kelly with both index fingers.

"Shut up!" Kelly's maturity gives way to the definitive all-purpose comeback.

"I'll tell you what!" I get their attention. "I'll tell you what we can do that's more fun than opening presents! Something we can do together right now on Christmas morning."

"What?" Kelly says limply.

"I'll give you just one hint," I say with raised eyebrows and a big smile. "It rhymes with fall line."

"I know," Kelly says dejectedly, "go fishing."

"Your brain went fishing," says Thomas predictably.

"Right!" I exclaim. "Wonderful, Kelly! Great idea! What we'll do is just put these presents aside and get on our coats and gloves and put the boat in at Ancarrow's and look for some fish! We can be there in less than 30 minutes!"

"Right, Dad." Kelly looks away.

"But the **big walleyes and smallmouths and blue catfish are swimming below the 95 Bridge right now just waiting for a fishing line.** And there probably won't be anyone there this morning to feed them." I pause, wait until their familiar anti-fishing disgust is at its low point, and crescendo, "So what do you say? Let's go!" And I stand and pretend to leave the living room and the blinking tree and the pile of presents.

"Dad, stop it." Thomas states matter-of-factly.

I do stop it and we do open presents and Janet reads Christmas poems and nobody except me thinks about fishing the whole Christmas day. It's been weeks, maybe months since I've wet a line in the James. I'll have to look at my calendar. I'll go next week if this weather keeps up. Perfect. Fifties. No wind. I'll cast big grubs, drift big minnows, bounce big spoons, try to catch big fish. Maybe even a striper or two. Some of them stay around all year. Even on Christmas if anyone's brain is smart enough to try the Fall Line.

Chapter Seven:
Climbing

I am indebted to Rob Carter and Jamie McGrath for allowing me to print their climbing guide here, and for letting me watch them climb. (See "The Wall" in this chapter.) They are Richmond climbing gurus, and their knowledge and advice are valuable.

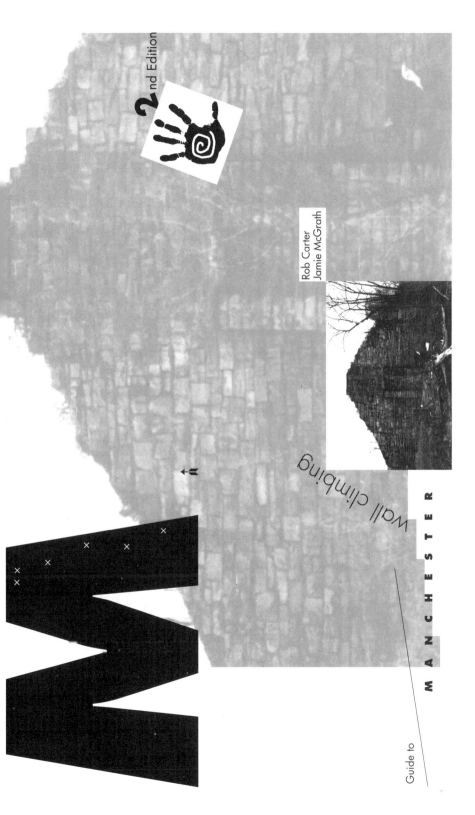

M

Guide to

MANCHESTER

Wall climbing

Rob Carter
Jamie McGrath

2nd Edition

In early spring of 1981,

four local climbers – Jamie McGrath, Les Newman, Rick Atkinson, and Ron Dawson – sauntered across Brown's Island in downtown Richmond to climb an imposing railroad pillar at the edge of the James River. Scrambling down a steep levy, and bushwacking through briars and underbrush the climbers came to the second pillar, and the east-facing wall rising 60 feet above the river. The climb they had established on this pillar was tenuously protected by quarter inch bolts and homemade hangers fashioned from angle iron. Peering out across the bouldery waters, the group spotted for the first time a triangular bridge abutment set into the earth on the opposite bank of the river. In the years to follow, this massive bridge support, known as the **M**anchester Wall, would become the center of climbing activity in Richmond.

Jamie McGrath high on Proctologist

"for most of us." Chris Craggs

"The grade people climb is a lot less important than the act of being there; the cleansing of the soul by a few hours of sport is still what it is all"

climbing

the days of quiet solitude

By 1993,

monoliths stretch across the entire width of the river. Only those pillars on the far sides of the river are accessible, the majority of them rising from the currents of the river, teasing climbers with unseen routes. The pillars are remnants of the Richmond-Petersburg railroad bridge, a 19th century engineering marvel, and while they are man-made, the nearly vertical pylons offer climbers challenging face

The first known route on the **Manchester** Wall, *The Proctologist*, was put up by Les Newman, Jamie McGrath, Rick Atkinson, and Ron Dawson around 1981. This 5.9 route was protected by the same 1/4" bolts and angle iron hangers that they had used on the north pillars. The bolts were driven only 1/2" into the rock. Over the years, these bolts took many falls.

While the **Manchester** Wall was first visited by climbers in the early 1980s, it was not until later in the decade that routes were vigorously established. From about 1986 to 1992, a handful of climbers visited the **Manchester** Wall on a regular basis, usually for practice and to hone their skills for climbing at Seneca Rocks and other substantial cliffs in surrounding states. It was during this time that most of the existing routes at the wall were established. This original group includes Jamie McGrath, Greg Elliott, Mossy Rowe, Keith Donovan, Barry McKenna, Rob Carter, Tyler Waybright, Mike Hutcheson, Keith Hall, Ed Wade, and Noel Swinburn. Other early **Manchester** Wall climbers may have inadvertantly been left out of this list.

wall had spread outside Richmond's boundaries, and the advent of sport climbing intensified activity.

The main **Manchester** Wall and most of the accessible pillars have been fully developed. Routes on pillars submerged in water, however, have yet to be explored. Development of these pillars will surely occur, but only with the aid of boats.

once enjoyed by climbers at the **Manchester** Wall were replaced by

Climbing

Climbing the Manchester Wall and surrounding pillars is a unique experience. Looking from the wall, the James River provides a scenic backdrop, with Richmond's skyline in the distance. Clean granite blocks stacked on top of one another provide delicate face climbing. All of the vertical or nearly vertical routes consist of tiny edges, and the irregular, fragmented mortar joints connecting the blocks furnish larger holds and cracks for protection. Monodoits scattered throughout the wall were originally drilled to enable the positioning of the massive granite stones. These provide single digit holds that regularly test finger strength. All of the routes can be top roped as well as led, and bouldering traverses provide great workouts. A majority of the routes are mixed, consisting of bolts and supplemental gear placements for protection. Unlike typical sport climbing areas, bolts are for the most part widely spaced. Sport climbers may find the routes uncomfortably runout.

All of the routes are highly recommended.

Ethics

Adding bolts to or removing bolts from existing routes is prohibited.

Use of pitons, rurps, bongs, copperheads, etc., is prohibited. Driving pitons into the mortar joints of the main wall and adjacent pillars weakens the structure and destroys the integrity of the rock. If aid climbing practice is desired, use passive protection such as nuts and cam-ming devices, or clip existing bolts.

Related to altering and scaring rock with pitons, chipping holds and removing mortar to create new holds is prohibited.

Please remember that the Manchester Wall is extremely fragile. Desecration of this historic site can lead to its closure.

The foregoing rules are determined by a general consensus of Manchester Wall climbers. Any style of climbing is accepted at the wall as long as it does not infringe upon the enjoyment and rights of other climbers, or alter the appearance and integrity of the rock.

> "There must be safer, saner ways to restore the spirit than by climbing, but I haven't found any yet."
>
> Susan E.B. Schwartz

Khanh man on Voodoo

Rick Ball bouldering on the *Buttress*

Safety

Climbing is an inherently dangerous activity. Anyone climbing in the **Manchester Wall** area is responsible for his or her own safety. Instruction in safe climbing technique is absolutely essential. The City of Richmond and the James River Park System are not responsible for accidents occurring at the site.

With growing numbers of people frequenting the **Manchester Wall**, it is crucial to abide by common climbing etiquette. When setting up topropes, please be careful not to knock loose rock onto climbers directly below. When dropping ropes onto the ground from above, please yell "rope," and wait for the response "clear" from climbers below.

Do not use the railing on top of the main wall for a rappel anchor. This is a dangerous practice prohibited by the James River Park System. The railing is not designed for this purpose.

When leading routes, beware that a fall before clipping the second bolt will most likely result in a ground fall. Using a single locking carabiner on the first bolt might save you from a broken ankle.

Double check that harnesses are doubled back, and that knots are appropriately tied.

All top ropes on the main wall can be set up by walking up a railroad tie stairway leading to the top. This is steep terrain, so be very careful.

Ratings

As at any climbing location, ratings are subjective at best. They are intended only as a rough guide. If anything, routes are underrated by the local climbing community. Test your limits by starting on climbs a grade or two below your ability. Ratings apply to the Yosemite Decimal System. Ratings for climbs are determined by a representational group of local climbers.

"Because if you lose control, you lose. Period."

Marc Twight

Tyler Waybright on Chalk It Up

Parking

Parking is available on Semmes Avenue at the trailhead of the Richmond Floodwall Walk.

Public Watering Hole

Just a long rope length away from the Manchester Wall on Perry Street is the Legend Brewery. This micro brewery is a gathering place for climbers at the end of the day. Four different, fantastic brews await you.

Getting there

From I-64, take Belvedere Road exit. Travel south and over the Lee Bridge. Turn left on Semmes Avenue. Go approximately two blocks to the Flood Wall Walk parking lot. Follow trail, pass over foot bridge and on to the overlook.

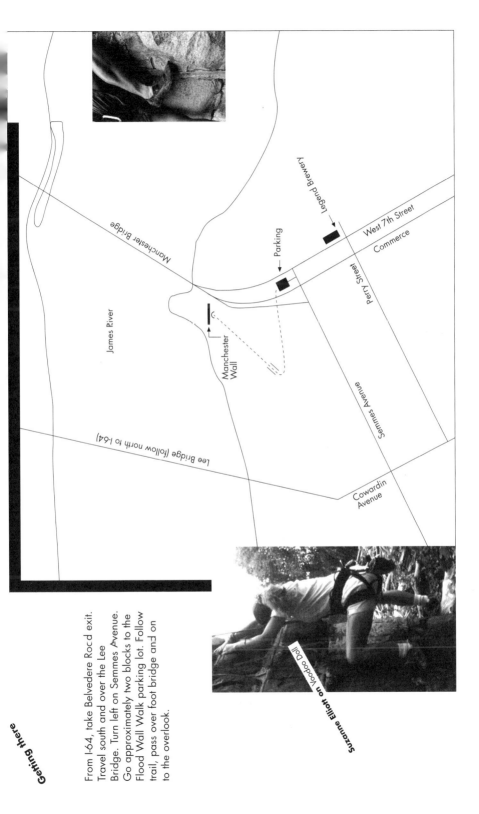

Suzzanne Elliott on Voodoo Doll

Main Wall

main wall

Note: Positions of bolt placements on the topos are approximations only.

Charles Igel on Lost Friend

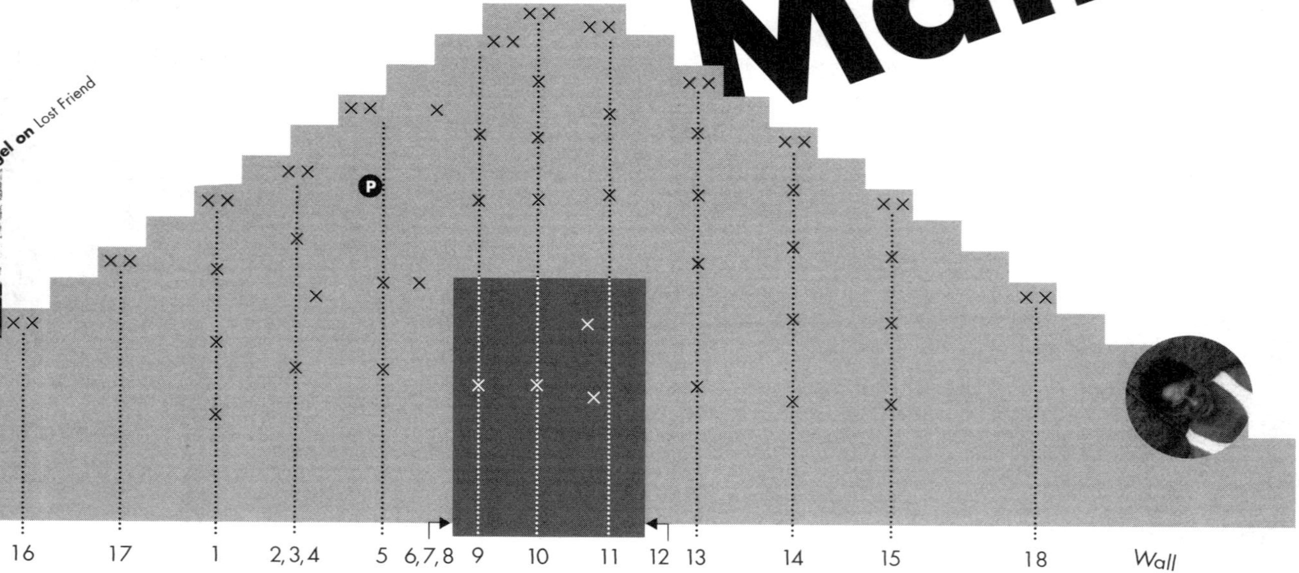

Peter Stücke on Proctologist

1. **Hooked on a Feeling** 5.7+
2. **Fun and Games** 5.8
3. **Berkley By-Pass** 5.9
   Start same as Fun and Games. Diagonal right after first bolt. Climb to fixed pin, finish at anchors on Proctologist.
4. **Piton Route** 5.9
   Start same as Fun and Games. Diagonal right after second bolt. Finish on anchors to Jamie's Connection. Back up fixed pin with gear
5. **Jamie's Connection** 5.9+ R
   Back up fixed pin with gear
6. **Gutter Ball** 5.4
   Left-facing corner of buttress.
7. **Bowling Alley** 5.10b
   Left-facing wall of buttress. Place pro after bolt.
8. **Reset Button** 5.10b
   Climb Bowling Alley, finish on Proctologist.
9. **Proctologist** 5.10a
   Beware of hard start and first clip. Place gear below ledge.
10. **Tendnitis** 5.10d R
    Protection needed between first bolt and ledge.
11. **Lost Friend** 5.10a
12. **Tostita** 5.5
    Right-facing corner of buttress.
13. **Top it or Drop it** 5.10b
    Pro between first and second bolt.
14. **Voodoo** 5.10a
15. **Bits and Pieces** 5.8
16. **The Mortar the Merrier** 5.8+ R
    Trad
17. **Take It For Granite** 5.9 R
    Trad
18. **Femme Fatale** 5.10a R
    Trad

Typical day at the Wall

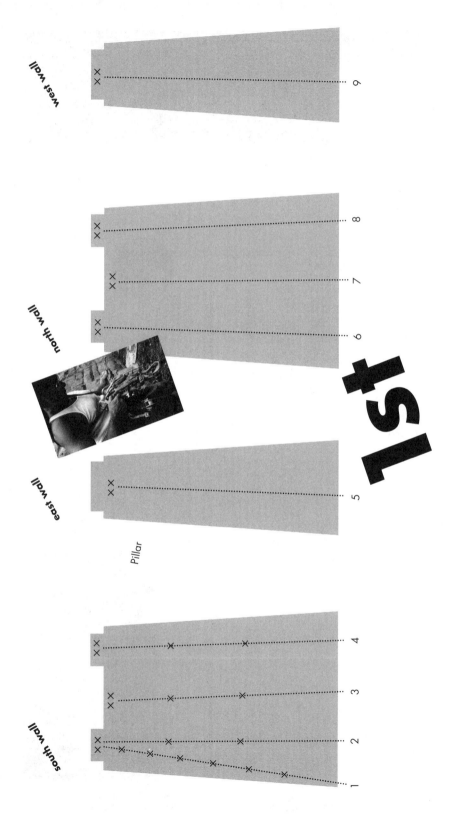

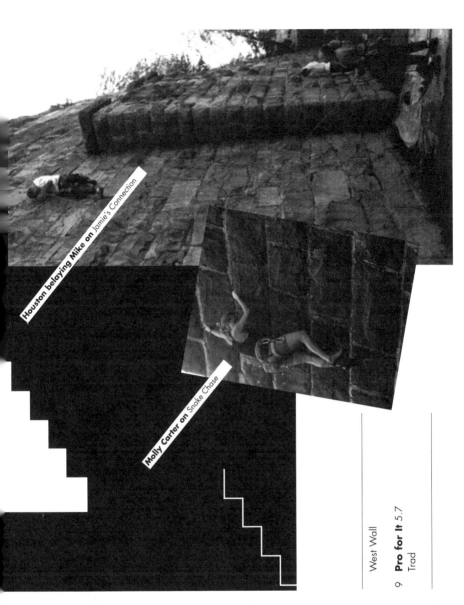

Houston belaying Mike on Jamie's Connection

Molly Carter on Snake Chase

South Wall

1. **Bolts from Heaven** 5.5
   Climb easy arete, finish on right face.

2. **Snake Chase** 5.7

3. **Snakes Above** 5.7

4. **Voodoo Doll** 5.7

East Wall

5. **Snakes Right** 5.7
   Trad

North Wall

6. **Proscuitto** 5.5
   Trad

7. **Pig Iron** 5.5
   Trad

8. **Potty Training** 5.4
   An easy route for a beginning leader to learn gear placements.

West Wall

9. **Pro for It** 5.7
   Trad

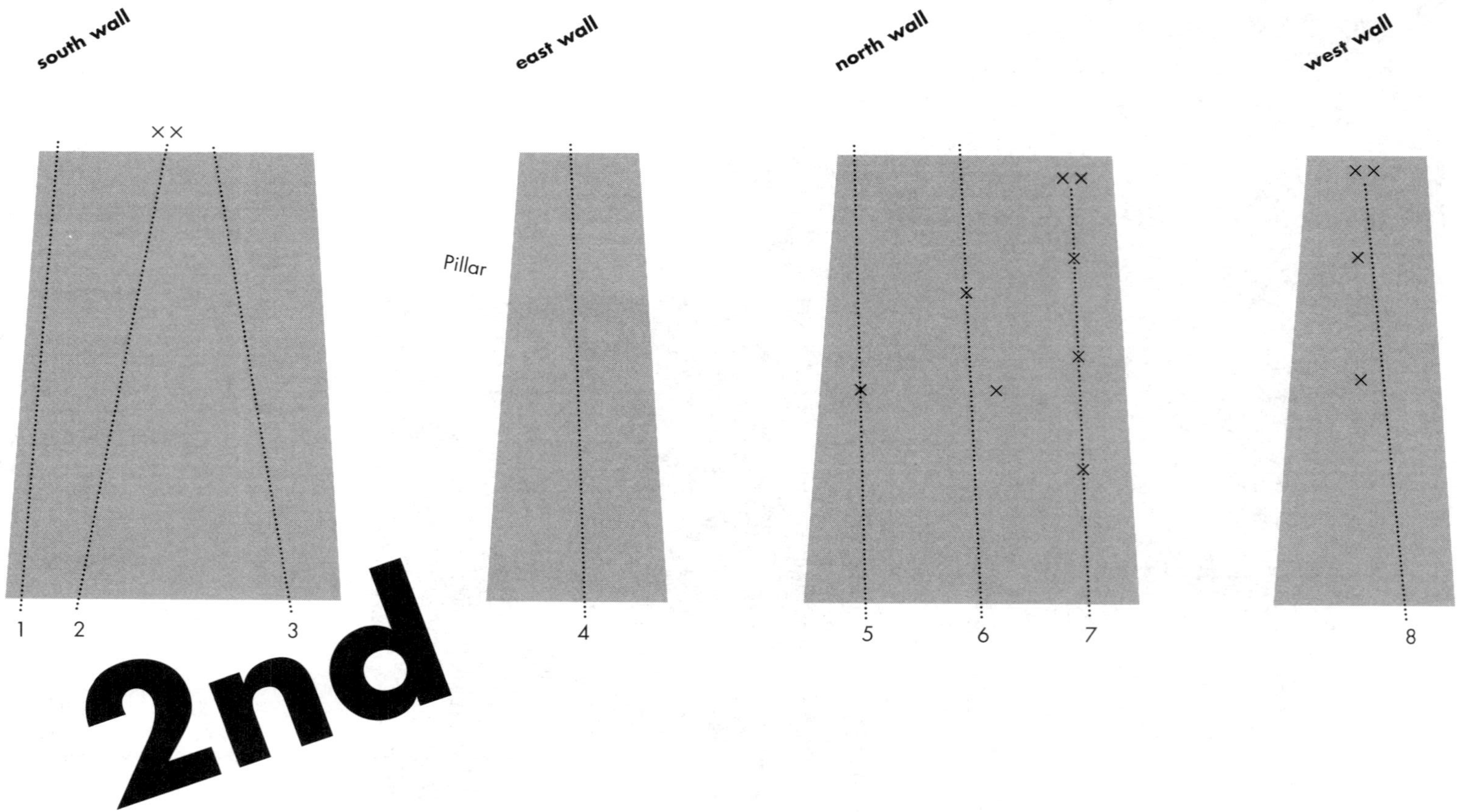

south wall | | east wall | north wall | west wall

1 2 3 | 4 | 5 6 7 | 8

Pillar

2nd

... But we lived to climb many more mountains. The critical task is separating one's ego from one's development. It is one of the hardest disciplines to live by."

Craig Berkley demonstrating the use of a monodot

South Wall

1 **Chipper** 5.10a R
   Trad, corner is not used

2 **Too Many Gins and Tonics** 5.9 Trad

3 **Chock it Up** 5.9
   Trad

East Wall

4 **Crown of Thorns** 5.8+ R
   Trad

North Wall

5 **Pulp Friction** 5.11a
   Mixed route; place gear before first bolt

6 **McKenna** 5.8+
   Climb the crack
   Trad or clip

7 **Nemesis** 5.11a

West Wall

8 **Iron Cross** 5.9
   Mixed pro

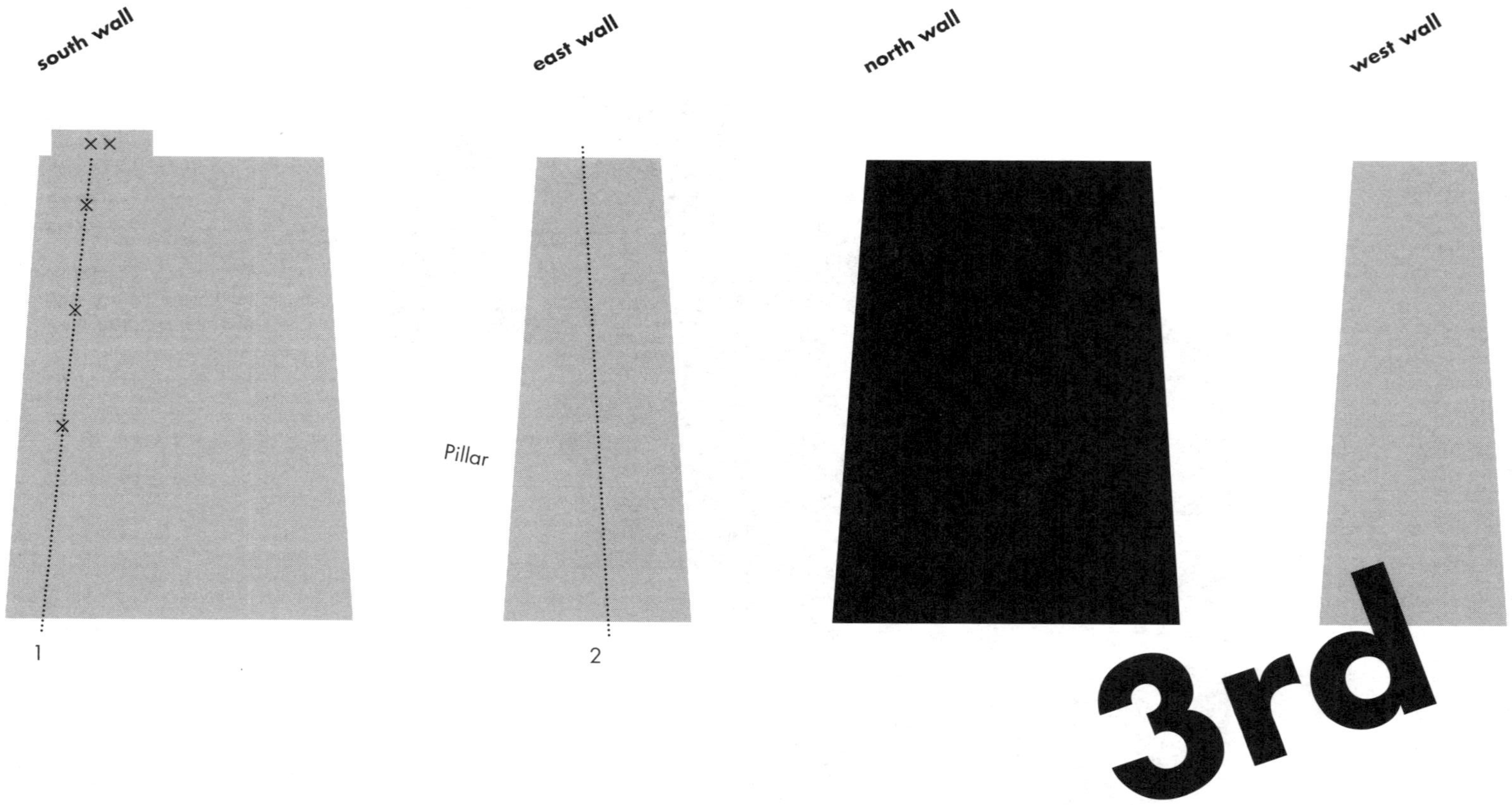

3rd

west wall

north wall

east wall

Pillar

2

south wall

1

"To truly appreciate the cliffs it doesn't seem right to chip. If you can't do it, don't chip. Wait for the future. We must build ourselves up, get stronger, with better technique, and train much. Don't take the challenge away."

Yuji Hirayama

Howard Doyle on Proctologist

South Wall

1 **Who Cares, Man?** 5.9 X

East Wall

2 **Mossie** 5.10b
   Trad

"You have a right to climb anywhere in any style you wish, as long as it does not alter the medium or infringe upon the next person's experience."

Yvon Chouinard

The Wall

It's May 4, 1996, sunny, 75 degrees, and I'm at The Wall. Near the south end of the Manchester Bridge are remnants of a long-ago bridge where climbers ascend the slabby tressels and the 65-foot vertical Wall. My friend Rob Carter started climbing here 10 years ago with a handful of his climbing friends. He's here today to provide my first in-person observation of the sport.

"What do you call these things stuck in the Wall?" I ask as I point.

"Three-quarter-inch bolts with Metolious hangers." Rob replies. "Carabiners, special aluminum clips, are clipped to the hangers to protect climbers in the event of a fall."

He has arrived casually, mellowly, slowly, placing his backpack on the ground and looking around. He greets a half-dozen other climbers who are here—some halfway up the Wall—some by name, others with only a nod and a smile. It's clear that Rob is at ease here; this is home territory.

Rob Carter and Jamie McGrath at The Wall.

"Who put them there?"

"We did," he says matter-of-factly. "Using a battery-operated drill. They're on the pillars beyond as well."

A friend walks past Rob towards one of the pillars, and tells him he is just going over there to boulder.

"What's bouldering?" I've never seen any of this before, and I'm here to learn some of the lingo and watch some of the expertise.

"Bouldering is climbing reasonably close to the ground without a rope," Rob points a raking arm at the Wall,

"just so that if you do come off you won't be seriously injured."

"Can you boulder without someone spotting for you?"

"Yeah. But if it gets into serious, difficult bouldering," Rob selects the phrase carefully, "then it would be wise to have a spotter. What we're doing today is free climbing or 5th-class climbing. 1st class is walking on flat ground. 2nd-class is easy hiking. 3rd-class is hiking over difficult terrain. 4th-class is serious scrambling—where if you fall and you don't have a rope, it could be fatal. Most experienced climbers do not rope up for 4th-class scrambling. 5th-class climbing requires the use of a rope with intermediate pieces of protection, because without them you will most likely die if you fall. **Rob says "you will most likely die if you fall" without flinching. It's a natural part of his climbing vocabulary.**

He continues, "Many climbers here at the Wall climb by means of a top rope. The rope goes through an anchor at the top of the climb. A belayer on the ground holds one end of the rope while the climber is tied into the other end. If the climber comes off the rock, the top anchor prevents a fall. This is a very safe method of climbing in which people are able to push their limits.

"Aid climbers use ropes and other gear to actually ascend. Another category—free soloing—is reserved for lunatics on the fringe. This is climbing at great heights without a rope." Rob pauses. "One does not make a mistake while free soloing. Climbers choose the games they want to play; some are safe, others are extremely dangerous."

"Do you ever see anyone doing that here?" I don't want to watch.

"Yeah, we all dabble occasionally, but it is not recommended." Rob doesn't spend any more time with the answer.

"**If someone wanted to get into climbing and lived here in Richmond and wasn't familiar with it, what would be the first steps?**"

"I guess the first thing would be to show some sort of interest." I can tell Rob likes this question. Back 15 years ago when he and I fished a lot together he had never climbed a rock. He was new to all this back then. Now climbing and being outdoors define his psyche.

"Do you need to take lessons?" I interrupt.

"It's very wise to take lessons from people with experience. I learned by just hanging out with good climbers. You should learn to climb safely whether you pay money or just hang out with friends."

A group of high school girls shows up. Maybe 10 or 15. Obviously some sort of weekend class activity. They carry backpacks and ropes and are about to swarm onto the Wall.

"We need to get moving," Rob says to his friend Jamie McGrath.

Jamie is Rob's climbing partner. I meet him for the first time today. He looks mid-forties like me and Rob, wears wire glasses like Rob, and has a huge chest and massive biceps, unlike Rob and me. They drop their packs at the base of the Wall.

For Rob and Jamie the Wall is a place to practice and to keep in shape for road trips to climbing sites in other areas of the country. "We're very fortunate to have the Wall," they both agree, "it is considered by many climbers to be the best Virginia has to offer. It is often visited by people passing through on their way to other climbing areas in the southeast."

"Most of the climbs at the Wall are moderate to difficult," Rob explains while looking upward. **The hardest route is Ten-d-nitis, which goes up the center of the buttress and beyond. It is rated 5.10d.** " He turns to the left and points. "This climb is Proctologist and is rated 5.10a. 5th-class climbing begins at 5.0 and progresses to 5.14. Climbing 5.14 is like climbing upside down on inverted wet glass. At 5.10, ratings are further broken down into increments of a, b, c, and d.

Rob begins to pull objects from his pack. Jamie is doing the same. They are not in a hurry.

He spreads a six-by-eight-foot ground cover at the base of the Wall. "This is to keep the rope clean."

I watch as he removes things from the pack—things I've never seen before. "We'll be here for about three hours, taking turns belaying and climbing."

The shoes fascinate me. All of the climbers' shoes fascinate me. The color combinations and designs are interesting, not mainstream like all the other shoes you see.

"The soles are made of a special sticky rubber," Rob says as he holds his shoes and contemplates them. "They cost anywhere from $100 to $150. They're usually pretty well designed and not too ugly. I had these shoes custom made in Utah."

Rob was born and raised in Utah. He goes west most summers to visit family members and to visit rocks. By profession he is a graphic designer. He's written books on design that are used internationally. My favorite research project of Rob's was a few summers ago when he documented petroglyphs out west. He got a grant to go. It was of course necessary for him to climb a few rocks in order to gain a proper perspective on and appreciation of the glyphs. I want to get a grant to go fishing.

"There are various kinds of sticky rubber and shoe designs for different kinds of climbing. Rubber can be either really soft and sticky for smearing, or harder for edging." Rob is a professional teacher too. "**Smearing is when you get as much rubber on the rock for friction. Edging is standing on minute holds like this one.**" He motions me to the Wall. He puts his hand on a slight outcropping the width of a quarter. "Yes, you stand on this."

Rob and Jamie join in conversation with a group of four climbers at the base of the adjacent route.

They discuss the Gunks and Seneca.

"The Gunks?" What are the Gunks?

"The Shawangunks in upstate New York. Sha-wan-gunks." Rob enunciates. He lists other abbreviated places that climbers know. "The New—New River Gorge. The City—City of Rocks, Idaho. Seneca—Seneca Rocks. The Valley—Yosemite Valley. The Winds—The Wind River Range."

I overhear another guy talking to Jamie, " . . . I was knocking a caterpillar off—glad I wasn't using an eight." What's a caterpillar? What's an eight?

Jamie answers me. "The caterpillar was an actual caterpillar. He knocked it off his shoulder and let go of the belay device. An eight is a figure eight—a device sometimes used to belay a climber." Jamie sorts through the metal hanging from his waist. "This is an eight." He shows me. Now he shows me a mechanical-looking device, "And a Grigri is designed so that if you accidentally let go completely the rope locks automatically. If he had let go of this," he holds the eight again, "it would have just slid on through and the climber would have zipped to the ground."

Rob continues my introduction to the equipment. "This is a carabiner or biner for short. These are wedges—or nuts. These are Black Diamond Stoppers, a form of nut." These Stoppers are slotted into cracks in the rock.

He lifts a complicated looking device. **"This is a camming unit. You pull on this trigger and insert it into a crack.** I'll show you." He scans the Wall and finds what he wants. "See this crack?" He inserts the device. "A lead climber artfully inserts this gear into cracks while ascending. Slings made of strong nylon webbing attached to two biners are then clipped to the gear in the rock. Finally, the end of the rope tied to the lead climber's harness is clipped to the runner. In theory and hopefully in practice, this protection system will stop a climber from falling to the ground—an ugly process known as cratering."

Rob sorts through more gadgets hanging from his harness. "This is a cleaning tool. It is a device to help the second climber get the nuts out of the cracks when they can't easily be removed with the fingers.

Rob explains that there are currently two forms of free climbing: traditional and sport. Traditional climbers place gear such as nuts and camming devices into the rock, while sport climbers simply clip short runners—called quick draws—into pre-placed bolt hangers. "Sport climbers typically climb in indoor climbing gyms on artificial holds. These are very safe, very controlled environments. **Traditional climbers prefer the outdoors, the mountains, natural settings.** The Wall is kind of a mixed area," he motions up to the Wall, "because traditional gear as well as bolts are used."

Ten years climbing the same Wall seems a long time to me without getting bored. I of course know you can fish a hundred years on the same pond without getting bored, but what about rock climbing?

Rob smiles at my question. "Hey Jamie. Has this gotten boring?" He answers before Jamie can. "This is never boring. Nah."

"It's odd," Jamie confirms, "because **you can climb here for 10 years, but continue to tackle climbs differently each time you're on them.** The other day I was doing a route and found some holds I'd never seen before."

"Yeah," Rob nods, "by using different holds, a climb can feel different every time you do it. Climbing is always exhilarating; moving vertically over stone sharpens the senses and heightens one's awareness of living and being."

Rob and Jamie are ready to climb, and each offers for the other to go first. "You want to do a route while I belay you?"

I ask about climbing etiquette, basic climbing rules. "Double-check everything," responds Jamie. "You check each other out—your knots, your harnesses." He thinks. "You never climb over top of anyone else."

"Adding bolts or removing bolts from existing rocks is prohibited," declares Rob. "The locals generally determine the ethics for every climbing area." He looks at Jamie who is now at the base of the Wall. "Okay, Jamie's going to put up the first lead. What're you going to do? Top It or Drop It or Voodoo?'"

"Top It or Drop It," smiles Jamie.

"Jamie is going to clip bolts and put in a little gear. If he falls—and I doubt that he will fall—he will only fall twice as far as his last piece of protection. In other words **if he falls before clipping that bolt,**" Rob points, "**he's going to fall to about here, about 15 feet.**"

"Three weeks ago I fell 20 feet while on this climb," Rob casually remarks. What about dying? What about breaking bones? What about cuts and bruises?

"Nah, nothing," he responds. "My toe just slipped."

"Momentary memory lapse," clarifies Jamie.

"A little too casual," says Rob with raised eyebrows.

I ask how often people fall here, and Rob explains that most people top-rope which eliminates fall potential. "People who do lead know how to climb here. Falls happen, but not as often as you might think. Falling and getting injured or dying are legitimate concerns, but the risk is minimized by experience and common sense. **Climbers use protection systems to transform a potentially fatal activity into a reasonable one.**"

I ask the value of the equipment he brought today.

"Probably $800 here—maybe more—" he scans the ground, "probably $1,000. The rope is $150 and the shoes are $150. These things are $65." He's showing me a camming device. "Average cost of a carabiner is $8. Only minimal gear is needed at the Wall."

A young friend of theirs is bouldering to the left. I ask how high people boulder. "As high as your confidence takes you," says Jamie. "Some people free solo all the way up. But here at the Wall it's not a polite or smart thing to do. Anything could happen." Jamie sits at the base of the Wall now, still fondling his equipment, preparing to put on his shoes.

"See how confidently and fluidly she moves on the rock?" Rob watches the friend boulder. "She has her finger in a monodot, a common feature found at the Wall. **I once had my finger in a monodot while bouldering and it popped. Blew out the tendons.** Couldn't climb for four months. Climbers' fingers take a lot of abuse."

I ask him how the round finger-size holes got into the rocks. "These holes were created because they drilled them when this bridge abutment was built. They were used to pick up the rocks. It's ethically wrong to create holds by chipping the rock."

Jamie's shoes look different from Rob's, and he struggles to put them on.

"Slippers," he tells me. "A generic term. These are Mocasyms and they are built on a shotgun last. The shoe is designed for incredibly technical face climbing. The foot is forced into a position to keep the big toe on the tiniest of holds.

"They're very uncomfortable. You can't walk in them but you can climb in them." Jamie winces as he stretches each shoe and bends each foot to go inside. "This is my third pair. They fit so incredibly tight that your foot cannot move at all inside the shoe."

"This is a kernmantle rope." Rob motions towards the rope onto which Jamie is tying. "It has an outside sheath with strands of nylon cords running through it. These are hi-tech, dynamic ropes and will hold around 6,000 pounds."

"They're fall rated," continues Jamie. "This is probably a seven-fall rope. After you take about seven falls—depending on the the length of fall—it would be wise to retire it. I use retired ropes to tie down my canoes—"

"Tow cars," Rob interrupts, "make hammocks. There was a sculptor in New York who had an ad in one of the climbing magazines wanting used climbing ropes for an installation.

"They have on the average maybe—what, 20% elongation? So if you fall they're going to stretch so you don't break your back. It's going to be an easy fall, a dynamic fall."

"That's how you took that head-first, 20-foot screamer not too long ago," Jamie winks at Rob.

Rob weaves an end of the rope through a device attached to his harness. "This is an air traffic controller—ATC. It is a belay device."

He tells me it's okay to continue our conversation as Jamie climbs.

211

"We give each other signals."
"BELAY ON."
"CLIMBING."
"CLIMB."
I see a chalk bag hanging on the back of Jamie's harness. Rob has a similar one. "I use chalk frequently while climbing. It improves your grip on the rock when your hands sweat."

Jamie starts up the Wall. His hands and fingers reach and take holds as his legs and feet move him upward. Rob narrates. "This is a 5.10c climb. A rather difficult climb with the most difficult moves towards the top. He's using a single, locking biner for the first clip because if he were to fall before clipping the second bolt, he would be less likely to hit the ground and break an ankle." Climbers sprinkle their conversation with falls and breaks. "So I'm letting out rope gradually and not putting any tension on him. He will never feel my belay."

What I'm watching is unbelievable. I've seen it on television, but in person it's different. Jamie is a fly climbing a vertical wall. How does he stay attached?

"My right hand is the break hand. The belayer never lets go of the rope with the break hand. **If Jamie comes off, the friction of the belay device and the securely held rope with the break hand will stop the fall."**

Rob's eyes stay on Jamie as he talks to me. Jamie is 30 feet up now, ascending steadily and quickly. "Yeah, Jamie's good.

"This is a single pitch climb, a single length of the rope."

He tells me about pitches. "Jamie and I often do multi-pitch climbs together, climbs that may range from several hundred to several thousand feet in height."

Even though Jamie is clipped into bolts, I am nervous watching him. He clips as he ascends—every 10 feet or so. So his rope is always attached to protection below him, not above him. If he were to fall now, he'd drop as far as 20 feet. The rope would stop him, but any number of things could happen on the way down. The top-ropers nearby are attached by rope to the top of the Wall. They can let go and lean back without losing an inch. If Jamie were to let go or lose control even for a blink of an eye he'd fall. I see that there is no room for loose concentration for lead climbers.

Jamie reaches the top of the Wall without incident. He clips two bolt hangers and starts his descent. "GOTCHA." Rob shouts up to Jamie. "I can easily let him down by allowing rope to slide through my break hand."

Jamie doesn't rappel as they do on those armed forces commercials. He just sort of walks down the Wall backwards, leaning out over the air, depending on the rope which Rob slowly lets out. When he arrives at the bottom he doesn't even seem winded.

"If somebody came to the Wall who'd never climbed here before, this would be much harder for them," Jamie modestly explains the apparent ease with which he climbed. "But when you do climbs over and over again, you get them 'wired.' I knew exactly what I was doing because I'm so familiar with the route. Climbing a route 'on sight'—having never seen it before—is much more difficult and challenging."

Jamie and Rob now prepare for Rob to climb while Jamie belays. Jamie continues to answer my questions about what I just watched. "You hold on with your hands but you actually climb with your feet."

"This 5.10 route is very sustained. It remains difficult all the way to the top. Climbs are rated on the basis of the hardest move. A 5.10 climb may have only one 5.10 move with all of the rest of the moves at 5.5."

I hear someone shout, "Rope!" People look up and a rope plummets to the ground. Climbers use many different warnings and signals to keep things as safe as possible. Jamie explains, "If a rock is accidentally dropped from the top of a cliff, you yell 'Rock!' If you drop anything you yell, 'Rock!'"

"If you don't, somebody's going to get killed." Rob says killed again.

"Rob and I go to Seneca Rocks at every chance. If Rob's leading and I want to talk to him and he's out of earshot, I scream, 'Rob!' and everybody scatters."

"They think I'm saying 'Rock!'" Rob laughs.

Rob and Jamie obviously enjoy what they're doing. And the enjoyment obviously reaches many levels. **"If you were to die and go to rock climber's heaven, what would be there?"**

Rob doesn't hesitate in his answer, "Jamie's going to give you the same answer I'm going to give."

"Seneca." Jamie doesn't hesitate either. Now he explains Rob's preparation at the foot of the Wall. "Rob's

tying a rethreaded figure eight which is a standard climbing knot for tying in."

"Also used for belay anchors." Rob looks up from his knot.

Rob boulders for a few brief minutes to warm up. He and I were born in the same year. We are older than the others I see here today. Rob's been athletic for the 15 years I've known him, but never competitive. Always modest, unassuming. We used to jog some together. He was always a lot faster, but ran at my pace when I was along. He was serious about biking too. Always good muscle tone. Which is apparent now. He wears a black tank top and khaki shorts. He wears socks with his climbing shoes, "because I sweat so much that my foot will sweat inside the shoe and it'll start moving around in slime."

His hands are white like a mime's face. Plenty of chalk.

Now he starts his climb and I get my camera and start working the angles and the sunlight. Jamie belays.

The Wall is dark against the sky and against the sun. If I stand close to the Wall the sun is behind it. A few steps back and the sun glares into my lens. Rob climbs slowly, lightly, methodically. Rob is several inches taller than Jamie, which is the reason he uses some different holds than Jamie. He makes it to the first bolt, clips, and ascends higher.

Rob constantly reaches behind him to chalk his hands. His body is flush with the Wall some of the time, but arches outward at other moments to achieve balance. Why doesn't gravity pull him off the Wall? He is lead climbing and there is no rope above him to counteract gravity. His feet stand and push up on invisi-

JOHN BRYAN

Rob Carter leading a 5.10.

ble outcroppings. His fingers hold onto ungrabbable surfaces. But he doesn't fall.

I watch half of his ascent through the lens of the camera. The camera puts him a thousand feet up, on the north face of the Eiger, the Grand Teton. But, as Rob would tell me, **you'd be just as dead falling 65 feet as 1,000 feet.** His silhouette composes beautifully in the frame of the camera lens. I move from one side of him to the other. From one direction he is a silhouette because of the sun. From the other direction I can recognize that it is Rob.

He makes it to the top without a problem—as Jamie did—and is lowered down, unclipping his quickdraws from the bolt hangers as he goes. "Wanna try?" He greets me at the bottom. "I have an extra harness." No, but thanks.

I ask him and Jamie about the fun factor. Is it fun every single inch of the way?

"Until you get scared." Rob's face goes solemn. "Like when you're about to fall because your forearms are blown and your last piece is 20 feet below you." He talks faster. "And you're gonna fall any second and you gotta get a piece of gear in. It get's scary, but it's part of the adventure." Climbers always have good stories to tell.

"What is the highest degree of difficulty you can climb?" I ask Jamie.

"Sport climbing? I can squeeze a 5.11 on a real good day, 5.10 for trad. Same with Rob."

"There is a lot of camaraderie among climbers. Most people are very friendly and will do anything to help another climber. A climber from out of town who was here for the first time fell a couple of weeks ago and broke his wrist because he didn't listen to Rob's advice." Jamie's voice quickens slightly.

"See that first bolt." He points at the Wall. "It's high, very high. In most climbing areas the first bolt is placed much closer to the ground. **But part of the Wall's tradition is to place the first bolts high off the ground.** This is a bold tradition that gives the Wall real personality.

"This climber was a gym climber unfamiliar with traditional protection, and he was accustomed to climbing routes with a first bolt nearer the ground. Because he was new to the area, Rob suggested that he put a piece of gear between the ground and the first bolt. But the guy said, 'I don't need it, I don't need it,' and he got all the way up to the first bolt and wigged out and came off before clipping.

215

Lost it." Jamie stops, thinking about the story. "Rob had suggested two other ways of climbing the lower section but he ignored the advice."

I say hello to a few other climbers and they all seem friendly. Everyone here appears to be considerate, aware of others, ready to assist. I have been told that's how it is here for most people. Nobody is in a hurry. Smiles. This is a comfortable club where most people are familiar with the code. I understand it's that way at other climbing locations too.

Jamie and Rob tell me that climbing has become trendy and even crowded in some places. Even at Seneca there are lines waiting for the most popular routes, as in an amusement park.

I watch a while, take a few more pictures, talk with some other climbers. I've seen what I came to see. But I have one other question. **The question about introspection. The question about the inner self. The question is whether people climb alone.**

Jamie answers. He tells me that there are days when there is nobody around and that he can come to the Wall and climb alone. He does it every now and then. "Sure, climbing can be a very solitary thing." He doesn't tell me why, nor what happens during one's solitude on the Wall.

Chapter Eight:
More Ways to Enjoy the Urban James

This chapter gives hints and glimpses of the real wealth of enjoyment potential the James River offers. I have left out a lot of things—like kite flying which is wonderful from the Floodwall Walk. There's always a breeze there and your kite can soar with the gulls. I've only barely mentioned biking and jogging; persons serious about these will want to explore for themselves. I didn't mention the poetry walk—currently in the works with Ralph White. When complete, it will provide a walking route through the James River Park System and poetry passages to read at the various stops along the way. If you spend any time at all along the river you'll make your own list of ways to enjoy it.

Catching butterflies near the James River Park System Visitor's Center.

September 6, 1982 ≋

The Labor Day James River was low and wide and clear and smattered with huge rocks and boulders. To escape the swimmers and picnickers I climbed down the steep path on the south side of the Nickel Bridge and waded upstream into a two-mile stretch of the river which has no access points on either bank.

That part of the river has two characters. One is a rocky, rolling, frothing, freestone stream; the other is a sandy, silent, smoothly gliding ribbon. The white-sanded flats swarming with darting schools of minnows remind me of the South Georgia Ohoopee. The bouldered rapids recall adolescent reminiscences of East Tennessee's Little Pigeon.

But the James has neither the largemouths of the Ohoopee nor the rainbows of the Little Pigeon; the star of the James is the smallmouth.

The bright Labor Day afternoon was absent of clouds, and the sun's beaming rays made it difficult for the large fish to summon the courage to venture from their secret hiding spots. Only a few yearlings were enticed by my artificial offerings.

I fished Beetle Spins—tiny ones—in greens and oranges. They produced dozens of redbreasts, some handsize, but none of the true giants I saw the year before. And they produced 10 small smallmouths, half of them stretching to 10 and 11 inches, none of them smaller than eight inches. I tagged and released each one.

The James had been high and dingy all summer, only settling into a blue-green clarity in the last week of August. Its summer-long swiftness had left massive deposits of small pebbles and shells high on sandy banks. I sifted through several promising piles, looking for fragments of Indian pottery. I found none. But I did find three especially round stones, each the size of one of those large marbles. I also found an eight-inch piece of ancient ceramic, perhaps from a 100-year-distant water works. And I found a palm-size stone with a fossil imprint of a segmented crustacean.

I saw a single banded water snake, only 12 inches. It swam towards the most awesome rapids I encountered, within which was a pair of kayakers. They bobbed and rolled and generally frightened any fish which would have been there to greet my lure.

The river was clear, but other than a million minnows I saw few fish. There were a few schools of shad, flattened against mid-current boulders. Occasionally I would surprise a fair smallmouth and send it darting into the nearest hideaway. And I saw three fish together that looked like walleyes. The newspaper had reported recent walleye catches in the James. The only other fish I saw was a 15-inch smallmouth, swimming slowly, and sporting a festering wound adjacent to its dorsal fin.

My Labor Day excursion into the James was two hours upstream and then a quick hour back down. I saw only one other fisher, but the river is so wide that we didn't come within 100 yards of one another.

An occasional jogger plodded across the Nickel Bridge downstream while an occasional freight train plodded across the railroad bridge upstream. Sycamores lined the banks and dropped leaves into the shoreline eddies. Hatches of delicate damsel flies clung close to the river's weeded pools. The afternoon was a splendid one, and my thoughts drifted with the breeze along the river.

Urban Siren ≈

How can I not stay here and fish when there are March fish jumping everywhere? What was going to be merely a reconnaissance is now going to be an all-out stretch of my brief break from chores: the roof, the yard, the basement, you name it. The river's probably high and muddy, so it'll be an all-day chore day. Patch that roof, clean that basement, trim that yard.

And take a 10-minute break to drive down to Great Shiplock Park to confirm the muddiness of the river while dunking a quick grub in the lock for crappie. Maybe 12 minutes. Maybe 15, max. "You go ahead and start on the yard," I told Janet, "I'll be back to join you in a few minutes."

The river is indeed high and muddy. That brief Richmond rain just two days ago didn't do it; it was the long rain a hundred miles upstream that did it. If you want to predict this urban river's condition, you learn to pay attention to the precipitation a hundred miles west. This old lock in Great Shiplock Park fills with the muddy water, but it is immune to the galloping currents, and the fish sometimes seek shelter here. They sometimes congregate here. They sometimes provide a quick midday fix here to my fishing habit. There are four hours of chores behind me, four more to go, and I now need a five-minute injection to satisfy my craving.

There has been no research on the chemistry of fishing—the actual oozy swirlings that surround the brain's synapses. **Are mysterious pleasure-enzymes released in my brain? And precisely when are they released? Is it when I reel in a fish? Is it when I make the first cast? Is it when I step out of my car and get my first glimpse of the river?**

No, it's before all that. It's when I allow myself to even think about this urban river. Like saliva being released in response to seeing a lemon being sliced. It'll happen just watching someone else taste a lemon. It'll even happen just thinking about squeezing a lemon. It'll happen even just punching five keys on a Macintosh Performa's keyboard: l e m o n.

I posit that fishing is like that for some of us. It's chemical. It's in our brains. It's a chemical addiction. The chemicals cause an involuntary takeover of our common sense. Of our logic. Of our ability to distinguish urgent chores from wait-until-tomorrow chores. Like now.

So what if I don't reattach those fence boards in the back yard today? So what if I don't prune those bushes today? So what if I don't pick up that Fan trash that the urban wind has deposited in my yard? And so what if I don't patch that rusty crack on the roof? It'll wait through another rain, won't it? I mean, what's the worst that could happen? A few drops in the living room, a few in the kitchen maybe. We have plenty of buckets. I'd have to ignore the crack another three years for the entire roof to disintegrate, wouldn't I?

I park in the Great Shiplock Park parking lot near the Valentine Bike Trail sign. The trail leads into the riverside woods. Maybe next time I'll bring a bike—if the fishing chemicals will allow. I walk over to the lock and look down: fish spatter the surface everywhere. Are they white perch? It's time for their spring run. Are they crappie? I've seen crappie splash the surface in muddy water before. No, now I see one clearly. They're shad, herring, menhaden—whatever these early spring arrivals are called. The locals refer to them as herring. They're sleek and silver and slimy, and they average a half-pound or so. And they're great bait for all the big fish: blue cats, bass, stripers. **Tomorrow I'll have to return with a big rig and use cut herring to attract a giant.**

I cross the lock gate and walk 100 feet down the trail to the island's point. There's a man with a white bucket on the tip of the point. I claim a spot 50 feet to the inside. From here I throw a chrome Rat-L-Trap across this inlet which feeds the lock. Fish are jumping everywhere. Herring. And Herring don't bite Rat-L-Traps. They don't bite anything except bare gold hooks. Empty hooks. They catch a million herring each year at Walker's Dam on gold hooks. They freeze the herring for unappetizing food purposes and for cut bait. Right now I'm interested in neither.

My Rat-L-Trap seeks a striper. Or a bass. Or maybe a catfish. Catfish have hit my lure plenty of times before.

I face the river's downstream flow; it's fast and ugly. It's the color of artist's mud—that awful color you get when you mix too many colors of paint. It's a stale brown. Not a rich, vibrant brown. Just a bland, featureless hue.

These shorelines are urban. To the left are two hulking loading cranes that service both the back-up trains and the side-loading barges that stop within feet of one another. Unload the barge and load the train in one motion. Or unload the train and load the barge. It goes both directions depending on the destination of the load. The cranes used to be painted deep sky-blue. It's a pretty blue, but it's now an urban-scarred blue—old and flaky and scabbed with rust everywhere. The cranes look long-abandoned. Ghost cranes.

Further to the left, back towards Shockoe Bottom, is the Lucky Strike smoke stack. A tall, slender, red brick smoke stack with Lucky Strike painted proudly in the sky. It's the tallest structure on the block. And it's as old as the cranes. A remnant of early industry in this neighborhood. No smoke comes out of the stack; I don't even know if it's used anymore. They've taken some of the industry buildings and turned them into upscale condos: Tobacco Row. Now that the Floodwall is complete, Shockoe Bottom will never be inundated with the river's mud again. A decade ago the James spread into Main Street Grill all the way up to the second floor.

Herring jump everywhere. My view captures at least 100 jumpers per second.

I hear a slow train coming. Slow trains use these tracks that cross next to and within Great Shiplock Park. If you disobey the signs and walk the short train tressel across the canal you can always get out of the way if a train comes. It will be a slow one. Like this one. It creaks and squeaks and groans as it makes the turn.

Now I notice the fish. They've quit. No more jumpers. Not even one. Sometimes they'll do that with a change of tide. But this is the first time I've seen a train put them down. The local fish are long accustomed to trains. But these herring come all the way from the ocean. For some of the new arrivals this must be their first train.

They stay down for almost 10 minutes. When they do start again, they do it slowly. **First one tiny, tentative splash. Then a few seconds later there's another. Eventually they're jumping everywhere like before.**

I catch some on my Rat-L-Trap. Not actually "catch." I snag them. In the back, in the tail, in the head, in the belly. They're so thick out there that I can't help but drag the Rat-L-Trap through them. I snag one every five or six casts. You can always tell it's not a bass or a striper. A snagged herring is sort of a dead weight that throbs a little. A fish can get better fighting leverage against a hook and line if he's caught in the mouth.

I watch the man on the point pull in a real fish. "Whatcha got?" I hail him.

"White perch." he shouts back and holds it up.

"That's a good one!" I respond. And it is. More than a half-pound.

The man is a brown Pillsbury Dough Boy. Deep brown. He wears an old, ragged gray puffy jacket , dark blue pants, and black tie-up shoes. There is a white bucket sitting next to him into which he drops the white perch. In front of him are three fishing rods pointing out towards the river and propped on y-sticks. I walk over to him.

"Mind if I take a look?" I ask as I lean towards the bucket.

"No, go ahead."

The bucket contains perhaps 20 fish—mostly white perch, a few catfish, one that looks like a crappie.

"You got some good ones in there."

"I had me one this big," he stretches his arms, "a while ago, but I lost him. I tried to drag him up right here," he points to the shoreline, "but he broke off. Should of stepped down there and got him. He was this big!"

"What was he?"

"One a them big catfish." His arms remain stretched apart.

"How many days have the white perch been biting?" I ask. It's now late March, and the white perch always arrive sometime in March.

"Don't know. This is my first time on the river this year."

"How long you been here today?"

"I been here all day." He looks at his watch.

"They been biting steady all day?"

"Off and on," he responds. "I gotta go in a few minutes. Make me some supper." And he looks down into the bucket.

"Well, good luck!" I walk back to my spot.

It is only after our conversation ends that I hear it. That I notice it. The urban roar. The urban drone. A steady bass cleft foundation of urban vehicles. Just upstream cars go 60 miles an hour across the I-95 Bridge. Their noise is constant. Just behind me cars go 20 and 30 miles an hour along Dock Street. And just beyond them is the bustle of the city: a murky jumble of all sorts of noises. And somewhere in the distance is a train. **In Richmond there is always somewhere in the distance a train.** These noises combine to form an urban hum.

I remember when we moved from 112th Street in New York City to no-name street in rural south Georgia. It took us a long time to become accustomed to the absence of noise. To the lack of an urban hum. Of course in New York City the hum was more of a roar, and in New York City the roar went 24 hours. In Richmond it's mostly a workday hum.

A flotilla of waterfowl drifts in the center of the river. A long row of them. I count 28, one by one, as they drift across my line of sight. I can't tell what they are. It's likely they are gulls, but their silhouettes look different—like Canada Geese. But I've never seen Geese on this stretch of the river. No, they must be gulls. With the sun positioned as it is, the birds are only dark gray silhouettes and I can't identify them. The scattered row of 28 begins and ends and drifts on down this high muddy river.

This spot where I stand was urban a long time ago too. Back in the days before railroads this was a busy spot. This spot right here was the beginning/end of the Kanawha Canal. Ocean-run freight would be transferred here. Active canal boats experienced traffic jams here. Tethered mules backed up and turned around alongside this canal. Merchants and workers swarmed all over every square foot of ground. Boxes and barrels and crates piled up everywhere. Ropes and riggings were coiled everywhere. Trash and mud carpeted every square inch. The urban hum was organic—quite different in hue from today's mechanical hum. This spot was surely too busy to allow a riverside fisher.

But just as surely the Urban James Siren did exist back then. It charmed and mesmerized fishers just as it does today. It lured them from their factories and their shops, from their homes and their hearths, from their work and their chores. **It is clear in fishing literature that these pleasure chemicals have been around for hundreds of years. Fishers back then were not immune to the addiction.**

There is a difference though—"Rrrrriiiiinng—rrriinng—ring—" my cellular phone interrupts from my jacket pocket.

"Hello, this is John Bryan," I answer. My office answering machine gives this number.

"Where are you?" It's Janet. She always begins like that.

"At the river," I reply honestly. "I'm leaving in two minutes," I lie.

"Two minutes?"

"Yep, I was just making the last cast."

"Would you pick up a clove of garlic on the way home?"

"Sure, glad to. See you soon."

Great! An on-the-way-home chore! Now I can still fish another 10 minutes and blame my lateness on the grocery store lines.

My cell phone confirms the difference in the 1996 fisher's response to the Urban James Siren to the response of the 1896 fisher. **The fisher of a century past could escape all ties to the real world. Back then the Siren could capture the fisher forever.** In 1996 I am always tethered.

A Walk on the Wall:
Interpretive Guide to the Richmond Floodwall

[*This section was written by Ralph White and published initially by the James River Park System.*]

Why the Wall? The Richmond Floodwall protects 750 acres of low-lying industrial land from flood impact. Several times a year the James River swells and overflows. Mountains in western Virginia trap clouds that dump rain into headwater streams. Since the James drains 25% of the state, moderate floods are estimated to occur every 3 1/2 years.

The Richmond Floodwall is a joint city and federal project that cost $135 million. In Richmond the clean-up for the Hurricane Agnes flood in 1972 alone cost $112 million. While there are environmental costs to the Floodwall, like the destruction of some wildlife habitat and the movement of flood impact further downstream, the benefits to Richmond include enhanced economic development, increased land values, and an improved tax base.

The Floodwall is located on both sides of the river. There is a 4,300-foot concrete wall on the north side and a 13,000-foot combination earthen levee and concrete wall on the south. It varies in height from 7 to 30 feet. The concrete wall sections are built with an underground ledge (an inverted T) so that the weight of the flood water actually helps brace the wall. The Floodwall Walk covers the first mile on the south side, starting at the Manchester Bridge.

Thomas Bryan in one of the "doors" of the Floodwall.
→

Floodwall Map

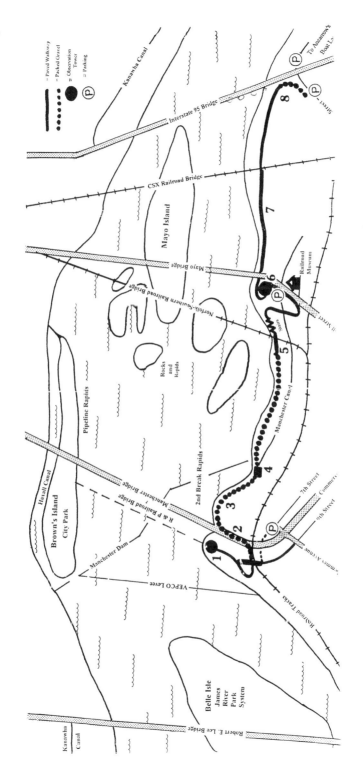

Scenic and accessible, this one-mile riverside tour runs from the Manchester Bridge Overlook at Semmes Avenue and 7th Street to the Mayo Bridge Overlook at First and Hull Streets and on to the I-95 Overpass at Maury Street. Parking is available at all three sites. The Old Dominion Railway Museum is located at Hull and 1st Streets and is at the midpoint of the walk.

The best views of rapids, historic structures and wildlife are during the first half of the walk. Most of this section is wheelchair-accessible with assistance. (There is a steep asphalt section below the Manchester Overlook and the rest is packed gravel.) A set of stairs three-fourths of the way to Mayo's Bridge blocks complete wheelchair passage. The second half, east of Mayo's Bridge, is entirely asphalt and parallels the flatwater. There is a moderate hill at the end near the I-95 Overpass.

TO BEGIN YOUR TOUR

From the Manchester Bridge Parking Lot, follow what used to be an old railroad grade, across the lawn and under the Manchester Bridge to a footbridge. Cross over the railroad tracks and follow the path to the right to the overlook.

1—The Manchester Overlook

You are standing on one of the abutments for the Richmond & Petersburg Railroad Bridge built in 1838. 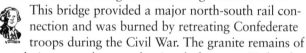 This bridge provided a major north-south rail connection and was burned by retreating Confederate troops during the Civil War. The granite remains of several piers extend across the river before you. **Today the rough texture and jointed surfaces make this a popular bouldering site for skilled climbers.** The shorter cement pillars that have fallen over show the power of the floods. These once supported a railroad bridge built in 1902.

To the left of the pillars is a long, low, bridge-like structure with handrails and narrow tracks. Metal spacers were wheeled out and dropped between the supports to create an adjustable dam called the VEPCO Levee and also called the Brown's Island Dam. The dam funneled water to the Haxall Canal on the north bank. This fed the now-abandoned steam and hydroelectric power plant identified by the three tall brick smoke stacks to your right. The canal now marks the perimeter of Brown's Island Park.

Further to the left, among the trees, is the eastern tip of Belle Isle, part of the James River Park System. It is the site of an infamous Civil War prison camp and has the remains of early iron and quarry industries. Today it is a popular place to view whitewater rapids, jog, climb and fish.

On the horizon and slightly to your left is the white mansion-like structure of Ethyl Corporation, the company that invented high-octane gasoline. The old brick buildings below Ethyl comprise the famed Tredegar Iron Works, once the largest iron foundry in the South. **It manufactured cannons during the Civil War and produced the armor plates for the Confederate ironclad, Virginia, better known as the Merrimac.**

The rapids in front of you and to the far right provide excellent habitat for fish and other wildlife. In the spring, shad, herring and rockfish migrate upriver to spawn. Fish-eating birds like Great Blue Herons, Cormorants and Fish Crows line the shore and islands, while anglers crowd Mayo's Bridge to your far right. At any time keep a lookout for rafts, kayaks and canoes shooting the rapids.

The jagged rocks and islands to your right were once part of a granite quarrying operation and were connected by bridges to the larger Mayo's Island downstream. Mayo's Island marks the lower edge of the Fall Line and the beginning of the flat tidewater area. The Fall Line in Richmond is a seven-mile-wide band of granite that created river rapids which begin west of here at Bosher's Dam near the Willey Bridge. The length of granite actually extends about 1,000 miles from New Jersey to Georgia. Most large eastern cities were located along it because early ships could not sail up through the rapids. The energy of the rapids was then harnessed to power early industry.

Turn around and follow the path down the hill. It leads under the footbridge and along the railroad to the underside of the Manchester Bridge.

2—Curving Arches Under the Manchester Bridge

The earthen levee you are walking on marks the start of the Floodwall. The squared-off rocks on your right are salvaged materials from the Kanawha Canal soon to be used in a restoration project. The open area beyond is the switch yard and repair station for the Norfolk Southern

Railroad. Ahead of you along the path you can see the top of the cement portion of the Floodwall.

3—Observations from Along the Wall

Looking at the river, you will notice a large flatwater area formed by a dam. This dam connects to the Floodwall at the machinery site about 200 feet down the path. Beyond the dam and below it are numerous rocks and rapids that provide feeding areas for birds such as Bald Eagles, Ospreys and Kingfishers. Also look for mammals like muskrats, beavers and otters in the river.

Looking toward the railroad is a large, open, earthen area without railroad tracks. It was the site of the Norfolk Southern Roundhouse where steam locomotives were turned around and repaired. Today you may see railcars on the tracks loaded with pulp wood, a commodity you would have also seen a hundred years ago. The lovely grass strip is maintained to prevent tree roots from undermining the wall.

4—Machinery Site Regulates Canal Flow

The pipes and machinery around you adjust the flow of water through the wall and into the Manchester Canal behind you. This mill race supplied water to power early flour, textile, and corn mills. William Byrd blasted out the first part in the 1730's. Paper mills and a hydroelectric power plant utilized water power from the canal. The canal reenters the river at the power line near the end of the walk.

The concrete wall that runs diagonally across the river is the Manchester Dam. A notch about 200 yards offshore, called Second Break Rapids, creates the only safe place for whitewater boaters to cross the dam. The rocks and rapids that continue to your right are known as Southside Rapids. These rapids are another good place to look for wildlife. The more famous Pipeline Rapids are on the north side of the river. The Devil's Kitchen Rapids are hidden among the islands in between.

5—Set of Stairs Rising Over Swinging Gate

Below this set of stairs is a Floodwall closure that allows Norfolk Southern trains to cross through the wall. Notice how it can be swung closed like a door in the event of a flood. Most other closures slide shut.

The walkway follows the canal to Hull Street and is paved from this point on to I-95.

6—Mayo's Bridge Overlook

A large sliding closure that seals off the Floodwall during floods is hidden in the thick concrete wall under you. On your right are the grain storage towers of Southern States Cooperative and to the left is the Richmond Paperboard Company.

Stairs to the Floodwall near Hull Street.

Ahead of you is Mayo's Island, Mayo's Bridge, and the end of the Fall Line, where the rapids cease and the flatwater begins. Mayo's Bridge, one of the first and most famous bridges in Richmond, was originally constructed of wood. Tolls paid for its frequent rebuilding and provided a good profit for Mr. Mayo, an early Mayor of Richmond. It was reputed to be so rickety though that teamsters did not want to pay because their horses would bolt as it swayed.

Near the end of the Civil War it was burned by retreating Confederate troops. The current Mayo's Bridge, built of concrete in 1913, has been totally submerged in floods and has not been damaged.

The asphalt path now goes under the bridge and follows the river at the base of the Floodwall.

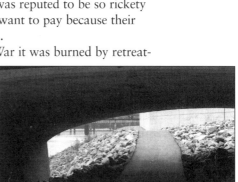

The Floodwall Walk beneath Mayo's Bridge.

7—Granite Surrounds You at Wall Base

The height of the wall, 30 feet here, gives you a sense of how much water the structure can hold back. The flatwater in front of you is an important resting site for striped bass and shad before they make their way through the rapids, and a popular spot for boaters and anglers in the spring. **The concentration of fishers is a modern view of what you might have seen 400 years ago with aboriginal Americans!**

The rocks (rip-rap) around you are designed to reduce erosion and may also serve as a home for harmless baby water snakes. Please do not hurt the snakes, but gently urge them off the path away from feet and bicycle wheels.

8—Flatwater View from Top of Hill

The I-95 Bridge looms to the east. Behind it along the south shore was located the first permanent English settlement at the Falls, (later known as William Byrd's trading post) and the site of Virginia's first railroad, a gravity-powered system that carried coal from Midlothian to the wharves on the river.

Across the river the low concrete platform with trees in front marks the largest underground concrete tank in the world—Richmond's Sewage Retention Basin. It fills with combined storm and sewage water during heavy rains, thereby protecting the river. Emergency overflow gates are also visible along the river. The restored brick buildings are former tobacco warehouses.

Behind the basin and to the left is the CSX Railroad Trestle. **At three miles it is the longest double track railroad trestle in the U.S. and the site of the only triple railroad crossing.**

Behind you on the south side are large pond areas that store storm water runoff during floods. The pond area at 4th Street is a six-acre man-made wetland and is being managed for wildlife. (Note the Purple Martin boxes on tall poles.) The concrete building houses a pumping station which removes rain water when the flood gates are closed. Behind these are cylindrical tanks which store gasoline and diesel fuel.

The Floodwall continues along I-95 for another 1 1/2 miles, but the walkway ends here at the intersection with Maury Street. It is about one mile back to the overlook at the Manchester Bridge.

Floodwall gate at Maury Street.

Annabel Lee

(804) 644-5700
1-800-752-7093 outside of Richmond
P.O. Box 7735
Richmond, VA 23231

The Annabel Lee is an old-time riverboat docked just downstream from downtown Richmond and features "lunch, brunch, dinner, party and plantation cruises on the historic James River." To get to the Annabel Lee from downtown Richmond take Broad Street east to 21st Street. Turn right on 21st to Dock Street. Turn left and follow Dock Street until you reach the Intermediate Terminal. Signs will assist you.

You really have to call and ask for a brochure to see all that the Annabel Lee offers. There are daily cruises at lunch and dinner plus special cruises for almost any occasion you can name or imagine. There are cruises for Valentine's Day, Wine tasting, St. Patrick's Day, Easter, Garden Week, Mother's Day, Father's Day, Halloween, New Year's Eve, and more. Plus there are "Summer Cruises for Kids" which include special entertainment. Prices for the vast variety range from $8.95 to $45.

Cross Country Skiing

Ralph White, Naturalist for the James River Park System—is the lone city official authorized to patrol by ski during whiteouts. Ralph reports that the one area along the river where cross-country skiing is good is on the main trail at the James River Park Visitor's Center. On Belle Isle there is also a trail, but it is not so good because the trails deteriorate quickly.

April, 1996

by Ralph White

Longer hours of daylight and fewer (and milder) episodes of freezing send plants back into a growth mode. A lot of other life forms take advantage of this new and tender food source to go into a breeding frenzy.

The Box Elder Beetles are massed by the the thousands on the sunny side of the James River Park System Visitor's Center walls. **Like college students hearkening to the call of Fort Lauderdale they are awaiting the right mix of light and heat to migrate.** The beetles go to Box Elder trees (Ash-leafed Maples) that will supply them with the liquid nourishment they need to carry on the species.

Box Elder Beetles.

By late March the first Mourning Cloak butterflies (brown wings with yellow edges) should be fluttering through the forest/field edges. Having overwintered as adults in the hollows of trees (or in butterfly boxes) they are searching for the sugary dampness oozing from trees' wounds caused by storms. It's an ill wind that blows nobody good.

The first Paper Wasps have come out from hiding in the cracks between the molding and siding of the building. All pregnant queens, they are awaiting the first wildflowers—not that they eat much pollen at first, but because the plant leaves feed caterpillars which are the food for larval wasps. Sun to sap to flesh and more flesh, all the while concentrating the sunshine. Meanwhile they soak up the sun and a few will begin their first nest building—a quarter-inch stalk hung from the ceiling with eight tiny cells fanning out from the end. Until there is a retinue of daughters the danger of wasp stings is negligible. It's interesting, and safe, to look at the tiny yellow eggs glued to the bottom of each cell, but you have to get up real close.

Sunlight is warming the river as well. The first larval stoneflies have crawled form underwater rocks and split their skins to merge as slow and awkward fliers—safe mostly because there are few warblers and flycatchers to eat them. **Like males of another species, newly adult male stoneflies spend hours courting the opposite sex, beating their heads against walls and branches.** With them, of course, it works. Fertilized eggs end up back in the water. The hatchlings scrape the tender diatoms that grow on the rocks now clear of the more coarse green algae that will come later in the season. The sap in this case is the nutritious slime on the rocks.

Jet Skiing

People regularly launch jet skis at Ancarrow's Landing during the warm months. The jet skis should be used only downriver from this point. Although some people attempt and succeed at running through and past the rapids upstream from Mayo's Bridge, this area—and all areas between Mayo's Bridge and Bosher's Dam—should be avoided by jet skis for three reasons. First, the water is shallow and rocky, and jet skis will hit the rocks. Second, it is improper to subject the city's rescue units to undue risks. Third, jet skis ruin the ambience of the unique natural setting of this area.

There is a popular and safe area for jet skis just upstream from Bosher's Dam—just beyond the portion of the river covered by this book.

Water Skiing

Although water skiing is possible from Ancarrow's Landing downstream, it is rarely done in this section. However, it is quite popular just above Bosher's Dam (beyond the scope of this book) in the long stretch of deep flatwater which has a ramp capable of launching appropriate boats.

Biking

The best bike route on the urban James River is the one-mile loop around Belle Isle. It is a well maintained path which has no very steep grades. The one difficulty is that on sunny weekend days throughout the year the path has plenty of walkers.

If you park in the lot on Tredegar Street, it is exactly 1 1/2 miles across the Footbridge, around Belle Isle, and back to the parking lot.

Biking is also available on the Floodwall Walk on the southside of the river. Park in the lot at 7th and Semmes or the one at 2nd and Hull. The Floodwall Walk is a mile long, but it

JOHN BRYAN

has a 47-step set of stairs over the railroad tracks at almost the midpoint.

Bikers also pedal along the trails at the Huguenot Woods, Wetlands, Main Area, and Great Shiplock Park areas of the James River Park System, although the trails there are neither graveled nor paved and can be difficult in wet conditions. Ralph White reports that a mountain bike trail from the 22nd Street area to Belle Isle will be built in 1997.

Bike Erosion on Belle Isle.

Although subject to erosion, the Buttermilk Trail through the Main Area of the James River Park System is used regularly by mountain bikers. (See the article on Jogging for details.)

One request for bikers: please use your good judgment in confining your biking to paths and conditions which do not promote erosion. (Biking on Belle Isle off the main pathway continues to cause significant erosion.)

Biking Along the Floodwall

It's March 31 and the urban James is elevated and discolored from upstream rains. Today I'm biking, not fishing, at the south end of the 14th Street Bridge. My bike glides along the paved path which you enter right there at the upstream side of of the south end of the bridge.

The first thing I see is a guy dipping herring with a long-handled green net. He stands on the rocks below and dips along the edge of the rapids. His colleague has a white bucket into which he deposits a fresh herring every couple of dips.

Downstream there is only one boat on the water—a blue and white cabin cruiser anchored just below the railroad bridge. Probably fishing for white perch.

My bike coasts effortlessly along the Floodwall. This path—maybe eight feet wide—is paved smooth with no cracks. I haven't been a recreational biker since I was a child, but the special feeling returns immediately. This path along the Floodwall coasts downhill beneath the railroad bridge where there are gorgeous deposits of driftwood on both sides of the path. The path is at its low point here and an area of dried mud covers it—left over from the recent high water. Ralph White has told me that sometimes harmless snakes are seen here on the path.

Once under the railroad bridge, the path is all uphill. I succeed in pedaling to the top of the hill—where the path changes to packed gravel—without having to get off and walk. But I am out of breath. I don't bike much, and this bike is a 30-year-old 3-speeder.

Up here I can see a lot of the river. There are no other fishers, but there is plenty of wind. I make a note to bring Thomas and his kite here. And I can see a lot of urban Richmond. This path ends alongside the south end of the I-95 Bridge.

A big billboard dominates I-95 drivers' entrance into the city: "Your Basic New Look"—an ad for Basic Cigarettes. Drivers also see Richmond's downtown skyline. The blue and red NationsBank letters form the most distinguishable building-top message. Drivers can also read Crestar on the top of another building.

I look at this view of the city as I would compose a painting. It's bordered by tall buildings on the right and left and the little blue and white boat down below. Shallow diagonals are formed by the railroad bridge and the 14th Street Bridge. Across the river there are the crisscrossing diagonals of the Downtown Expressway and the Interstate above Shockoe Bottom. These are contrasted with the verticals of the I-95 pilings—smooth and round with T's on the tops, 20 of them between here and the island.

A second boat motors slowly upstream carefully and hopefully, avoiding the rocks which the elevated river has hidden.

The river is brown and gray. The sky is a weak blue. Spring foliage is just barely awakening; tiny swatches of green spatter the mostly gray landscape.

A family of four walks past me on the path. The little girl, perhaps nine, has dirty blonde hair, jeans, white sneakers, and a white tee shirt over a long-sleeve yellow shirt.

The skies reveal only three gulls and a single Great Blue Heron. It's midday, 12:45.

The slow motorboat is one of those windshield/deck runabouts. Four people sit in it poking fishing poles into the air. I assume the boat will eventually stop and anchor.

The season's first wildflowers have blossomed on this slope up here near the I-95 Bridge. There are Dandelions—both the yellow flowers and the white seed pods—and there are tiny white clustered flowers.

Beneath the I-95 Bridge at the river's edge is the cache of driftwood Thomas and Hank and I explored several weeks ago when there was still some snow on the ground. And below it is the small inlet where Hank's dad and I wet a spring fishing line from my little cartop boat last year.

Just as my eyes alight on the inlet a carp breaks the surface. His entire yellow/orange body leaves the water and splashes down like a whale. It's not all that big, maybe five pounds. The carp surfaces five times over the next minute and then disappears. My eyes shift to a lone orange traffic cone deposited among the driftwood.

This trail ends atop the Maury Street Floodwall Gate. The gate is tall and looks like something built to keep King Kong out. This spot is the same elevation as the I-95 Bridge and only 20 feet away. I count the cars—two or three per second. They contribute to the city's urban hum.

Sitting on my bike this high above the river with the city stretched out beyond gives me a regal feeling as if this is my kingdom. It's only an old bicycle, but it feels like a throne, or like a magic carpet on which I can glide at will along this river.

The slope behind me, away from the river and towards Manchester, has blue-purple clover flowers everywhere. Bordering them is the industrial water treatment plant. I think of Alice Walker's bright admonition to notice the color purple.

I glide back to the 14th Street Bridge, cross 14th Street, and then pedal up the spiraling ramp to the lookout. The ramp has smooth concrete and smooth railing and lights within central pilings. At the top the lookout area is about 10' x 50' and is carpeted with brick pavers. This is a spectacular view of the city and the river. On my tiptoes I can see the Lee Bridge and its underslung footbridge upstream. Below I watch the herring dippers. Traffic crosses the 14th Street Bridge at a rate of one car per second. Four fishers fish from the bridge.

Again an almost mystical feeling of power arrives. Atop my bicycle atop this lookout atop the city and the river I somehow transcend earthly constrictions and limits.

This is only slightly akin to the feeling you imagine when you look down at a city from an airliner. In the airliner you're at someone else's mercy. On my bike I'm the singular potentate. I decide where I go, how fast I fly, which direction I look. I wonder if other bikers think this way.

About 100 feet upstream is a brown sign, "Floodwall Western Half." A paved pathway leads to a bridge walkway which crosses the railroad. There is a canal alongside the path and on its shores I see two female Cardinals, four Starlings, some wildflowers, and five Milkweed pods hanging lifelessly. This canal looks bassy—fallen trees and deep water. But it's too industrial as it creeps alongside train tracks and manufacturers. I've tried for bass here, but never a bite.

I carry the bike up 47 risers to the top of the bridge that passes over the railroad, then down 17 steps to get to the top of the Floodwall. This view of the river and the city is unsurpassed. What makes it so stunning is that the Floodwall completely blocks your view of the river until you get to the top of the stairs. **Then you are suddenly confronted with a vista of the river's rocks and rapids spread out beneath the city's tall buildings.**

Behind me, on the other side of the Floodwall on which I'm standing, is a metal utility tower with a red, black and white sign that reads "Danger High Voltage." The bottom of the tower rests on concrete footing on the edge of the canal, and on the footing are two Mallard ducks.

This path on top of the Floodwall is meant for walkers and joggers and bikers. The gravel is mostly fine, but is sometimes golf ball size and could be challenging in places to bike tires.

I see only one gull right now. No Great Blue Herons.

I see the Manchester Bridge upstream. It is supported by a series of St. Louis arches with T's on top. Way upstream the Lee Bridge looks almost futuristic with its footbridge suspended beneath.

When my top-of-the wall bike path reaches the Manchester Bridge it takes a left turn and goes up under the bridge over a rocky and gravelly pathway. I reach the path's end and turn right on a paved pathway which leads up the hill towards the rear of Crestar's new building. At the top are two signs: "Floodwall" and "Overlook." The Floodwall sign points back towards where I came from.

The other sign leads me to the overlook wall where the rock climbers climb. Another spectacular view.

Across the river I can see James River Corporation and Hollywood Cemetery. Pairs of ducks paddle across still water just upstream. This time of the year—prior to the emergence of foliage—the river looks old and dead and lifeless. Driftwood and flotsam and driftbottles and driftfoam are easily seen—not yet hidden by under- or overgrowth.

A long black train crosses at the base of the city on the other side of the river. The engine is yellow and red; all the cars are black. The train's engine disappears to the right, and its end is still beyond my sight to the left. In the panorama I am able to see 60 train cars at any given time. They are all filled with coal.

I watch and count the cars crossing the Lee Bridge in the near lane: one car every two seconds.

A climber down below starts up one of the old bridge supports. A woman belays below. He wears Easter egg green climbing shoes and a backwards baseball cap. His rope is yellow and black. The support he is climbing is 15 stones high, and each stone is perhaps 18 inches tall. He attaches protection every two stones. He looks up then down, reaches, pushes up with his legs. He reaches the top with no trouble at all, and I leave to coast back down along the top of the Floodwall.

Jogging

The one-mile loop around Belle Isle is the best jogging route on the urban James. Another scenic section is the one-mile Floodwall Walk on the southside. (See the Biking article.) Most of the trails in the James River Park System are used to some degree by joggers, but they are not made specifically for joggers and they do not have distance markers. These trails are located at the Main Area, Pony Pasture, Huguenot Woods and Wetlands areas. A popular trail for some joggers is the "Buttermilk" Trail which is a wooded path through the James River Park System from 42nd Street to 22nd Street. From the 22nd Street lot the trail leads upstream from the western end of the parking lot. To reach the trail from the 42nd Street parking lot, take the steps down towards the walkway which crosses the railroad, but take the path to the left just before going onto the walkway. The path circles below the walkway and heads east. Buttermilk Trail crosses varied terrain, has uncertain footing, and changes in quality according to weather and maintenance. It has some steps, a couple of soggy areas, and crosses Reedy Creek at the Hillcrest lot for the James River Park System. The Trail is approximately 1.2 miles long.

Swimming

No formal swimming—laps, diving, lifeguards—is available on the urban James. However, many people do "swim." They wear their swimsuits and protective footwear and wade in and sort of drift around. Anywhere upstream from 14th Street is okay for this as long as you're not near any dangerous rapids. The most popular places for this are the Pony Pasture, Belle Isle, and 42nd Street sections of the James River Park System. Another good area is the Northbank section, although this area is less populated and seemingly more remote. These areas have common attributes: plenty of flat rocks for sunbathing and picnicking and plenty of non-dangerous water.

The Pipeline

Although technically closed, there are those who venture onto the pipeline which traverses along the north side of the river from the 14th Street Bridge upstream to the Manchester Bridge. This shoreline has spectacular views of the river, excellent fishing, and a wonderful feeling of isolation.

To reach the pipeline, walk across the railroad tracks through the Floodwall gate just upstream from the 14th Street Bridge. (At this writing there is no nearby parking; you'll have to park on one of the streets a couple of blocks northeast.) Once through the Floodwall, walk down the rocks over to your right and climb down the steel ladder onto the metal grade walkway on top of the pipeline. The railroad tracks will be above you. If a train comes, there is the remote chance of hot oil or coal falling on you, but I have never heard of this happening to anyone.

The metal walkway goes for 250 yards upstream alongside the Pipeline Rapids. Then the metal walkway ends and the pipeline continues for 200 yards encased in concrete. When the concrete ends, you can continue walking upstream along the shoreline to the Manchester Bridge.

Rowing

The Virginia Boat Club's written materials begin: "We are a diverse group of men and women who are dedicated to the challenges, elegance, and joys of the sport of rowing. We proudly claim descent from the original Virginia Boat Club, one of the nation's oldest rowing clubs, which was founded in 1876 and flourished until it foundered on successive natural and financial disasters in the early 1970s. We reformed in 1986 and incorporated under its historic banner in 1987.

"Our facilities [4710 East Main Street, just downstream from the Annabel Lee] include a dock, a boathouse in the basement of leased premises with a shower, boat racks, and maintenance space for shells. The Club owns two eights, three fours, a convertible pair/double, and two singles with plans to acquire more shells as funds and membership dictate. Individual members own and store a number of shells and oars for their own private use." [This passage was written a few years ago, and the Club now owns more shells.]

The VBC's mailing address is The Virginia Boat Club, P.O. box 26051, Richmond, VA 23260-6051. The Spring 1996 issue of the Club's newsletter, "The Blade," listed 68 members. Membership is open to anyone who is interested including novices.

The VBC offers a variety of coaching sessions for its members. The Club participates in several regional races each year, and hosts the annual Deepwater Run race from the VBC dock to the Deepwater Terminal and back (nine miles).

VBC member Cindy Donnell talked with me about the sport and showed me the VBC's facilities. The VBC leases a building along the James just downstream from the Annabel Lee. The boats are stored on racks in the basement and are carried down a short hill to the Club's dock. There is a grassy parking area behind the building, and every foot of that area is needed to maneuver the 60-foot shells as they are carried from the building. Sometimes people not affiliated with the Club mistakenly park there thinking the area is not used for anything.

Cindy showed me the shells. They range from "eights" (eight rowers plus a coxswain) to singles. They are made of different materials including contemporary carbon fibers and kevlar. The thing all have in common is that they are sleek and beautiful. They are steered by pressure on the oars and by foot pressure. The largest shells have postcard-size rudders.

VBC members generally row in the mornings before work (6:00 a.m. until 7:00 a.m.) or in the evenings. Problems on the river can include wind and tide, but the most common difficulties are caused by the wakes of powerboats.

People of all ages can row, but the regattas are geared towards youth. The Masters Level usually begins at age 27. The Virginia Boat Club currently has no members older than the Baby Boomer generation.

The VBC members built their own floating dock, and they strive for "peaceful coexistence" with trespassers. Fishers often use the dock, and VBC members generally don't bother them. However fishers should be mindful of two very important things. First, they should keep the dock clean. It is not a cutting board for bait. It is not a picnic table. It is not a depository for rusted hooks. The rowers step onto the dock in their stocking feet as they get out of the shells and as they prepare to board the shells.

Second, fishers should exit the dock anytime a shell is

using it. The boats are delicate, and docking is always a careful maneuver. The rowers need full concentration without the distraction of fishers.

Cindy and other members often row upstream past the Annabel Lee in that area between Mayo's Island and the bridge. It's shallow enough there that the powerboats go only slowly. The common downstream run—to the Deepwater Terminal and back—has the potential of traffic, and rowers must be continually vigilant.

Cindy gave me copies of newspaper articles from 1929 and 1931. 1929: "In 1876 seven young men interested in rowing organized a boat club, and built a one-story house on the old canal bank at the foot of Second Street, on the site of the present Chesapeake and Ohio Round House. The equipment consisted of a six-oared boat, and in the words of one of the seven, 'When the crew went rowing, it took the entire membership of the club to man the boat.'"

1931: "Formal opening of the new Virginia Boat Club, located on Mayo's Island on the site of the old structure, which was destroyed by fire last Christmas, will be held on Saturday afternoon, with boat races, swimming events and the finals of a handball tournament on the program."

JOHN BRYAN

First Day of Spring

It's Saturday, April 13, mid-80's, and sunny. I have lifted my bike from my car which I parked near Brown's Island, and I shall now narrate a bike-riding tour for you of Belle Isle and Brown's Island.

I pedal upriver and on my right is the vacated Valentine Riverside and the parking lot designated for this area. The lot is full and 50 cars have parked on the grass. On my left the urban James is full and green.

I stop at the base of the ramp up to the Footbridge. This view always amazes me. **Looking across to Belle Isle the Footbridge suspended below the Lee Bridge seems to be a futuristic construction.** The concrete and steel are clean and new, and the lines are both geometric and organic. This would be an ideal setting for a final showdown in "Terminator III."

December 13, 1984

This December 13th is a glistening gem of a day. The fish are out there grinning; I'm sure of it. **I'm stuck in this urban university, grabbing hunks of this 70-degree sunshiny day during sidewalk walks between meetings.**

I'm out here on Harrison Street now, drifting north towards Broad. With me is a colleague, an occasional fisher himself.

"You know where we ought to be right now?" I smile as we walk, our faces and shoulders swallowing through springtime airs. "The James is out there just waiting—not another fisher on it. It's smooth and ripply and rolling; its trees have lost their leaves and its banks are bare.

"A fishing line would cast just fine today—just lift the rod," I raise my arms, "sweep it back, fling it forward, and the line launches out across the water. **The lure touches down with a proper plop; wavelets circle around it and calm ever so slowly. Fish cruise below.**"

My partner's eyes twinkle as he listens. Still walking up Harrison in our coats and ties we transcend urban commotion. We're on the water, adrift and content. My monologue continues.

"There's a brace of diving ducks ahead. They squirt over and under and disappear and won't reappear until we count to 20. They grab a breath and go down again for another 20.

"We don't get bites; merely casting and knowing the lure is doing something down below is enough. The air is so comfortable, so different from the hard-teen-frostiness of past weeks—that we're aloft in it. Our lures are airborne and do Olympic tripple-dives."

"Let's go fishing," my colleague snatches us back to Harrison Street.

"Can't. Too much to do. Too many meetings and papers."

"Let's do some planning for next spring. Some smallmouth outings. All day. Leave early and get back late."

"Great."

Last year's buds of Indian summer, and those of the year before and the year before, sprouted the same promises. They're bright now; they'll fade though.

We're set for north winds tomorrow morning, rain then cold. My walks between meetings will be quick and dirty with thoughts of red cheeks and numb nose. My fish and my river will settle into winter freeze.

I read the sign at the start of the ramp: "Park Rules—No glass, leashes required, closed at night, no alcohol, illegal to dig, no bows or slingshots, no fires, no camping, no guns." There is another sign: "Bicycles yield to pedestrians." Bicycles love Belle Isle.

I pedal up the ramp and enter the suspended bridge. Halfway across I see a helicopter—a low helicopter. It's very low. It almost shaves the top of the Lee Bridge as it speeds upriver. Then it dips low, almost skimming the surface of the river as it u-turns back towards us. It curves, slows, hovers, and lands on Belle Isle.

Now I see the flashing police light. There are vehicles near the helicopter. Someone must be injured. There are kayaks and rafts pulled up on the shore. A rescue vehicle stands with its back doors open. I stop on the bridge and watch along with 30 other people. This is a good vantage point to see what's happening.

There is a police car, a red pickup truck, a yellow park truck, the rescue truck, and the helicopter—all on the grassy field on the north side of Belle Isle. There is also a man with a huge video camera.

I now notice that the helicopter is painted red, white and blue, and it rests on sled-type runners. Its back cargo entrance is now open. Four men lift a stretcher from the rear of the rescue vehicle and carry it towards the helicopter. I can see a head immobilized with cushions, and a body tied down with sheets. It takes less than 60 seconds to move the person from the rescue vehicle to the helicopter.

The helicopter takes off immediately, scattering dust everywhere. It flies low to the horizon towards downtown Richmond and disappears behind the Richmond skyline—I assume to MCV Hospitals. Tomorrow I will scour the newspapers for information on what I have seen—but will find nothing. That's a good sign.

There are dogs everywhere. All have leashes. And there are rafters and kayakers and tubers everywhere. All have wetsuits. A flotilla of blue and yellow and gray and black and red rafts is grouped down to the left, and the video cameraman is interviewing one of the rafters. I bike down there, but I can't hear what's being said.

A big American Crow lifts off from the trees ahead of me as I enter the path along the river's north bank. The Crow flies smooth and level across the river. There are rapids to my right, woods to my left—

fallen logs and vines and undergrowth and overgrowth. These rapids are the dangerous ones—called Hollywood Rapids because of the cemetery on the bluff across the river. These are the rapids that people have died in.

This path is good for walking and biking. This section has fresh gray gravel. Today the path is crowded with walkers and bikers.

A little girl sits pathside with her bike. She looks at the palm of her hand and cries while her dad lifts a bandage from his cooler.

There are huge flat boulders along these rapids, and on one of them people have a water fight. They use black combat boots to scoop and slosh water on each other. A wide lady in a violet bikini shouts from the path, "Do it, do it!" She turns and laughs when they score a watery hit.

Young love is in the air. People hold hands and swing arms while walking. They turn and smile while biking. For many of the men it's no-shirt weather. Women in two-piece swimsuits lounge on the flat rocks.

This path is a one-mile loop around the island. On this north shore there is a slight uphill grade, and on the opposite shore it's downhill. The path is smooth, and there are no deadfalls or boulders blocking the way. When it's not crowded, it's possible to go fairly fast.

Near the north end of the island is the quarry pond. Today a single fisher stands on the dock. He fishes with a float and a live worm. He hasn't caught anything, but has "seen something lurking down deep." I see a few handsize bluegill.

He tells me he's new here and asks if I've fished here much. I lie my reply, "Yeah," like a seasoned professional, like I know how to crack the code on this difficult pond, like I've caught a million fish here. In truth I've just had that one good bass day here a few years ago when I caught some on a blue Power Craw.

I leave my bike next to the dock and walk 50 feet to the bluff side of the pond. There is a fallen tree, big enough to walk out on, stretching 20 feet out into the pond. I look below it through my Polaroids, but I still see only bluegills.

Back on the path I watch as the yellow James River Park System pickup truck stops to empty the trash can. Belle Isle—as well as the other James River Park System lands—has adequate trash containers which are well attended. You don't see many people littering anymore. Most of the trash along the river floats down from upstream. And most of that gets its start during high water.

I scan the flat water northeast of the island. A Cormorant flies parallel to the island. Two more follow it. A lone gull circles above. Small birds whistle invisibly in the trees above me, and another Crow launches and glides towards Hollywood Cemetery.

Birches border the upriver side of the quarry pond. Their bark peels up and down their trunks as if they've been used to brush dinosaur teeth. The tree birds now chatter like a Sunday picnic. I decide I'm going to bring my blow-up raft here and float the quarry pond.

At the upstream tip of the island is a sign: "Observation Area Class 3 Access." There is a Portolet here.

Around the tip I come to the huge logjam that marks the northeast tip of the island. Grackles fly above the acre of drifted and jammed wood. **Three dozen people scatter across the boulders that rest south of the wood—people hiking and exploring and looking.** Here on the side of the path is a left-behind baby stroller. To climb over onto the boulders and rocks that stretch to the southside you have to leave behind bikes and strollers.

In front of me on this path is a couple with two dogs. He walks a huge white long-hair; she walks a tiny white short-hair. Beside me, to my left, is the steep hill to the crest of Belle Isle. Fancy bikers zoom paths up and down the hilly parts of the island, and I am frightened for some of them as they jump over ledges and crash down through vertical trails. Their bikes—off the official bike trail—contribute to significant erosion.

On this southwest side of Belle Isle the path gently slopes downhill, and I have to constantly slow down to dodge pedestrians. Usually the island is not this crowded, but this is the first warm and sunny Saturday of the year, and it follows a record-snow winter.

The man now in front of me wears a black baseball hat and a backpack. In the backpack is a baby wearing a purple and white striped outfit. The baby looks like a tiny prisoner.

Spring is busting out all over and crayon green is the color of the day both on the ground and in the air on the vinery climbing the trees.

The path increases its downhill grade and a golden-haired guy whizzes by me gaining speed with his shirt flying from his belt loop. At the bottom of the hill is a dogleg turn to the right towards the Lee Bridge above. Then you can turn left back towards the Footbridge or right to the Access Road for Emergency Vehicles. The sign says, "Emergency Access Bridge—Pedestrians Prohibited."

I head back to the Footbridge, past the old Armored Storage Shed. This huge field below the Lee Bridge has been plowed and probably planted. There are other bikers here—most like me, but some wearing helmets, gloves and backpacks. One guy walks a wet brown dog and a wet brown-butted child.

There is a great view of the city here—framed by the Lee Bridge, the Footbridge and the river—three horizontals against the verticals of the city.

I bike up the ramp onto the Footbridge and I recall how frightened Thomas was years ago when he first crossed it. He stayed in the exact center and walked slowly. Today I feel a bit of his fright as this bike seems to wobble as if something's come loose. I imagine myself taking a spill over the edge. It's a long way to the river below. And the water's still cold.

Across the river I glide from the ramp into the parking lot of James River Corporation; the natural drift of the bike takes me almost to the company's parking deck. I lazily turn back to the left and back to the road.

A couple lies in the riverside grass on a blanket kissing in blue jeans. Their embrace is a copy of the beach embrace in "From Here to Eternity."

It's after 5:00 p.m. and the parking lot has thinned. This is a smooth area of the river no rapids. There must be thousands of smallmouths out there—fish which will awaken when the river warms in another month or two.

A Mockingbird hops along the grass only six feet from my bike along the river's edge. He lifts and lands on a riverside Sycamore limb just five inches off the water. The Sycamore still has its balls although new foliage is starting to sprout. Fifty yards downstream is a still wintry River Birch.

This little path from the Footbridge has a brown pebble surface about four feet wide. It takes me down to the boat launch area where a little white butterfly the size of a half-dollar flutters by himself among Dandelions.

The tip of Brown's Island approaches and I see that the canal is dry except for a few stagnant inches. I pause in the middle of the bridge that arches over to the island and remember when Thomas was afraid of this bridge too. Below in the canal sand is a grocery cart, bottles, footprints, a tire, some coiled fencing, oily water, and various trash. Last year when this canal was full I could see fish down there. And I caught them downstream along the canal walkway—small smallmouths and bluegill.

Once across the bridge I carry my bike down the 17 stairs to the surface of Brown's Island. Immediately to my right is Paul DiPasquale's statue, "The Headman." The plaque says, "**This statue commemorates the contributions of African-American men as skilled boatmen on the James River and its canals and in the development of industry and commerce in the city of Richmond.** Designer and sculptor P. DiPasquale." The bronze dedication was in 1992 and the original dedication was in 1988. This is a wonderful work of art. You can move around it and silhouette it against Ethyl's white headquarters on the hill, against the Radisson Hotel, and against downtown's skyscrapers.

The pathway around the perimeter of Brown's Island is paved and embedded with brown gravel. As I start biking the pathway a Mourning Dove immediately flies across not five feet away. A train passes by on the nearby tracks and bangs its bell. A grove of Cherry trees is at the upstream end of the island, and it provides the border of a heliport facility. A white, red and black sign proclaims: "Stand well back during all helicopter operations. Beware of strong rotor downwash." The Cherry blossoms are falling and snowflaking the ground.

On the southwest side of the island—the river side of the island—there is an interesting view of the river. The view is bordered above by an elevated train track.

A pair of Mallards lands below me in the gentle rapids. Directly above me a train rolls along. Across to the right cars speed across the Manchester Bridge. And out across the river Grackles fly and land on big rocks.

My two Mallards face upstream in a little stretch of current, obviously having fun. One lifts its neck and flaps its wings like it's drying itself, then lifts off the water and skims across the surface, out across midriver rocks and lands beyond. Now a very big bird—a hawk of some sort—hovers and glides and looks. It circles towards the other side of the river.

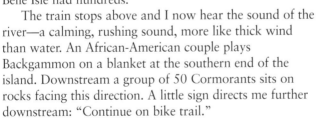

There is a canoe 100 yards out from the island, and the blue-vested canoer negotiates a tricky set of rapids. He is followed by a kayaker who also makes it through without difficulty.

View from Brown's Island.

This is a magnificent juxtaposition: train above, automobiles above and across, ducks below, Grackles out beyond, a hawk way up there, a kayaker drifting quickly, and noises. There is the screech of the train, the call of an unseen Crow, and laughter of passing strollers.

An obviously homeless man sleeps at one of the metal picnic tables that dot the island. He is one of only 10 people on Brown's Island. Belle Isle had hundreds.

The train stops above and I now hear the sound of the river—a calming, rushing sound, more like thick wind than water. An African-American couple plays Backgammon on a blanket at the southern end of the island. Downstream a group of 50 Cormorants sits on rocks facing this direction. A little sign directs me further downstream: "Continue on bike trail."

Now at this downstream tip of the island I encounter the canal again to my left. It's dry. **In past years schools of huge carp swam this canal in the spring.** Now there are Grackles in the trees that buffer the canal from the city. There's also an occasional Robin.

I pedal past the maroon and green and blue Canal Walk banners. But the canal is dry and dirty and forgotten-looking. The city is in the midst of a huge improvement project for the canal, and it is necessary for it to be dry during the process.

Down this path there are old buildings on the right and one has an open area with a display of a packet boat. I'll look more closely on my way back. The path continues between the canal and the buildings until the canal merges with the river at what is called the "Pipeline Overlook." This is indeed an overlook, although the elevated train track blocks much of the view of the river.

These are the Pipeline Rapids, "named because they flow by the major interceptor pipe which transports wastewater to the city's wastewater treatment plant. With the increased recreational use of the river this area has one of the most challenging canoeing and kayaking runs in any American city."

Standing on the Pipeline Overlook I can look down into a basin pool where kayaks are put in and taken out of the river. Now there are two men fishing here. One wears a baseball cap, blue jeans, and a fresh white t-shirt and throws a white grub on a spinning rod. The water is clear and I hope to see a fish silhouetted down there but I don't. The other fisher wears no shirt. He fishes with a live minnow below a float on braided line. I can see a yearling largemouth on his stringer dangling in the water at his feet.

Now two boats enter this basin. They are the canoe and kayak I watched earlier negotiate the rapids out beyond Brown's Island. They greet the shoreline fishers with considerate smiles, tell them they're coming into the basin, and exchange conversation about what's biting.

A man now walks down the rocks towards the basin carrying an olive kayak. He wears slippers, a yellow helmet, a black life vest and a black and blue wetsuit. He balances himself with the doublesided paddle as he carefully boards the kayak and pushes off. He paddles quickly across the 75-foot basin, climbs out on the opposite side, and walks upstream carrying his kayak on his right shoulder and paddle in his left hand. A single Mallard swims 10 feet from where he exited the basin.

On the way back to Brown's Island I stop to look at the packet boat exhibit. "**From the Depths of the Great Basin—an exhibit by the Archeological Society of Virginia and the Virginia Canals and Navigations Society.**"

The Pipeline Overlook.

JOHN BRYAN

"Iron Hulled Packet Boat—This was the first boat to be recovered in the basin far down in the silt 23 feet below street level. It was one of the few iron hulled boats on the canal and possibly the oldest considering its depth in the silt, its wooden keel and the fragile condition of the metal. An unexpected find was the bathroom fitting in the ladies' cabin in the bow. Note the tube through the bottom! Packet boats carried passengers, baggage and mail as far as Lynchburg, Buchanan and Lexington with connections to points west. This is only the bow half of the boat which was probably 90 feet long. **The stern half is still buried 23 feet under 9th Street.**"

I see huge nails sticking out of the metal hull and there are parts of the wooden keel still on the boat.

There is another sign: "Gallego Mills—Once the largest flour mill in the world, Gallego Mills was powered by water flowing from the Great Basin where the Omni Hotel is now. This turbine was found deep in the mill ruins. You are standing on the site of Hexall-Crenshaw Mills—Richmond's other major flour mills. It was powered by the Hexall Canal behind you which was not navigated by canal boats."

Other signs give more information and I don't transcribe them: "Canal Lock Sluice Gates," "Bow Timber of a Freight Boat."

This mid-80's day has made me hot, and my shirt is damp. A few pedals on the bike and the breeze cools me as I coast back alongside the canal. **Four Grackles down in the sand peck at something the size of a golf ball.** It looks like a dented ping pong ball. One picks it up and drops it. A Robin stands high nearby with his neck in the air, and so does another 20 feet away.

There is a sign at this downstream tip of Brown's Island: "Johnson's Island was originally a small separate island located surrounding this plaque. Over time it was 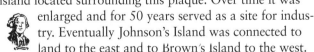enlarged and for 50 years served as a site for industry. Eventually Johnson's Island was connected to land to the east and to Brown's Island to the west. Ross's Mill Race, begun in 1778 ran west, from the foot of 12th Street to Johnson's Island. In 1835 as the embankment which separated Ross's Mill Race from the James River was improved the island could be reached by land from the east. By 1848 the island itself had been expanded enough to hold the steel works of Virginia Steel Company. By 1869 John R. Johnson & Company operated the

Richmond Steam Forge on the island which is recognized as Johnson's Island on a map in 1876. In 1893 Richmond Railway and Electric opened a coal fired electric generating plant on the island which was active until 1901. Johnson's Island was joined to Brown's Island to the west in 1972 by filling in the Vepco Spillway which ran slightly west of the Manchester Bridge supports." There is a little map and photograph ("Richmond from the south, 1873") on the metal engraved plaque.

"Two Pulleys and a Gear" on Brown's Island.

You can't miss the huge wheels here at the tip of Brown's Island. A sign tells that Brown's Island generated power to run the 1894 streetcars. Another sign says that Albemarle Paper's mill on Brown's Island operated until 1967, completely filling the island with buildings. There is a photograph confirming that the island was completely covered.

Finally, the sign about the wheels: "Two Pulleys and a Gear—Preserved here from the papermill's machinery are a breaker beater driven pulley—the large one—a floor beater driven pulley and a cast core mortise gear."

Brown's Island is gorgeous now. Three little Magnolias stand near the pulleys and gear. Purple Clover and yellow Dandelions are 10 feet away. There are tiny blue flowers also, and white clover, and another white butterfly—all near the sign showing that the island was all industry just a few years ago.

I bike back over the plank bridge that connects Brown's Island to Richmond. The bridge is introduced by brick pavers with names on them—names of persons whose support created this little oasis. The fountain in the drive circle—entitled "The Falls of the James," proclaims four things on its perimeter: "Nourishment, Energy, Community, Trade."

This is a blue, blue day. I look up and see a white contrail in a wispy sky, and wonder if the jet knows I'm looking at him.

At the Bottom of the Canal—
Spring, 1996 ≋

This one goes out to Tanya R. And to faraway lonely lovers everywhere.

The four of us—Thomas and I and Trevor and his dad Morrie—have a purpose: to scour the bottom of the 100-year-old canal. To set foot on the bottom of the now dry entrance to the Kanawha Canal. To comb those first thousand yards above which boats hauled turn-of-the-century cargo. **To go where no twentieth-centuryers have gone. To boldly discover old worlds. To encounter the maxim: The past is another country; people live differently there.**

And we will indeed encounter it.

The city has pulled the plug on this all-important stretch of the Kanawha Canal—the brief first leg of the canal from Great Shiplock Park to the I-95 Bridge. The only water in it now is the few inches which creep in through the open lock every six hours with high tide. Supposedly there are a few years of repairs and renovations and reconstructions ahead as the city transforms the canal into an urban nicety.

But today it looks like what it is: an old, forgotten, trash- and debris-laden, dry, deep ditch—an urban ditch nestled between set-aside slivers of trees and bushes and undergrowth and overgrowth claimed as public land.

We come prepared. We wear our mud shoes, we carry a metal detector to find treasures, we carry a bucket to haul treasures.

Trevor, the youngest, gets first turn with the detector. It beeps immediately. Just a beer can. There are cans everywhere. It beeps immediately again—a rusted hunk of metal. There are rusted hunks of metal everywhere. Most are castoffs from the still-live train tracks which run alongside the length of the canal: spikes and couplings and links of chain and other heavy-duty pieces. Thomas picks up one which is the shape and size of a crowbar. He'll carry it during the rest of our venture, using it to poke and dig.

The dry Kanawha Canal near Great Shiplock Park.

Years ago I used to occasionally float my Jon boat in this canal and catch bass and bluegill. The water was always dark and murky and although my lures told me the canal's depth reached 10 feet, I had no way to visualize the configuration of the canal's floor. Now of course I see it. It is deep: 10 feet near the lock, gradually shallower—due to silt deposits—upstream towards the I-95 Bridge. Some of the shorelines still drop straight down. Others have caved in and now offer gentle slopes. The middle of the canal is wet from the high tide. Its mud still sinks fast: Thomas learns that as he tests a dark brown area which almost swallows his calf-high boot.

Fallen trees and overhanging bushes line the sides of the canal. Occasional groups of pilings are planted along the sides: tie-ups for canal boats. **And the canal's current trophy is the 100-foot rusty metal boat which lists precariously along the opposite shoreline.** "No," I tell Thomas and Trevor, "we can't go on the boat. First, there's no way to climb into it, and second, it would be too dangerous."

We walk along and kick among piles of debris hoping to find something of interest. We have turned off the detector; the abundance of metal has diffused its usefulness. There are plenty of bottles. I wish for bottle expertise. The only bottles I know are the old Coke bottles with the cities on the bottoms. And I haven't found one of those in years.

"Trevor," I ask, "you know what I'd like to find?"

"What?"

"A fat wallet."

Trevor smiles and thinks. Then he looks up at me. "I'd like to find a gold coin."

"What would you do if we looked right over there next to that log and saw a gold coin on one side and a fat wallet on the other? Which would you choose if you got one and I got the other?"

"I'd take the gold coin," Trevor didn't hesitate, "because you wouldn't know what was in the fat wallet."

"But my fat wallet might contain a bunch of hundred-dollar bills."

"I don't care; I'd still take the gold coin."

We find neither. Our first unusual find is a lot worse.

"Mr. Bryan!" Trevor shouts from 100 feet up in front of me.

"Hey Dad!" Thomas joins him. "It's something dead!"

We determine it's a possum carcass. Not much left but skin and bones. A rotted remnant of aroma still lingers.

"Did he drown?" asks Trevor.

"I don't know," I reply. "Looks like he's been here a long time."

We move on without any young urges to poke it or kick it or turn it over.

"Hey Trevor!" We hear a distant shout.

"It's my dad!" Trevor jubilantly exclaims as he points. "He's in the boat!"

Morrie is back down on the other side of the canal, and he has somehow scaled the 12-foot metal side of the old boat, and he is hailing us from atop its slanting deck.

"Hey, you guys," he shouts. "This is really neat!"

"Can we go there?" Thomas and Trevor ask me in unison.

"Yeah, but there's no way to cross the canal here. We'll cross over when we get to the I-95 Bridge. Then we'll walk back along the other side of the canal and get in the boat."

"We'll be there later!" Trevor shouts. He has a fine shouting voice.

This canal floor has fewer treasures than I had expected. Mostly it's cans and bottles—new cans and bottles. I was hoping for castoffs from the previous century—maybe a cannonball or a rifle or a dish or a piece of silver. And I was anticipating contraband from the present century: handguns, bags of drug money, headless gangsters.

"Hey Dad!" Thomas shouts. "It's a CASH REGISTER!"

"Mr. Bryan!" Trevor shouts even louder. "We found a CASH REGISTER! A CASH REGISTER!"

Sure enough, it appears that they are leveraging a cash register from the sandy mud. Maybe it's filled with money. Maybe old money: real silver, mercury dimes, buffalo nickels, wheat pennies, liberty half-dollars, Silver Certificates. I walk quickly to join them. Maybe the crooks couldn't get it open and had to toss it in the canal as the police got closer. They had to toss their bounty, toss the evidence. But we'll get it open. We'll use Thomas' crowbar if we have to. No cops chasing us today.

I arrive at the cash register and tilt it over. It's too heavy to lift. But it's not a cash register. It's some sort of electronic scale. It's the size of a cash register, and I guess it would appear to be a cash register to children searching for gold coins. But it's not a cash register. We walk on.

The boys' next find will seem equally provocative—in the other direction.

A single Kingfisher emits brief screams and alights on an overhanging branch a hundred yards ahead. I hear a Chickadee—too high to see amid one of the taller trees. The driftwood in this canal is awful; it doesn't have the swirling, gnarled character that you find on the main river. I pick up a seemingly old bottle every now and then and drop it into my bucket. I see continual stray pieces of metal. One looks like a discus; another round one with a hole is a huge washer.

"Where's my dad?" shouts Trevor.

He's no longer visible on the distant boat.

"Probably behind the boat," I assure him.

There are shoes sprinkled in the canal. There are always abandoned shoes along rivers and oceans and creeks and canals. I see only sneakers today, maybe a total of 10. Only two match, and I see them 100 yards apart.

"A BODY!" I hear from one of the boys.

They're up there on one of the slopes leaning tentatively over something on the ground.

"Dad!" Thomas shouts. "We found a body!"

Thoughts stream into my head. Will I telephone the police immediately? Will this be the solution to some long-ago murder? Will there be a fat wallet next to the body?

As I walk closer I see a ribcage. It's a body alright. Thomas and Trevor are standing back a couple of feet—unfamiliar with the rules for encountering a body. If there's a diamond ring on its finger, will I remove it? I find myself thinking about material things rather than having sympathy for the body's owner.

I arrive and look closely and see that the ribcage does appear to belong to a human, but the tail doesn't. Neither do the jaw and fangs. I turn to Thomas and Trevor, "It's a dog."

"Oh." They're disappointed. "Did he drown?"

I don't explain that not everything that ends up at the bottom of this canal necessarily drowned. We'll soon find another dead dog that definitely did not drown.

Morrie appears from behind us and hustles to join us in time to see the dog bones. He marvels at how interesting the canal is and tells me he's going to add this to his list of places to regularly visit.

The next dog we find is different. It has decayed like the last, but there is something different about the skeleton. There is no head. The boys don't notice this and I don't tell them. I've seen photos of headless dogs—photos of freshly headless dogs. The photos I've seen have been documentations of religious ceremonies—religions which worship frightening deities. My friend Thomas Daniel has such photos as part of his "Jesus Saves" series. He has photographed all sorts of religious ceremonies—from tent revivals to snake handlings to dog sacrifices. The dog sacrifices are the most haunting. They're the photos I turned away from. They're the photos I declined seeing more of. The poor dog we see now in this dry Kanawha Canal likely gave his life in the name of a deity. I now turn away again and move on.

Thomas—my son—finds an old Coke bottle. "Look, Dad," he holds it upside down as he reads, "Cincinnati, Ohio." It goes into the bucket.

The religious dog is left behind and true love is on the way.

We arrive at the I-95 Bridge and cross over to the other side of the canal and start back towards the boat. This side of the canal is next to Canal Street. Cars can pull over on the grass alongside the canal and easily dump things. We find an old washing machine, an old television, a sink, a toilet. "Someone must have been living down here!" Trevor concludes.

I lean over and pick up an old audio cassette tape. "Look Trevor," I show him. **"I bet this cassette has the instructions to the buried treasure."**

"Lemme see!" Trevor reaches and I hand him the cassette. It's of course dirty with dried mud.

"I bet the guy who buried the treasure in this canal recorded the instructions how to find it on this cassette. I bet if we play that cassette we'll all be rich. I think we have just found a most amazing discovery!"

Trevor's eyes are wide as he looks at the old cassette in his hands. Morrie stands behind him smiling and shaking his head. "That's right, Trevor," Morrie adds, "that can show us the way to the treasure."

"I tell you what, Trevor," I lean closely. "You take that cassette home and put it in YOUR cassette player and listen carefully."

"Can we Dad?" he turns and asks Morrie.

We both smile and explain the joke to little Trevor.

"But it might have something good on it," he attempts to salvage some hope.

I explain that dirt and mud are not good for a tape player and we discard the tape and move on. But I will save the next cassette tape we find.

"Hey Dad!" Thomas waves a bottled hand at me. "Enid, Oklahoma!" Another old Coke bottle! Enid was one of those cities that all of us heard of when we were kids via the Coke bottles. Enid's bottling plant must have shipped a lot of Cokes to Nashville. I haven't thought of Enid in years. A flood of thoughts about playing the Coke bottle game come to me. The game of whose bottle came from farthest away was the most common one. But my favorite was always the bluff game. You'd find a discarded bottle somewhere and then name three cities. The other person had to guess which one was on the bottle.

"Hey Dad!" Trevor shouts. "Here's a hubcap!" he shouts even louder.

"Trevor," Morrie says, "I can hear you without shouting. Let's try not to shout so loud."

"That's right Trevor," I tease. **"Out here in this canal we use our quiet voices. You should always save your shouting voice for the library."**

Morrie laughs—thank goodness. "Yeah Trevor, shout only in the library," he confirms.

"Trevor has a pretty healthy little shout there, doesn't he?" I ask Morrie.

"Geeeez!" is his reply as he stops smiling and shakes his head. "I can't stand it when he does it at home."

"When he's in your back yard we can always hear a Trevor shout at our house."

"I bet you can even hear him when he's indoors."

"I don't think so."

Trevor is listening to us and he responds with a very loud piercing scream, "HEYYYY, LISTEN TO THIIIIISSSS!"

"Trevor!" Morrie doesn't smile.

"Hey Trevor," I get his attention. "If there were a screaming contest, would you enter?"

"I don't know."

"If there were a William Fox School Screaming Competition, do you think you'd want to enter?"

"He'd win," Morrie says.

"If we held a screaming competition at the Strawberry Street Festival," I look at Morrie, "do you think any kids could get their parents to pay a dollar for the entry fee?"

"I think every kid there would enter," he concludes.

"I think I'll do that." My wheels turn. "That'll be my volunteer job this year. I'll set up a table with a sign and the Festival will raise some money from the screaming competition."

Morrie is shaking his head.

"Who would be good judges?" I look at him.

"Not me," he responds without hesitation. "I won't be there."

"You don't want to watch Trevor win?"

"Nope."

"You think a lot of parents would leave during the competition?"

"Yep."

"Well, maybe it's not such a good idea then." Then I have an idea. "I know, the judges could wear those headsets that block out noise!"

"That'd be good," Morrie nods.

"Hey Dad," Thomas gets my attention. "Listen to this." **And he emits a high-pitched scream that could curdle this canal water.** Morrie winces and tilts his head.

"How do you do that, Thomas?" Morrie can't believe what he just heard.

"Like this," Thomas grins, and does it again.

"How does he do that?" Morrie turns to me.

"Okay Thomas, that's enough," I say. "We'll enter you in the competition too."

We are almost to the boat when I see another cassette tape. This one is in its plastic case. There is a label. I pick it up to read the label, but everything has faded away. Except for an ink message someone wrote on a piece of paper in the plastic case: "Eric, I'll miss you this summer. I can't wait til next summer. All my love, Tanya."

True love. Young love. Tanya and Eric. True love forever. The tape is too dirty to play, and we'll never know what's on it. Probably the Righteous Brothers. Unchained Melody. Or maybe Johnny Mathis. I show Morrie.

"Yeah," Morrie says as he hands the note back to me. "But look where we found the tape: at the bottom of this canal."

"You think Eric tossed it here?"

"Sure," Morrie nods and looks around. "Tanya gave him the tape, and as soon as she left town he tossed it. He was glad to be free of her."

"Holy smokes!" I realize. "Eric was just waiting for summer so Tanya would leave. I bet he dropped her off at the bus station and drove by here and rolled down his window and just let it fly. **'Good Riddance!' 'Adios Muchacha!' he probably said. Poor Tanya."**

"Yeah, and then he drove on over to see his other little honey."

"His summer honey."

"Just tossed Tanya's tape into the canal—note and everything."

"Tanya probably wrote him every day all summer ."

"And Eric probably tossed her letters without reading them."

"Tanya probably still thinks about him even after all these years."

"Her one true love. She's probably got a bunch of kids and a car pool and dog or two, and late at night she still sometimes thinks about Eric."

"And I bet she thinks he still has that tape and plays it late at night when he thinks about her."

"Secret lovers now—secret lovers separated by years and miles. That's what Tanya probably thinks."

"We ought to put an ad in the Personals."

"Yeah. 'Tanya, I still have the tape. Eric.'"

"Or, 'Tanya, no matter what anybody says, I didn't throw the tape into the canal. Eric.'"

We arrive at the old boat and Thomas and Trevor beg us to let them climb on board. It takes some doing. Morrie finds foot- and hand-holds on the side of the boat and scales to the top and over the rail onto the deck. While I push from below, he pulls from

above, and we enable Thomas and Trevor to join him. I follow. The boat is huge and old and rusty and metal and heavy. Not much left. This canal stopped being used 75 years ago, and I assume that is the age of the boat. **There are only two sights of interest: the old bathroom—with toilet—and the old inscription engraved into one of the interior walls: "Dead Annabel."** I try to persuade Thomas and Trevor that this is a ghost ship, but they don't bite. They're much more interested in the bathroom.

There is a rickety ladder down to a lower deck, but there is a foot of water at the bottom. Nothing to see down there either. The main source of fun is just standing on the boat and realizing that it's old. We climb out after a few minutes. Morrie and I marvel at the four-blade propeller which has a six-foot diameter.

Thomas and Trevor have discovered a dirt bike—a motorized dirt bike—a motocross-type bike. It's on its side at the bottom of the canal near the boat. They lift it and discuss the virtues of taking it home and cleaning it and riding it. Morrie and I of course squash their dreams. I'm not putting that nasty bike in my car.

It's past the time when I told Janet we'd be back and we climb out of the canal and walk under the tracks towards the parking lot. Under the tracks are scattered pieces of coal. **Amid the coal I find the final treasure of the day:** a little white plastic packet, the size of a packet of ketchup, of a product called "Grime-Free." The front of the packet says it is "Waterless antiseptic skin cleaner." The back of the packet says it is "Tough on grime, gentle on skin. Quickly cleans most substances from most body areas." It contains 1/4 ounce and was packaged in Louisville, Kentucky.

I show it to Morrie and we both look up at the coal-dusted railroad track above us. **"Can you imagine a big, burly railroad worker finishing a hard day of loading coal and then opening a dainty little packet of this stuff?"**

"That's exactly what happened."

"Somehow I imagined those guys with big cakes of Lava sudsing down under an industrial shower somewhere."

"I guess not."

We drive home without having found a fat wallet or a gold coin. My bucket now contains three Coke bottles—one of them a 10-ouncer—a handful of other bottles, Tanya's tape, and the 1/4-ounce packet of cleaner. Thomas wanted to take his "crowbar," but I made him leave it. You don't take old metal objects from these old lands that border the urban James.

"Did you have fun?" Carol and Janet greet us when we drive up.

"Hey mom, listen to this!" Thomas and Trevor chime. And they begin a screaming competition.

James River Batteau Festival

Although batteaux were once commonly floated all the way to Richmond, this modern-day week-long float trip ends a few miles west of Richmond at Maidens Adventure. The Festival features replicas of the original water craft which capably floated through the river's most challenging rapids.

The Festival begins at Lynchburg and features seven stops along the way—Galt's Mill, Bent Creek/Gladstone, Wingina, Scottsville, Slate River, Columbia, and Cartersville—before arriving at Maidens Adventure. At the stops along the way the public is invited to join and witness music, storytelling, costumes, and other traditions of the period.

The goals of the James River Batteau Festival are:
1. To promote the building and operation of authentic replicas of James River Batteaux.
2. To promote awareness of the James River as an important natural resource.
3. To call attention to the James River basin as a geographical community of special significance to Virginia and the nation.

James River Batteau Festival, Inc., P.O. Box 10564, Lynchburg, VA 24506

Individual and family memberships are available.

Bill Trout and the "Lord Chesterfield" batteau.

June 14, 1983

There was a baptism at the James River on Sunday evening. Rob and I waded in at 5:00 beneath the Nickel Bridge, and by dusk we had voluntarily plumbed the river's depths. We had waded deeply, over our heads, so we could reach the mid-river shoals and rapids, and so we could also reach the swift rocky currents of the far bank.

We swam like a brace of moose, rods above our heads like antlers. Our tiptoes searched anxiously for absent footholds. Our heads bobbed and grinned in a whitewater ritual. Our baptism was like all baptisms: it sparked new life, excitement, expectation.

Inaccessible fishing holes were accessible to us on Sunday. We tossed Beetle Spins and Meppses into eddies we had previously only admired from a hundred feet above—from the Nickel Bridge. Our lines played among boulders unaccustomed to wading shoes and dripping jeans. We gazed into the center-stream silver currents and watched bright teaming schools of minnows. And we caught fish.

Rob caught the first bass of the evening: a deep, bronze-green, 10-inch smallmouth. Dozens of redbreasts followed, most of them hand-size. We caught other bass too. My pound-and-a-halfer was the largest; I teased it from beneath a mid-current boulder. The others all flirted with a pound, and they were all that rich oak-green of strong, clearwater smallmouths.

In the midst of our baptism we watched, our eyes barely above the water, as a Blue Heron flapped lazily overhead. The bird flew seaward along the center of the river, seemingly in no hurry.

Among the midstream boulders we watched schools of hickory shad skim sideways along the rocks, using the currents to aid their upstream glides. Their flat bodies paralleled the underwater stones, and they were flashy silver coins in the late-day sunshine.

We saw a pair of Mallards circle only a few yards overhead. They flew on upstream, beyond the tree-sheltered bend. And we saw fat catfish spawning in thick, inundated grasses, quiet and solitary.

The James is full of gars, needlenose gars, long menacing torpedoes. Rob has seen giants from the bridge. We didn't see any on Sunday. Perhaps their presence would have inhibited our baptism.

The James has been high since February. Only on Sunday—the first Sunday of June—did the river reach that slender margin between high and low. **The water's temperature was cool enough to offer a brief chill, warm enough to relax the bones, swift enough to offer precarious excitement, and slow enough to immerse the angler in summer's wet angling ritual.**

Maymont

Located just on the north side of the Boulevard Bridge, this wonderful and free natural area offers a variety of pleasures including animals and gardens and a house museum. Although it is located adjacent to the James River, it offers no access to the river. Maymont visitors are separated from the James by a fence, a canal, railroad tracks and woods.

Maymont's inclusion in this book is predicated on its promise for the year 2000: a spectacular new nature center which has the Falls of the James as its theme.

"The new nature center will be a remarkable resource for students and the general public with interpretive exhibits centered around the fall line of the James River, including the geological formation of the region, indigenous animals and plants and the causes and impacts of flooding. Each individual's role as a good steward of our environment will be emphasized. In a 100-foot terraced river aquarium exhibit, visitors will 'walk the fall line' to view fish and other aquatic life and see and touch the plants and animals that live along the river. A large Discovery Room and enhanced learning spaces will delight young and old. The transition exhibit from the center to Maymont's 100-acre living laboratory will be a wondrous river otter habitat."

At this writing Maymont's goal is to raise $10 million for this project which they intend to complete by December 31, 1999.

Passages

Passages is an organization which offers special programs in "outdoor skills." The following information is printed in Passages' brochure for summer programs.

CANOEING
We will start to build your skills by teaching you to master the basic strokes and techniques on the flatwater of the quarry on Belle Isle. We then advance to the James River where we will use the river's current to learn ferries, eddy turns, and dynamic peel outs! The finale will be a half-day canoeing trip on the beautiful and exciting upper section of the James River.

KAYAKING
We will learn all of the basic strokes and safety techniques involved in kayaking, including the Eskimo Roll and Rescue. The one-week camp provides a great introduction to this exciting sport, while the two-week session develops a solid foundation of skills.

ROCK CLIMBING & RAPPELLING
Your climbing experience begins with an introduction to the basic knots and safety skills that will give you a safe and fun climbing experience. We will rappel down cliffs over 40 feet high, right down to the edge of the quarry, and then climb up some tough climbing routes. We will also climb the difficult Manchester Wall. Be prepared for a real challenge!

ROPES COURSE
Our Ropes Course brings the whole group together for a morning of tough team challenges. These are fun events that push you to work together, trust each other, and be creative.

Passages, 3030 Grove Avenue, First Floor, Richmond, VA 23221 (804) 358-0577.

March 29, 1985 ≋

The Cedar Waxwings came last Sunday. They herald spring's arrival. Hundreds of them swarmed the big American Holly in the back yard and ate the ripe red berries. Kelly and I watched and pointed from the window. We saw their perky, crested tops and their flickery, yellow-banded tails. They came for only a day; when they left, the berries were gone.

The sunbathers have arrived at school. They sprinkle the urban university's tiny lawns, and they crowd the adjacent blossoming parks. Their companions are towels and radios and sunglasses and coolers and books. Above them sail Frisbees and baseballs.

Minnows will soon arrive in the urban James' shallows. They'll dart among rocks, school along the shorelines, go this way and that, always swimming in unison.

White perch have already arrived to push their way up to the river's spawning bars. They're small and delicious and agreeable to most baits and lures. White crappie have moved into the shallows of Swift Creek Reservoir. They roam the flats in bunches and crowd tiny minnows to the surface.

K-Mart's fishing shelves have filled. Pinched to nothing during the winter, they balloon and expand each spring to feature everything new and old. There is a dozen of everything in every color. The rows are straight, the packages are fresh, nothing is picked over.

Boats all over town are being repaired and readied. I've cut a hole in the carpeting of mine and have sanded the spot so my depth finder will read right through the hull.

Spring is the time when my strawberry patch has more strawberry plants than weeds. Yesterday Kelly and I spent an hour disarming the frail advance troops that the weed army has sent. In another month or two hoards of well-drilled weed soldiers will cripple and strangle and attempt genocide on my poor berries.

And with spring arrives a flow of melancholy. My remembrances are of the green winding Harpeth, its rock bass and smallmouths and suckers, and its trophies that I never caught. I think of the Buffalo—that blue, unharnessed head-shaking scoundrel of a stream, filled to the brim with somersaulting smallmouths that strain to attack rapid Meppses. There's the West Branch of the Croton with its waist-deep pools of brown trout and rainbows, and its pine-needled, pathy shorelines that twist among boulders and deadfalls. The Ohoopee, stained black with tannic acid, shouldered with clean white bands, moves lazily among Georgia Pines and Willows and Horse Chestnuts, and harbors pickerel and crappie and bass and catfish and spring-spawning mullet. And of course there's the Duck. Duck River teams with white bass and white crappie and long-nose gar. Its mistletoed banks are muddy and unkempt, its waters are brown and thick, its fish are gems.

Today is March's final day and it will reach 80 degrees. An "emergency" will likely require me to miss an afternoon committee meeting.

Chapter Nine:
The Environment, Conservation, Politics, The Future

In this chapter there is a variety of information dealing with these topics. Ralph White's "Disaster Zone" article provides a great look at the river's power to shape its environment. There are articles about some of the organizations which work to preserve the river. And you will find plenty of things you can personally do to help the river.

The Breeze Along the River

"Here in Switzerland we do not pick the wildflowers," is the smiling phrase repeated to each tourist who pauses to collect a bouquet or a boutonniere. Wildflowers generously sprinkle Switzerland's hills and fields. The Swiss ethos regards picking wildflowers is as we regard shoplifting: you don't do it.

We Richmonders are learning not to pick or destroy the bounty of the urban James: the rainbow-colored rocks, the swirling organic driftwood, the scraps of ancient metal, the wildflowers. Even the snakes. We discover them, we enjoy them, we observe them, we allow their natural metamorphoses, we leave them undisturbed. They spice the beauty of this urban river. And because we have this attitude of protecting the resource, our river will continue its progression as our city's most valued amenity.

Our urban James is a most amazing resource. Today, in 1997, we enjoy it in many ways, but I envision a future day when we will enjoy it more. All of us. The river's

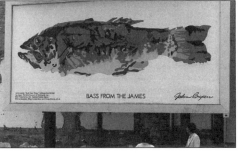

The author's 22-foot "Bass from the James" on a 1986 Cary Street billboard as part of the Arts Council's "Rush Hour Art Show."

267

beauty will be an important ingredient in our recreation, our education, our commerce.

Urban James access parking will be at remote locations—locations from which we will hike, bike and shuttle to the river. Our mass transit system—the city buses—will have proudly marked stops at river locations. And our urban streets will be laced with bikeways and walkways which lead to the river.

Commerce will focus on the river. The Cormorant Cafe will be perched high atop a downtown building. Diners there will take turns at the binoculars stationed along the glass wall facing the river. They'll take after-meal strolls along riverside walkways, and will patronize The Otter Gallery, The Rockfish Confectionery, and The Mallard Blues Bar.

Corporations will profit from the beauty of the urban James. They'll change their names to public-friendly names such as The First Bank of the Urban James, Natural River Law Firm, and River Rapids Technology. In their buildings their customers will see photographs of what the companies are doing to preserve the river's beauty, and will be ushered by proud corporate guides to rooftop observation stations.

The urban James will be an educational site not only for biology classes, but also for math and language and history and sociology. Seventh-graders will learn poetry along the James; twelvth-graders will discuss Greek mythology within a corporate riverview education center; university students will base their dissertations in urban planning on the miracle of the James.

Our city will embrace the Great Blue Heron as its official symbol—its easily recognizable reminder that Richmond's urban river is special. Its symbol of the citizens' respect for nature, the citizens' appreciation of the beautiful resource, and its symbol of our recognition that our welfare and our enjoyment derive from the urban James.

The breeze along the river will spread wildflower seeds, will loft waterfowl, will enrich businesses, will provoke intellectual thought, will sway branches, will drift leaves, and will continually refresh us.

Disaster Zone: Ecology of a Floodplain

[*This section was written by Ralph White and published initially by the James River Park System*]

Introduction: Your tour begins on the deck of the Visitor's Center at the Reedy Creek entrance to the Main Area of the park. The walk should last between one half to one hour. You will be guided through the unique ecosystem of the Floodplain—the flat land bordering rivers that is prone to regular flooding. You will explore how plants and animals have become adapted to this changing environment and you will see how humans have impacted and changed the area.

Bridge to Saw Mill Island with flood debris.

1—The Changing Environment

As you stand on the Visitor's Center deck, look for a pile of logs in the river. Is this a beaver lodge? The large size of the logs and the jumbled placement tells you the answer. Floods carry dead trees from upstream and deposit them on rocks or at the tips of islands. You can tell at least how high the water came by looking for the highest log. Remember, wood floats.

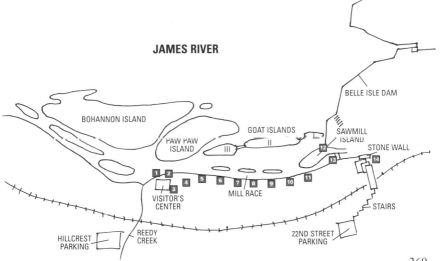

2—Mother Nature's Sneeze

Note how the trees along the shore are leaning as they grow, reaching out for sunlight. Even without a flood, these trees will ultimately fall into the river! Indeed, they would clog the channels without a cleansing pulse of water

now and then. (A pulse of air does the same thing when you get pollen or dust in your nose and sneeze).

As you walk along the trails, beware of poison ivy growing as a low shrub or as a thick, hairy vine. "Leaves of three, let it be." (There are no poisonous snakes along the floodplain.)

3—The Cradle of Civilization

Walk along the deck towards the parking lot and the wildflower meadow, stopping at the cement ramp that leads to the building. Flood waters carry mud from upstream fields and mountainsides. This leaves a thin, rich deposit which tends to smooth out bumps and make the land level. (The building is higher because it is built on an artificial hill of rocks and fill dirt.) Notice that the railroad chose this flat land for its route. Plants grow very well here. (The earliest recorded civilization developed on a broad floodplain between two rivers—the Tigris and Euphrates in what is now Iraq.) Where the land rises up on the other side of the railroad tracks is a different environment—the ancient banks of the James River.

4—Harvesting the Forest

Follow the trail back into the woods, past the trail sign marked "Riverside Trail East," heading towards the river and take your first right. There are many small tree stumps and maybe a fallen tree or two.

Welcome to the Beaver Super Market! Beavers cut trees here to get at the soft, sap-filled, energy-rich growing parts. Too fat to climb up to the tender twigs, they bring the entire tree down, cut off branches, and drag them into the river to eat safe from bothersome animals like dogs, bobcats and people. Their favorite part of the tree is the same as you like. Think breakfast, think pancakes.

Examine some of the stumps. Notice the teeth marks. Even though they cut down some of the trees (whose roots would hold the soil and reduce erosion), beavers actually make the land more protected against floods. When stumps sprout again, they grow back in a "bushy" form. This dense growth traps flood debris and slows down the flood waters. Take another look at some stumps and you will see that beavers often come back to harvest some of these new tender shoots in a process something like farming.

A note on beaver sociology. They live and work as a family (two parents, last year's two kits and this year's two). A new set of babies means that mom drives the two oldest away by biting them on their rear ends to search for their own home sites. **Beavers do not make dams or lodges along the river, because flood waters would tear them away. Instead, they dig holes in the river bank.** If you are visiting when the water is low, look for signs of their abandoned "high water homes" as you walk along the trail.

Look for "beaver highways," places where beavers drag branches and small logs to the water. Can you find ten of these sites along the edge of the trail?

Walk down the trail for about five minutes until you come to the sound of rushing water and the first good view of many rocks.

5—Shaping a Rock Garden

Before you is an interesting view of both human and natural history. The smooth, rounded rocks on the distant shore were shaped by moving water carrying fine sand. The more squared-off, sharp-sided rocks nearby were all cut by humans. This represents the remains of a small dam. Water was allowed to flow down a six- or eight-foot-wide opening near the shore. It led one quarter-mile down to a water-powered sawmill. The long narrow islands about 20 feet from shore are all that remain of this "millrace."

6—Footbridge Blowout

Walk about 50 feet to a cement platform. It is all that remains of a low footbridge that led out to one of the three lovely Goat Islands. It lasted only about a year when it was hit by a flood. Do you think the water alone knocked it out? A glance across the river will reveal what smashed against the structure. (What do you suppose knocked out the little dam we saw earlier?)

7—Fooling the Floods

Continue east on the trail, about 200 paces from the bridge blowout, until you are opposite a footbridge connecting Goat Islands II and III. Be careful of the many sharp thorns on the blackberry bushes that stick out onto the trail. This bridge was built at the same time and in the same manner as the washed-out bridge. However, this one has resisted many floods. Can you think of the reason why?

8—Fooling Around with Nature

Water comes over a low spot along the bank a few feet behind you. Racing down the trail, it gouged out a deep gully which had to be filled with rocks before a new island was formed. The erosion began when the trail surface was dug up with a tiller in order to plant grass. Since tree and shrub roots are the skeleton of the river bank, their removal caused the earthen skin to wash away during floods. What would have been a better way to make the trail?

9—Body Building

What the river takes, it also gives back. The islands in the channel to your left are growing in size. At low-water times in the summer, it is easy to see that sand is deposited at the downstream end of each island—the part of the island that is out of the current. Shrub and tree roots bind the loose sand and new land is formed.

Certain trees are especially adapted to this new land with broad, shallow, net-like roots and fast growth. Two examples of this would be the River Birch with thin, peeling, reddish bark and Sycamore with bark falling off in patches revealing white, green and tan, camouflage-like bark below. Sycamores can grow much larger than most other trees here but develop rotten spots where limbs fall off, creating homes for many animals. Neither the River Birch nor the Sycamore serves as a food tree for beavers. Instead, beavers prefer trees such as Cottonwood, Green Ash and Ash-leaf Maple.

10—River Cleanup

Walk ahead along the service road about 100 yards to a big cement box-like structure on the right side of the road. If you look carefully into the water on your left (beware, it's a steep drop-off), you will notice a huge door. This is a "safety valve" for the Richmond Storm and Sanitary Sewer System. When it rains heavily in Southside Richmond, water from the streets is added to the sewer pipes. Heavy rain fills them to bursting. This Combined Storm and Sewer Water Overflow gate—CSO for short—relieves the pressure by dumping the mix into the river. It keeps the system from exploding, but it also pollutes the river and degrades recreation. Since Federal laws have made it illegal now to pollute rivers, the city is constructing an additional pipe. It will be placed underground beside the railroad tracks. All four CSO's in the park will eventually be closed.

11—Water Powered Industry

Continue on the service road about 150 paces to a flat wooden bridge. Cross halfway onto the bridge and look to the left, upstream. The eastern tip of the island you are about to enter is a stone wall. Part of the island is obviously manmade. A wooden gate ran from the wall to the shore. It controlled water flow down the channel to a water wheel at the saw mill. The rest of the water was sent back to the river.

Walk straight ahead to a set of steps along the river's edge. These steps mark the site of a recent park ferry boat. Attached to a cable, it could be pulled by hand across to Goat Island #1. It was frequently damaged by floods. The only way to get to the island is by walking across the dam when it is dry. Access to the dam is just beyond the picnic shelter. (If water level permits you may cross the dam and explore the three Goat Islands or go ahead to the footbridge that lies past the dam.}

12—Helping Fish

Standing with your back to the footbridge stairs, you will be looking out at the usually dry rocks and can observe again the way that nature and humans shape rocks differently.

The solid rock riverbed explains why there are river rapids. While a mud or sand bottom would create a smooth flow, rocks push water up and around. At high river flows in the spring, water often comes over the dam and covers these rocks, creating rapids and whitewater. Note that most rocks are rounded and natural.

Migrating fish like shad and herring can make it upstream only as far as the dam. Since they cannot jump like salmon, the Virginia Electric Power Company, who built the dam, also built a fish ladder. Look for a long, open-topped cement trough which can be best viewed by crossing the dam. Water ran through it and cement baffles slowed it down. It did not work well because it was not in the main flow and the fish were unable to find it. (Even if it were easier to find, they would not tend to navigate through the holes in the baffles.) Nonetheless, it was a serious attempt by humans to get along with nature. (A modern, effective fish ladder will be built at Bosher's Dam.)

13—The River Runs This Way

From the middle of the footbridge looking east, you can barely see where the rock wall once closed off this millrace. (Note the stones jutting out at right angles from the wall on the left side.) A notch in the bottom of the wall probably let water shoot out to turn an "undershot" water wheel. This powered a long, straight saw which cut planks from logs. Just beyond the bridge on shore there was a chair factory.

14—Nearing the End of Your Journey

You may end your tour here and loop back to the Visitor's Center heading west along the service road. Or you may wish to continue east towards the spiral pedestrian tower.

Continuing downstream to the foot of the 22nd Street pedestrian tower, you will notice a stone wall. This was the "headgate" for a water-powered cotton mill. If you walk further along a very narrow, rock path for about 50 paces you will come to a cement walkway that forms the top of the sewer line. Along this walkway you will find the remains of an old granite quarry full of drill holes and pieces of cut curbstone.

On your way back pick up a piece of litter to make the park an even better place to visit!

In River Time ≋
(*Originally written and published in July, 1986*)

Last fall on a rainy afternoon I stopped on the way home from work and looked at the James River from atop the bluff at the south end of Richmond's Lee Bridge. The river was cresting at one of its highest flood levels of the century. Businesses and homes and crops and livestock were lost.

Today I stand atop the same bluff amid what may end up being the worst drought in Virginia's history. It's July, it's 98 degrees, and the James stretches down there with all of her rocks and boulders and nooks and crannies exposed and drying. I stand here now not to see the thinning river that has made the 6:30 news, but to see the wonderful river that has flowed among the pages of the book I finished reading last night: *In River Time: The Way of the James*, by Dr. Ann Woodlief.

Not since Robert Boyle's *The Hudson River* have I enjoyed a river book so much. *In River Time* incorporates all of the currents that run through Boyle's book, but they're mingled with an extra added attraction: philosophy, metaphysics, heart and soul—poetry. As Dr. Woodlief guides us along the James' twisting paths, shows us its history and geography and sociology, stops at every significant marker buoy from Pocohontas to Kepone, pauses to wet our toes and scent our nostrils and muddy our fingers. She also throws in a little Thoreau and Eliot and Woodlief: "Once, as I paddled in a rainstorm, jumping with each distant thunder clap, I heard under the pounding raindrops a low steady hum which penetrated and calmed my shivering body. I can still hear this hum of the river's 'valv'd voice' in my dreams, and I wonder if it might be the same soul that Walt Whitman invited into his body in 'Song of Myself.' Perhaps, for me, it is."

I stand here now, without my customary fishing rod, to think about the river. Dr. Woodlief's book has so compelled me. What, besides fishing, does the river have for me? I've sat in a 60-mile-an-hour bass boat and pulled 3-pounders from the mile-wide stretch near Hopewell. I've floated a 6-hour inner tube above the Falls near Goochland. And I've rolled up my after-meeting suit pants to catch a brace of before-dark smallmouths near the Natural Bridge exit of I-64. For 5 years the James River has been an irretractable part of my life, but seemingly only because of its fish. Dr. Woodlief's *In River Time* now embarrasses me, convicts me of sins of omission—omission of the river's other currents. The book is a look at the James' Indians, its settlers, its river barons, its factories, its public services, its messy chore of "absorbing and flushing, floating and nourishing." Dr. Woodlief is a historian, a researcher, an observer, but also a thinker and a ponderer. Her James is a river, but also a metaphor: "All our accumulating knowledge must be tempered by the wise ignorance which knows that the ways and rhythms of the river, like those of our lives, sometimes reach beyond the limits of our understanding. When the river loses its freedom to run freely, to be itself, usually it is we who eventually lose."

It interests me that smallmouth bass were stocked in the James less than a hundred years ago, that Richmond didn't get a sewage treatment system until the fifties, that little organisms are breaking down at least some of the killer Kepone, and that there are at least a hundred organizations whose charge is the welfare of the James River. But the book's best gift to me is a new look at the river—at all rivers—so that during future dusk and dawn angling outings I may pause a time or two and repeat Ann Woodlief's words: "Here I forget what I know about rivers so that I can see the seamless river time which promises perpetual beginnings in the midst of entropy." (Algonquin Books of Chapel Hill, 1985)

20-Year Projection for Park Needs & Development

[This document was prepared by Ralph White for the James River Park System and dated April 4, 1996]

Assumption: The James River will continue becoming clean. An increasingly rich and diverse mix of wildlife combined with an attractive downtown shoreline and an increasing interest in water-related recreation means that there will be a need to expand public access to the river. The riverside park system will be considered an increasingly valuable asset to the quality of life in Richmond and the surrounding metropolitan area.

Problems: African-Americans comprise over 50% of the population in Richmond, but are very light users of much of the riverside park system. (The areas used by this group tend to be the flatwater sections, especially those areas east of the 14th Street Bridge.) The "natural area" park concept of which the riverside parks are the primary component have been systematically underfunded and understaffed ever since federal funding was eliminated. (Resource deterioration and potential public safety issues have grown at the same time that public interest and use has increased.) Parking and public transportation to river park areas are inadequate now and are projected to be increasingly so in the future. The public school system and university communities make only moderate use of the river in Richmond. (Private high schools do use it for education.)

Workers who built the kiosk at Reedy Creek in 1992: Michael Barnes, Jonathan Batzli, Brian James, and Michael Malarkey.

Projected Developments for the Riverside Park System: Expansion of park land and public access in the areas just below the Fall Line (east of the 14th Street Bridge) should be a major goal to attract a greater racial mix to the river. (Mayo's Island would be of great value since it marks the end of the rapids, is an important fishery, and is accessible by public transportation. The gravel pits east of Ancarrow's Landing are potentially valuable marina and fishing areas. Small parcels of unused land just above and below the Port of Richmond/Deepwater Terminal may be of value as special parks bringing people close to exciting views of big ships.) **Expansion of commercial development that fosters recreational use of the river should be incorporated into the long-term park plan—e.g., restaurants, marinas, fishing docks, etc.**

Public transportation and jogger/walker/bicycle routes should be overlaid onto existing streets—especially with inexpensive signage, curb cuts, route striping, bicycle parking, and bus stop shelters. Commercial parking lots should be encouraged to take the place of city parking in public parks and along roads. Muscle-powered access should be especially encouraged as most compatible with the qualities of a natural area park system and is projected to be of increasing interest to a health-conscious population.

Universities and/or private foundations should be encouraged to set up environmental education facilities along the river, probably in city parks. (Belle Isle offers opportunities for this in the underutilized triangular building wistfully referred to as the Environmental Center. Mayo's Island offers structures that would also serve this purpose. Virginia Commonwealth University is the closest and most likely source for educational efforts along the river, but the Math & Science Center is another strong candidate. Virginia Union University might expand more into recreation management and the University of Richmond is another possible participant.) Expansion of educational/interpretive services by city park staff does not seem likely given the history of tight budgets. **More privately run tours and educational experiences should be encouraged: kayak lessons, boat tours, nature painting classes, history walks, fishing lessons, etc.**

The most important facilities that the current and long-term riverside parks lack are continuous and well-marked pedestrian access routes.

James River Association

"Join us on the James" is the title of the brochure published by the James River Association, an organization which promotes conservation of the river's natural and historic resources consistent with orderly development.

The goals of the Association are: to ensure the quality and effective use of the James and related natural resources; to support sustainable development and creative land use policies throughout the James River Watershed; to enhance the quality, quantity, and diversity of aquatic resources in the James River; and to increase public education and information for greater appreciation of the James River.

Memberships in the Association are available, and members receive the quarterly newsletter, the annual report, and can participate in field trips, seminars and other special events.

The Association lists the following available publications: "Lower James River Corridor Study," "Watershed Resources Management Plan," "Virginia Byway Route 5 Study," "An action Plan for Sustainable Development Brochure," "Historic Landmarks Brochure," "Reflections on the James" (videotape), and "Protecting the James: A Watershed Management Plan" (videotape).

The brochure states that you should join the James River Association, "if you want to help preserve the natural beauty and historic landscape of the James River, if you want to improve air quality and water quality, if you are concerned about the loss of wetlands and wildlife habitat, if you are interested in restoring fish and shellfish in the James River, if you are concerned about the impact of actions by upstream localities on the downstream portion of the James, if you believe in coordinated planning for development along the River, and if you want to be actively involved in shaping the future of the James."

And the Association lists 19 accomplishments, among them the following: Historic River Designation for 25 miles of the Lower James, Scholarship Program, fish passages on James River Dams, keeping Harrison Lake National Fish Hatchery open and producing rockfish for restocking, passage of the Chesapeake Bay Preservation Act, legislation to protect instream river uses such as habitat and recreation, and presentations to schools and civic groups.

James River Association, P.O. Box 110, Richmond, VA 23201

Alliance for the Chesapeake Bay

The Alliance for the Chesapeake Bay has published a James River fact sheet, "as part of its commitment to responsible use of natural resources." The fact sheet was made possible "by a generous grant from Virginia Power and by a donation from the Lower James River Association." The following is a summary, with excerpts from, the comprehensive publication.

"The falls of the James occur in the heart of Richmond—over seven miles the river drops 105 feet in elevation. When Captain John Smith explored the river in May of 1607 he was stopped by the 'great craggy stones in the midst of the river, where the water falleth so rudely, and with such a violence, as not any boat can pass.' Settlers, quick to recognize the potential power of the falls for flour mills, paper mills, and iron works, built the nation's first industries. **Richmond became a transportation center where goods were unloaded from oceangoing ships and taken farther inland by other means.** Today's kayakers and whitewater enthusiasts relish the Falls of the James as some of the finest whitewater on the

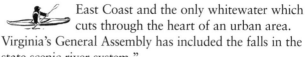 East Coast and the only whitewater which cuts through the heart of an urban area. Virginia's General Assembly has included the falls in the state scenic river system."

By the year 2000, 2.3 million people will live in the watershed for the James River. The Virginia State Water Control Board lists 21 significant municipal and 28 major industrial dischargers on the James River—with most of the industrial activity concentrated in Richmond and below. Phosphorous, nitrogen and other nutrients—mainly from sewage plants, industrial outlets, agriculture and urban sources—continually threaten the river. Nutrients cause excessive algae growth which can choke oxygen from the water.

Sewage flow systems have a particular threat to the river. In Richmond there are two types of pipes—one group which carries sewage to treatment plants and another group—fed by storm drains—which carries stormwater directly to the river. However there are 11,000 acres in Richmond which are serviced only by the sewer pipes, and when storms overfill those pipes, the excess goes directly into the river carrying untreated sewage. Currently the city is undergoing a multi-year construction project to route the excess runoff downstream from Richmond, away from recreational areas. Ideally, hundreds of millions of dollars should be spent to install new systems to eliminate the problem.

Another potential problem for the James is not enough water. By the year 2030 critical water shortages are predicted for Richmond and the surrounding counties. Planning for this water supply problem is underway now, and hopefully enough water will be left in the James "to protect water quality, aquatic life, wildlife habitat, recreation, and aesthetics."

Water flow is also important to migratory fish on the James. **As of this writing, all the dams in Richmond except one—Bosher's Dam—have been made passable for migratory fish.** Plans are in place to make this dam passable too. This is important for the full restoration of the fisheries in the river and the Bay.

"THE FUTURE OF THE JAMES RIVER DEPENDS IN PART ON HOW THE RAPID GROWTH OF ITS URBAN AND INDUSTRIAL AREAS IS HANDLED."
With growth, urban development, and industrialization comes runoff, erosion, and the need for control programs.

"Significant work has been done and money spent on improving the water quality of the James River. For the James to be clean in the future, it will take a continued effort by the Commonwealth, local governments and James River citizens."

Alliance for the Chesapeake Bay: (804) 775-0951

Falls of the James Scenic River Advisory Board

Dr. Reuben B. Young has chaired the Falls of the James Scenic River Advisory Board since its inception in 1972. The Board meets monthly and reviews all projects along the river to assure that they pay attention to aesthetics, history, recreation, and environmental concerns. The Board is an advisory board, and provides advice on city, state, and federal levels. It has nine members: five appointed by the Richmond City Council and four by the Governor. The Board receives no funding and its members are volunteers.

The Board began as the Richmond Scenic James Council—a group of citizens who successfully opposed a plan to construct a major expressway along the southwest bank of the urban James. Since then the Board has played key roles in the establishment of the James River Park System and the hiring of its full-time naturalist, the designation of the James as a scenic river, the construction of the pedestrian bridge slung beneath the Lee Bridge, the Combined Sewer Overflow Project, and other projects.

At this writing **the Board is recommending that the urban James be considered as a separate planning district rather than the current status in which portions of the urban river are claimed by several districts.**

On May 3, 1996, the Board submitted a memorandum to the City Manager's office which included, "We therefore recommend to the City of Richmond that the James River, within the city limits as well as its banks, its parks and canals be designated as the James River Corridor Planning District, and We further recommend a review of the river parks, historic sites, natural areas, open spaces and vistas, recreational opportunities, canals, and urban riverfront in this new James River Corridor Planning District." The City Manager's reply was encouraging.

The Falls of the James Scenic River Advisory Board has received national recognition. At a 1995 ceremony at the National Press Club the American Rivers organization presented its Urban Rivers Restoration Award for Lifetime Achievement to the Board for its 25 years of dedicated vigilance to, "conservation, protection, and appropriate utilization of the James River and its environs in Richmond."

In 1982 Dr. Young received the Virginia Wildlife Federation's River Conservationist of the Year Award for his work on behalf of the urban James.

The Board's objectives are:
- Preserve and protect the natural qualities of the river, including its banks and islands.
- Rehabilitate downtown Richmond riverfront areas, including Mayo's Island.
- Control and eventually eliminate combined sewer overflows.
- Add appropriate sites to the James River Park System where feasible. Create greenways where appropriate, feasible, and acceptable to neighbors.
- Insure adequate funding for managing the James River Park System, as well as recreational and interpretive programs.
- Assure fish passage through the various James River dams.
- Assure flows adequate to maintain a healthy ecosystem, water supply, and river recreation during drought conditions—and in view of projected population growth in the counties.
- Restore the historic 18th century Kanawha and Haxall Canals.
- Promote environmental education and cleanup projects along the river.

A 1995 printed article from the Board states: "Urban rivers and their environs need to be protected by public policies written into federal and state laws, local ordinances, and master plans. River conservation organizations should not only make sure that existing laws (such as the Clean Water Act) are properly carried out, but also lobby for additional policies (such as scenic river designations) when these are found to be needed. Follow-through should be continued indefinitely! Members should be vigilant and alert to problems, as well as opportunities for enhancing the rivers and their environs, and should respond accordingly. This requires long term commitments on the part of the organization. An officially designated advisory board has the same responsibilities plus the advantages of greater influence owing to its status, and regular communications with all interested parties including conservation organizations. Properly constituted, advisory boards can play an important role in the long term protection of urban rivers."

Center for Environmental Studies

Under the direction of Dr. Greg C. Garman, Virginia Commonwealth University's Center for Environmental Studies—formed in 1993—presents a "truly interdisciplinary approach to understanding the structure and function of ecological systems."

The cover of the Center's brochure features the Richmond skyline above the urban James River, and presents this caption: **"The James River is the dominant focus, both physiographic and cultural, for the City of Richmond.** . . . Because of its unique urban mission, VCU's Center for Environmental Studies maintains a strong commitment to the study of urban-dominated landscapes."

The Center not only presents areas of study as part of the university's curriculum, but also provides educational opportunities for the general public. One of the Center's missions is to "foster the creation of an informed public on environmental issues, and to make scientific data readily available to decision-makers and their constituents."

The Center presents seminars on such controversial topics as private property rights, air quality issues, and multiple-use of water resources. The Center also offers training classes designed for professionals. The following are three examples:

THE ECOLOGY AND MANAGEMENT OF
WETLAND ENVIRONMENTS

"The three-day course will focus on the ecological structure and function of wetland ecosystems, the identification of indicator plant species, current state and federal regulatory policies relating to wetlands, and a description of the methods used to delineate wetland habitat boundaries. Extensive time will be spent in the field, allowing students to participate directly in data collection and delineation protocols. The workshop will conclude with an exercise in the wetland permit process for proposed development."

RAPID BIOASSESSMENT PROTOCOLS
"The three-day workshop will provide an overview of environmental monitoring and assessment principles, and describe the use of ecological indicators for aquatic environments. The course will focus on the use of EPA Rapid Bioassessment Protocols (RBP's) for macroinvertebrate communities and stream habitat. The Index of Biotic Integrity (IBI), a rapid bioassessment tool for fish assemblages, will also be presented. In the field, participants will be involved in all aspects of data collection, and will use recently-developed computer software to calculate bioassessment indices."

WATER QUALITY ASSESSMENT
"Participants will be trained in EPA- and Virginia DEQ-accepted procedures for the evaluation of surface water quality. Topics covered will include: sample and data collection for the most widely-measured chemical and microbial parameters, calibration and maintenance of field and laboratory equipment, QA/QC protocols, and the use of in-situ dataloggers for long-term monitoring of temperature, dissolved oxygen, pH, and turbidity in lakes, streams, and rivers."

Virginia Commonwealth University
Center for Environmental Studies
(804) 828-7202

Volunteer Projects in the James River Park

[*The following was prepared in 1995 by the James River Park System. These lists demonstrate that there are endless ways we can all help make the James River Park System more enjoyable. Surely there are new projects available as you read this.*]

Chester Brazzell, Michael Dwiefel, Jason Stephens, Austin Brazzell, Robin Wilhelm and Chris Knoop spread wood chips at Pony Pasture.

1. Construct a boardwalk out of railroad ties or telephone poles across muddy area of trail at Northbank Park (Texas Avenue Beach) like that on Buttermilk Trail . . . good for large group of fairly strong people, carry long distance or arrange with CSX Railroad for supply access.
2. Construct at least 3 flood proof benches at Huguenot Woods (like those on Belle Isle) for fishermen and walkers.
3. Construct R.R. Tie steps to top of Belle Isle at eroded site beside quarry. Use 1/2 lengths of R.R. Tie and stake down.
4. Prepare soil and plant wildflower seeds at selected sites (esp. at meadows near Visitor's Center and perhaps on Belle Isle . . . could become an Eagle project). Purchase seeds.
5. Design and construct a small observation deck above the quarry on Belle Isle. Requires woodworking skills.
6. Construct an additional boardwalk on top of the earthworks at the Civil War gun emplacement at the western end of Belle Isle.
7. Remove the underbrush and lower limbs on all the trees in the mill race on Belle Isle so that the stone work can be seen. (Possible Eagle) . . . a big job.
8. Construct an information kiosk at the Floodwall parking lot at Semmes/7th Street like those on Belle Isle and 3 Mile Locks ("Pumphouse"). Requires woodworking skills.
9. Construct an information kiosk on Belle Isle at the western end—like the one at the east end. Requires woodworking skills.
10. Remove all underbrush at site of Civil War Cemetery on Belle Isle, stack and chip (or remove). Big job!

11. Construct steps from 1/2 length of R.R. Ties along fenceline at Manchester wall. Climbing site.
12. Clear fallen trees from fenceline in main area of park. (Requires use of chainsaws and ladders.)
13. Cut down telephone poles on Belle Isle and winch to edge of maintenance road or to nearby storage site. (Winter)

SMALL GROUP PROJECTS

A. Spread wood chips on trails and shrub beds (esp. Pony Pasture and 43rd Street).
B. Pick up litter on rocks and shoreline (esp. 22nd St. area and Great Shiplock).
C. Cut back brush at scenic vistas and quarry walls (also around factory sites on Belle Isle).
D. Wade for cans in river (esp. in front of Visitor's Center) summer and early fall.
E. Cover graffiti with black paint on rocks in river (esp. at 22nd St. and Hydro Plant Belle Isle).
F. Mow and clip grassy trails (esp. near Visitor's Center and Pony Pasture). Spring and fall.
G. Adopt-A-Trail and maintain monthly for one year (esp. Buttermilk, Goat Island, Pony Pasture Meadow and V.C. Meadow).
H. Make and install distance markers along Maintenance Road/River Trail.
I. Clip ivy on trees along Riverside Drive or herbicide.
J. Replace railroad ties around walkway at Visitor's Center.
K. Re-pile rocks along Riverside Trail on Belle Isle.
L. Paint base of Lee Bridge supports on Belle Isle.
M. Plant Red Bud trees along Riverside Drive.
N. Remove rocks from turbine opening in mill race wall.
O. Construct stairway out of R.R. Ties on top of Belle Isle.
P. Paint some doors and walls in the Visitor's Center.

PROJECTS REQUIRING MONEY

- Engraving marker stones on Belle Isle for historic sites (approx. $200 each).
- Publishing park coloring book (approx. $1,000).
- Fabricating temporary interpretive signs (approx. $75 each) for Belle Isle.
- Preparation and seeding of wildflower meadows (3 sites, approx. $500 each).

- Purchase of a small tractor (new $8,000) with mower and grader.
- Purchase of a small copying machine (new $400).
- Purchase of a computer.

The Honorable Becky Norton Dunlop

[*Secretary Dunlop provided the following information during a 1996 interview.*]

Virginia's Secretary of Natural Resources Becky Norton Dunlop believes that the James River is Richmond's best natural amenity. She maintains a logical and optimistic philosophy about the urban James and about other natural resources: *a growing economy and an improving environment are mutually dependent.*

As people move beyond an economic level sufficient for their basic needs, their interests then turn towards quality of life: education, the arts, and especially their neighborhoods, their parks, and enhancing their community's natural resources.

The same is true with businesses. As they profit, they seek ways to be better neighbors and ways to have a better impact on the environment.

Translation: the better the economy, the more resources and energies can and will be devoted to maintaining and even enhancing the natural resources. **As Richmond's economy grows, we will give more and more attention to making the urban James even better.**

Secretary Dunlop's Secretariat of Natural Resources includes not only Recreation and Parks and Game and Fish, but also Historic Resources and Water Quality. Although the water quality of the urban James is already remarkably good, Richmond's Combined Sewer Overflow Project is proceeding, and will help maintain the water quality during times of heavy rainfall.

Secretary Dunlop is interested in new technologies which can help protect water quality—such as the permeable concrete developed by TARMAC. Water—but not trash and debris—will be able to seep directly through cemented areas, thus eliminating some of the waste problems currently associated with storm drains.

The Honorable Becky Norton Dunlop

Secretary Dunlop is a proponent of the James River not only because it is her Cabinet-level responsibility, but also because she has floated through its urban rapids and experienced the river first-hand.

She expects Richmond's citizens and businesses to continue devoting their energies towards enhancing the natural beauty of the urban James River and maintaining its historic resources. She foresees a day when Richmond's James River will receive national attention as a tourist destination. She sees the urban James continuing to blossom as a provider of recreation, ambiance, and natural beauty in a way that strengthens the city's economy.

August 23, 1981

I cross the Nickel Bridge each day to and from work, and as traffic slows, my eyes are a hundred yards below, counting crisscrossing currents, supposing somersaulting smallmouths, and wading waist-high waters.

I waded into Richmond's urban James on a sunny August Sunday. I was just downstream from the Nickel Bridge. The area is spattered with a maze of boulders and rocks and rapids of all sizes. And smallmouth bass.

In minutes I had leaped my way to the river's center and was casting a tiny green Beetle Spin on 4-pound line. Far and fine is the way to fish the James when it's low and clear.

Everywhere I looked were eddies and rapids and undercut boulders. I threw the tiny spinner to a swift upstream glide and after only two swift turns of the reel handle the line stretched and a giant smallmouth salmon-jumped amid the churning waters.

It was a large fish, surely three or four pounds. **I held the rod high as the drag hummed briefly. The fish went around one boulder, then another as I maneuvered him towards me.** I stood high on a flattened stone three feet above the river's surface. My position was fortunate.

At last the fish tired and came towards me, but with another effort he zigzagged among a trio of deep rocks and my line froze. The fish had succeeded in wedging the fragile line.

Quickly I entered the waist-deep water and somehow managed to free the line and the fish. I put my left thumb in the fish's mouth and lifted him onto my standing rock.

Brenton S. Halsey

Comments from an interview in November, 1996:

"The foremost value of the James is recreation and nature and of course the aesthetics—what the river does for you when you look at it, and that's a lot.

"The primary focus of the Richmond Riverfront Development Project will be on the canals. From 7th Street east the railroads present an inherent barrier that's not going to change. With the Floodwall and the railroads there will be little development right on the river. But it's close, and you can walk. This is a key area for whitewater kayaking and rafting, and hopefully we'll even see the shad fishery come back.

The fish was not four pounds. The excitement of that first jump had magnified him. Nor three. Only two, maybe plus a couple of ounces. I took an instant photograph and released him.

I caught seven more bass during the rest of my two-hour wade, but none as large as the first. Not nearly.

The James' boulders are sprinkled not only with fish but with treasures of all sorts.

My bounty included a practice golf ball; a flat, yellow rock with a black square on it; a thin, curved black stone which may be a pottery remnant; and a green and yellow Nike running shoe. At first the shoe looked as if it had a human toe emerging from the hole in it and I was afraid to pick it up. But it was just an illusion.

As I climbed the 72 steps to the platform that exits James River Park I passed the mid-afternoon flow of rivergoers.

Two women, followed by two husbands, talked literature. "Well, it's the perfect thing for summertime reading," one of them said.

Another two-couple group, carrying four small coolers, spoke of flashlights. "No, you keep your flashlight, I don't want it," offered a bermuda-shorted woman. "There's just no way I'm getting out of my car after dark. I'll just sit there and wait for the police to arrive."

At home I discarded the golf ball and the shoe. I had left the two rocks in the river where I discovered them.

After getting into some dry clothes I sat down in front of a television football game and put new batteries in my flashlight.

"But tourists will be attracted to the canals, and a significant theme will be historic interpretation. Hopefully Valentine Riverside [Tredegar Iron Works] will be back in action as a Civil War center where people will come first to find out about the War's impact in the whole region.

"While the Richmond Riverfront Development Project is currently focused on the downtown portion of the canals, the next phase will redevelop the canal from Valentine Riverside all of the way up to Maymont where there could be a beautiful landing area at the Japanese Gardens.

"The five property owners between here [James River Corporation] and 17th Street are all very sensitive to the aesthetics of the entire area, and want to ensure that development occurs in a carefully controlled manner.

"I don't foresee any new industry coming which will have any adverse effect on the river. I see nothing but improvements."

Brenton S. Halsey is Chairman Emeritus of James River Corporation and has leadership roles with the Richmond Riverfront Development Project and the Virginia Historical Society. He devotes much of his energy to Richmond's James River.

Virginia Canal Museum?

The Virginia Canals and Navigation Society has published a brochure which makes an exciting case for Pump House Park being turned into a museum devoted to Virginia's canal system. The brochure features George W. Bagby's quote from canal days: "Of all the locks from Lynchburg down, the Three-Mile Locks pleased me most. It is a pretty place, as every one will own on seeing it. It is so clean and green, and white and thrifty-looking. To me it was simply beautiful. I wanted to live there; I ought to have lived there. I was built for a lock-keeper . . . . What more could the soul ask?"

The brochure's vision includes an archives and

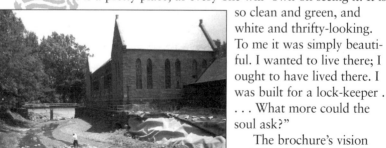

JOHN BRYAN

library, exhibits, a meeting hall, chamber music in the Pump House Pavilion (where dances used to take place), operational turbines and pumps, gift shop, bateau rides on the canal, mule-drawn boat rides through the locks, hiking trails, and the famous "Lower Arch."

Mayo's Island

Mayo's Island Park officially opened on April 11, 1921, with a capacity crowd of 7,500 persons in the new grandstands to see a baseball game between the Richmond Colts and the Petersburg Goobers. The following year major league exhibition games came to Mayo's Island, and fans got to see Babe Ruth hit a 378-foot home run. There were many other major league exhibition games in future years featuring the Detroit Tigers, the New York Giants, the Baltimore Orioles, and the Dodgers and Yankees. Although the official home of the Richmond Colts baseball team, Mayo's Island Park also hosted football games of William and Mary, the University of Richmond, Virginia Polytechnic Institute, the University of North Carolina and other colleges.

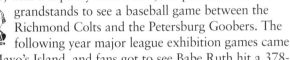

The field was highly susceptible to intense sogginess from rain and high water, and games were often played in mud. Floods damaged the stands from time to time, and a 1941 fire destroyed the stands for good, thus ending all sports activities on the island.

Today there is an effort to revitalize Mayo's Island.

Greg Weatherford's article, "Party Island," in the October 1, 1996 issue of *STYLE Weekly*, describes Mark Brown's work and vision to establish an entertainment complex on Mayo's Island. Brown and partners have signed a 20-year lease for the 14-acre property which includes easy access from Mayo's Bridge and enough parking for 700 cars.

The vision calls for outdoor concerts, a 400-seat restaurant, a concert hall, offices, and unfenced open-to-the-public parts of the island available to fishers and kayakers and others who go there to enjoy the river.

There is still plenty of cleaning and developing to do. Already they've hauled away 40 old trucks and school buses, 50 trash bins, have cut back overgrown areas, and have planted grass. There are warehouses on the island which the developers hope to renovate for other uses, and there is the chore of making the parking area hospitable for cars.

There was a concert on the island on September 22, 1996 which drew 2,000 persons—a benefit for Feed the Future. A month earlier 1,500 persons attended a dance party on the island.

Mark Brown envisions the time when Mayo's Island will be the most exciting entertainment area in the city.

Appendix

Your 99 Most-Asked Questions About the Urban James

1. What about snakes?
   THERE ARE NO POISONOUS WATER MOCCASINS ON THE URBAN JAMES. NONE. You can count the people who have been injured by snakes on your little finger and still have one finger left over. Nobody is ever harmed by any snake on the urban James.
2. Are there really Bald Eagles in Richmond?
   Yes, and you'll see them if you frequent the river.
3. Is it okay to take home a nice piece of driftwood?
   No. Everything along the river is protected—the animals, the flowers, the driftwood, even the rocks. Leave all of it undisturbed for everyone to enjoy.
4. Can I safely go to the river alone?
   This is an urban river and you should use the same precautions you'd use anywhere else in the inner city. I'm a tall man and have never had any problems going to the river alone during the 15 years I've lived here. On sunny weekend days there are many areas of the river that have enough people that anyone would be safe alone.
5. Will my car be safe?
   If you leave anything anyone would want to steal visible in your car, there's a chance of a broken window. But it's rare that anyone breaks into an empty car. About 10 years ago someone broke one of my windows and took a fishing rod. I have had no problems since.

Devil's Kitchen, 1988: Phil Frederick, Ralph White and Bill Trout.

6. Is it safe to swim in the river?
   Yes, but use common sense. Don't try to swim or wade near swift water. The river is much more powerful than it looks. Life jackets are legally required when the river level reaches five feet at Westham Gauge. After very heavy rains there is a chance of

some raw sewage draining directly into the river. It's best to wait two or three days to swim. Always wear shoes for protection from broken glass, metal, and rocks.
7. **Can I let my children swim in the river?**
Again, use common sense. Children should be watched and life guarded ANYWHERE they swim, and especially in a lake or river. Be sure they wear life jackets and shoes. And don't allow them to dive—the urban James is full of rocks.
8. **Is it safe to eat the fish?**
In a word, yes.
9. **Do I need a fishing license?**
Yes, state regulations apply. Licenses can be purchased from most retail tackle dealers. They expire every December 31.
10. **Can I camp on the river?**
Camping and fires are not allowed along the urban James.
11. **Is it safe to go to the river at night?**
The James River Park System is open only during daylight hours. Some people safely fish at night near the Annabel Lee and from the 14th Street Bridge. Generally you should enjoy the river only during daylight.
12. **Is there really a herd of albino deer along the river?**
No. Up until 1994 there were reported sightings of albinos in the Williams Island area. But pibaldism is the real characteristic. A true albino deer rarely lives past infancy. It not only has severe vision problems and other physical disabilities, but it is highly susceptible to disease and predators. A pibald deer (some white areas, but without the pink hooves and eyes) also has physical problems, and usually reaches adulthood only in isolated areas which are free of predators. It is probable that one or two pibald deer have existed, but not a herd.
13. **Is it okay to picnic along the river?**
Sure. But glass containers are not allowed.
14. **Can I take my dog?**
Yes. But leashes and clean-up are required.
15. **Was there really a Civil War Prison on Belle Isle?**
Yes. See the section on Belle Isle.

JOHN BRYAN

16. **Are there really Class V rapids in the city?**

    No. They are Class IV and lower. At certain high water levels, some can be considered Class V.
17. **Have people really drowned in Hollywood Rapids?**
    Unfortunately, yes. Those Class IV rapids are safe only for experienced rafters and paddlers with proper safety equipment.
18. **Can I fish everywhere along the river at any time of the year?**
    Yes, as long as you're not on private property. There are no closed seasons except for stripers (rockfish).
19. **Can I keep the fish I catch?**
    Yes, but state restrictions apply—size and number restrictions on some fish. You'll want to get a copy of the regulations from the Virginia Department of Game and Inland Fisheries. The game wardens are extremely enthusiastic about the establishment of stripers (rockfish), and if you plan to keep a striper, be certain to know that it falls within the size and seasonal restrictions.

20. **Who maintains James River Park?**
    Ralph White (Chief Naturalist for the James River Park System) and his limited staff and limited budget. In order to maintain the Park properly, our city needs at least 10 times the resources and personnel currently available. Ralph always has a list of volunteer projects—big and small—available for those who want to help. There are good projects for children and adults—some that take a couple of hours, some that can last a season.
21. **Were there Indians here?**

    Yes. When Christopher Newport was the first white person to arrive here in 1607, this was important site for the Algonquins.
22. **Where is the best view of the river?**
    Good question. There are dozens of answers. Try the mausoleum at Hollywood Cemetery, the Confederate Soldiers and Sailors Monument at the intersection of North 29th and Libby Terrace, any of the bridges or lookouts, or most any of the tall office buildings in Richmond.

Morrie Piersol viewing the river at flood stage from the Floodwall.

23. Is this really the best smallmouth fishing in the nation?
No. Twenty years ago before it was "discovered" the smallmouth fishing was indeed phenomenal with four-pounders common in the urban James.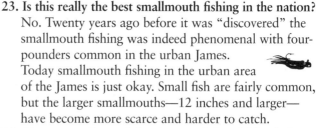
Today smallmouth fishing in the urban area of the James is just okay. Small fish are fairly common, but the larger smallmouths—12 inches and larger—have become more scarce and harder to catch.

24. Can you really catch herring on plain gold hooks?
Yes. Drop a line with a gold hook below the 14th Street Bridge in April and you'll quickly find out.

25. Are there animals on Belle Isle?

Muskrat prints.

If you mean mammals, yes. There are no deer, but there are muskrats, beaver, river otter, and a red fox family. Don't worry, they're shy.

26. Can I just grab a tube and float on the river through the city?
No. You MUST accompany someone who knows the routes. If not, 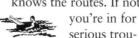 you're in for serious trouble. There are rapids which do take lives.

27. When were the canals built?
They were continually being built and maintained from the 1770s until the 1870s when the railroads took over.

28. What should I do if I see a problem in the James River Park System—such as an obstructed trail, a pile of litter, vandalism, or a dangerous fallen tree?
Please call and report it immediately: (804) 780-5311.

29. Are there any projects for my scout troop?
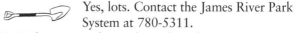 Yes, lots. Contact the James River Park System at 780-5311.

30. Is there a newsletter about the urban James?
Yes. It's new. See the information at the back of this book.

31. Is it okay to drink the water in the urban James River?
Although the James River is extremely clean, it's not a good idea to drink water from any urban waterway.

32. Is it okay to take home some nice rocks?
No. Everything—living and not living—is protected. The rocks, the flowers, the driftwood, and all else is there for all of us to enjoy.

33. **How deep is the urban James?**
    At normal flow it averages three or four feet deep upstream from Mayo's Bridge (with some areas as deep as 10 feet), and 15 or 20 feet deep near the Annabel Lee. However, the relatively shallow water should not imply a lack of danger. The river is quite powerful upstream from Mayo's Bridge.
34. **Does a flood wash the fish away?**
    No. They merely seek calm waters behind boulders and among inundated shorelines.
35. **When did settlers arrive here?**
    Christopher Newport "discovered" this area on May 24, 1607.
36. **What kinds of fish can you catch in the urban James?**
    Smallmouth bass, redbreasts and catfish are common above 14th Street; largemouth bass, crappie, catfish, stripers, white perch, and herring are common below 14th Street.
37. **How big is the James River Park System?**
    Almost 400 acres on both sides of the river and Belle Isle.
38. **Is there much poison ivy along the urban James?**
    Yes, a moderate amount. It has three leaves and its vines have little hairs which hold to tree bark.
39. **Can you eat the clams in the river?**
    It's not wise. The clams' filtering systems allow impurities to accumulate.
40. **What are those finger-size holes in some of the bigger rocks in the river?**
     They were to hold fish traps and quarry equipment.
41. **How many prisoners were on Belle Isle?**
    A total of 30,000, usually no more than 5,000 at a time.
42. **Are there beaver dams here?**
    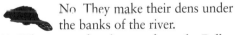 No. They make their dens under the banks of the river.
43. **What type of rock came from the Belle Isle Quarry Pond?**
    Granite.
44. **Are there Hummingbirds along the river?**
    Sure. They arrive in the spring.

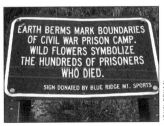

45. Is it too crowded to float or paddle on summer weekends?
No. The urban James is wide and is never "crowded" for paddlers and floaters.

46. How high have floods gotten?
Hurricane Agnes raised the river to 36.5 feet in 1972; normal flow is three feet.

47. Are there presidents buried in Hollywood Cemetery?
Yes, James Monroe and John Tyler.

48. Is the water deep enough to paddle during the summer?
Yes. Even in times of drought the James maintains enough water for floating and paddling.

49. Where can I rent a raft?
In the city, you can rent a ride on a raft: Richmond Raft Company, (800) 540-7238.

50. Why do they call it Hollywood Rapids?
From Hollywood Cemetery which overlooks it from the north. The cemetery got its name from its Holly trees.

51. How deep is the Belle Isle Quarry Pond?
19 feet.

52. Do fish bite in the winter on the urban James?
Below 14th Street, yes; above 14th street, it's not worth it.

53. How big do the fish get in the urban James?
Blue catfish reach 50 pounds; stripers reach 20 pounds; gars reach 20 pounds; carp reach 20 pounds.

54. Will the gars bite you?
They do have vicious teeth, but they won't bite you.

55. Can you fly fish in the urban James?
Of course. It's perfect for fly fishers.

56. What can you catch from the 14th Street Bridge?
In April and May that area is full of herring, white perch, yellow perch and stripers. During the rest of the year you'll catch bass, crappie and catfish.

57. Is it good to fish near Great Blue Herons?
Yes. They stay where the fish are.

58. Did people ever play baseball on Mayo's Island?
Sure did. Even Babe Ruth played some exhibition games there in the 7,000-seat stadium.

59. Were there really sturgeon in the urban James?
Plenty. When Christopher Newport arrived in 1607 the Algonquin Indians were catching eight- and nine-footers.

60. Are there sturgeon here now?
Yes, but they're rare. One is seen every few years.

61. Can fish go upstream past the dams?
Almost. All the dams except for Bosher's now have fish passages. The passage through Bosher's Dam is in the planning stages.

62. How many different birds can you see along the urban James?
Well over 100.

63. How many kinds of wildflowers grow along the urban James?
In David Ryan's 1975 book, *The Falls of the James*, he printed Newton Ancarrow's list of 471 species.

64. Does the river ever freeze?
It gets ice on it, but it almost never freezes all the way across.

65. Can I ride my bike on the Belle Isle hills?
Please stay on the loop around the perimeter of Belle Isle. Bikers who leave the loop contribute significantly to erosion on the island.

66. Can I row on the urban James?
Yes. Contact the Virginia Boat Club, P.O. Box 26051, Richmond, VA 23260.

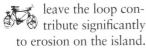

67. Can I take beer to the river?
Alcohol is prohibited in the James River Park System.

68. Does anyone live on Belle Isle?
No.

69. Can I jet ski on the urban James?
Some people do, but there are rocks. A jet ski not only endangers the rider but also degrades the natural ambience of the urban James. There are good locations above Bosher's Dam and below Ancarrow's Landing.

70. Where can I get a good guidebook on the urban James?
This is the only one.

71. Is there an organization I can join to help preserve the urban James?
The James River Association's mission is the welfare of the entire river: P.O. Box 110, Richmond, VA 23201.

72. Are there fishing tournaments on the urban James?
No. There are some upstream and downstream.

73. Are there concession stands or drink machines in James River Park?
No.

74. Can I buy bait along the river?
No. Pony Pasture Tackle on Forest Hill Drive is the closest place.

75. Is it okay to catch my own bait?
Yes, but you are limited to 50 live baits in aggregate.

76. Where can I take my kids to fish?
Try the 14th Street Bridge in the spring, and the Belle Isle Quarry Pond in the summer and fall.

77. Do you think I could take a camera with me on a professional raft trip down the urban James?
Not a good idea. It will get wet, and there is always the chance that you'll fall out (one in twenty persons does) or the whole raft could turn over in the Hollywood or Pipeline Rapids. (This happens sometimes in the summer when the river guides try some interesting techniques such as "surfing.")

Testing life jackets in 1988—Hatcher Memorial Baptist Church.

78. Should I wear a life jacket if I'm just wading?
Life jackets are required when the river level reaches five feet at Westham Gauge. Below that, adults who can swim and who stay away from dangerous rapids don't need to wear life jackets.

79. What do I do if I see a snake?
Nothing. Just leave it alone. The snakes along the urban James have never hurt anyone, and they are quite beneficial.

80. Can I wade barefoot?
Not a good idea. There is broken glass, rocks, and manmade debris from past years.

81. Are there any "nude beaches" on the urban James?
   Not officially. But ask around.
82. Where can I change into my swimsuit?
   Behind a tree. There are no changing facilities along the James.
83. Can you fish from any of the bridges?
   Just two: the 14th Street Bridge, and the Footbridge which hangs beneath the Lee Bridge.
84. Can you catch fish when the river is high and muddy?
   Yes. Catfish sometimes bite well then. Try cut bait or chicken livers fished in eddies.
85. Is there anywhere to rollerblade along the urban James?
   The downstream portion of the Floodwall Walk is great. Park at 2nd and Hull Streets.

86. Is it okay to pick a bouquet of flowers along the James?
   No. Everything is protected. The flowers are for everyone to enjoy.
87. What's the "fall line," and is it dangerous that Richmond is on it?
   No, it's not dangerous. The fall line is simply the place where a river's downhill path reaches tidal water. In Richmond, it's at 14th Street.
88. Are there any trout in the urban James?
   Every few years somebody will catch one, but no, there is no trout population.
89. Isn't the James poisoned by a chemical called kepone?
   Not anymore. There was a problem years ago downstream.
90. Is there anywhere I can launch my boat in the urban James?
   The only place you can launch a trailered boat is at Ancarrow's Landing, across the river from the Annabel Lee.
91. Do they enforce the No Parking signs on Riverside Drive?
   Yes. Park only in the designated parking areas at Pony Pasture and Huguenot Woods.

92. Where are the best sunbathing spots on the urban James?

The rocks at Pony Pasture and at the 42nd Street area of the James River Park System.

93. Is there any buried treasure along the James in Richmond?

None that anyone knows about.

94. Are there any good walking trails?

There are several throughout the James River Park System.

95. Do I need hiking boots for the trails in the James River Park System?

No. Even sandals will work fine in the summer.

96. Do they stock the James River with fish?

No. However they are reintroducing American shad with the hope that they will one day be plentiful again. From time to time certain species will be "introduced" or "reintroduced"—as has been done with blue catfish and rockfish.

97. Are there mayfly hatches on the urban James?

Yes. But they are not significant as they are on some of the famous trout streams. Caddis flies are more numerous than mayflies.

98. How much does it cost to enter the James River Park System?

It's free.

99. Is there any way for me to do some volunteer work for the James River Park System?

Certainly. Call Ralph White at (804) 780-5311.

Take the Urban River Challenge

I'll put Richmond's urban James up against any urban river in the country based on how much fun it is. Funability. Ability to have fun on an urban river. Any river in any metropolis anywhere in the United States. Our urban river's FQ (funability quotient) is higher than your urban river's FQ.

First your city has to qualify as urban. Simple: it must have its own airport and it must have three local television stations affiliated with NBC, ABC and CBS. Those ingredients make it urban; a lack of any of them means your city doesn't qualify for my Urban River Challenge.

Second, you have to determine which area of which river is your "urban" river. This is also simple. Pinpoint your city's mayor's office and draw a city-limit radius around it on your city map. You can use any portion of river within that circle as your urban river. Activities which take place beyond that radius don't count.

Third, add/subtract points to determine your river's FQ according to the following:

IN THE RIVER

Fishing
1. Add 1 point for each month of the year which begins with the letter R during which you can actually catch fish from your river.
2. Add 1 point for each species of fish which is commonly caught in your river.

3. Add 1 point for each of the following types of fishing which are common in your river:
fishing from the shore
wading
tubing
canoeing
Jon boat
motor boat
50+hp engine boat
20+foot boat
bridge fishing
ice fishing
4. Add 1 point if people commonly fly fish in your river.
5. Subtract 3 points if there are current laws (based on water quality) prohibiting sale of any single species of fish commercially caught in your urban river.
6. Subtract 2 additional points if there are current laws (based on water quality) prohibiting sale of all fish commercially caught in your urban river.
7. Subtract 2 additional points if there are laws or official warnings prohibiting the consumption of fish you catch in the river.

Swimming, etc.
8. Add 1 point for each R-month during which people commonly swim in your river.
9. Add 1 point if on an average sunny summer Saturday there will be 100 or more persons tubing or swimming in/on your river.
10. Add 1 point if scuba diving is common in your river.
11. Add 1 point if snorkeling is common in your river.
12. Add 1 point if there are any paid lifeguards on your river.
13. Add 1 point if your river has an abundance (25 or more) of mid-river rocks or islands or platforms on which people picnic/sun/relax.
14. Add 1 point if there are areas larger than a football field that are at least 20 feet deep.
15. Add 1 point if there are areas larger than a football field that are shallower than 5 feet.

Boats, etc.
16. Add 1 point for each R-month during which people commonly use kayaks.
17. Add 1 point for each R-month during which people

commonly use canoes.
18. Add 1 point for each R-month during which people commonly use motor-powered boats.
19. Add 1 point for each R-month during which people commonly use sailboats.
20. Add 1 point for each R-month during which rowing crews practice on your river.
21. Add 1 point for each class of rapids on your urban river.

ALONGSIDE THE RIVER

22. Add 5 points if an adequate (your judgment) amount of riverside land is accessible and public-owned.
23. Add 5 points if the public-owned riverside land is generally well-managed (your judgment) for the enjoyment of the public.
24. Add 2 points for each of the following items appropriately (your judgment) represented on public-owned riverside land:
picnic tables
trash containers
restrooms
parking
boat ramps/access
kayak/canoe access
signage (maps, rules, information)
25. Add 2 points if camping is allowed on public land alongside your river.
26. Add 2 points if there is more than 1 mile of designated bike trails alongside the river.
27. Add 2 points if technical rock climbing commonly takes place alongside your river.
28. Add 2 points if jogging commonly takes place alongside your river.

Flora, fauna
29. Add 2 points if Eagles are regularly seen alongside your river.
30. Add 2 points if antlered wildlife is regularly seen alongside your river.
31. Add 2 points if alligators are regularly seen in your river.
32. Add 2 points if there have been published writings describing wildflowers alongside your river.

33. Add 2 points if there have been published writings describing birds alongside your river.
34. Add 2 points if there have been published writings describing geology alongside your river.
35. Add 2 points if there have been published writings describing historical things alongside your river.

OTHER

36. Add 2 points for each major (50,000 people attend) public riverside festival or celebration that takes place on an annual basis.
37. Add 2 points for each pedestrian bridge that crosses your river or that crosses to a mid-river island.
38. Subtract 3 points if your river commonly floods (into occupied buildings or streets) at least every 10 years.
39. Add 3 points if there is a volunteer club/society whose purpose it is to protect your urban river.
40. Add 2 points if there is a published guide to children's activities on the river.
41. Subtract 2 points if your river's level fluctuates according to the activities of an upstream dam.

My score for Richmond's urban James is 114.

Resources

The following is list of just some of the resources which will assist you in enjoying the urban James River.

Adventure Challenge
8225 Oxer Road, Richmond, VA 23235, (804) 276-7600
Lessons/trips in whitewater kayaking, canoeing, rafting, and more.

Alliance for the Chesapeake Bay
600 York Road, Baltimore, MD 21212, (804) 775-0951
You receive lots of goodies when you join at the $25 or higher level, including the newsletter, "Bay Journal." "We'll throw your money directly into the Bay—planting trees, testing water, restoring wetlands, and educating policy-makers and teaching citizens about their individual responsibility for a healthy Chesapeake Bay watershed."

Alliance for the Chesapeake Bay, Richmond Office
P.O. Box 1981, Richmond, VA 23216, (804) 775-0951

The American Canal Society
117 Main Street, Freemansburg, PA 18017

American Fishing Tackle Manufacturers Association
1250 Grove Ave., Suite 300, Barrington, IL 60010, (708) 381-9490

American Whitewater Affiliation
P.O. Box 636
Margaretville, NY 12544
(914) 586-2355

"American Whitewater Affiliation Safety Code"
This is a wonderful and detailed set of guidelines for paddlers: personal preparedness, water hazards, rescue equipment and skills, boat equipment, group trips, river signals, rapids difficulty ratings, and more. All paddlers should have this. Write for copies from American Whitewater Affiliation, P.O. Box 636, Margaretville, IN 12544.

Archeological Society of Virginia, Greater Richmond Chapter
P.O. Box 711, Mechanicsville, VA 23111, (804) 746-9745, Dick Griffith

BASS Federation
7901 Wood Mill Drive, Richmond, VA 23231, (804) 795-5918

"Beginning Angler Education Kit"
Available for $15 from Anne Skalski, Aquatic Education Coordinator, Virginia Department of Game and Inland Fisheries, 4010 West Broad Street, Richmond, VA 23230-1104. This kit contains basic information about fishing, including a video.

Bicycle Organization of the Southside
P.O. Box 36458, Richmond, VA 23235

"BIRDS OF THE JAMES RIVER PARK"
Available from the Richmond Audubon Society, P.O. Box 804, Richmond, VA 23207

This little brochure presents a comprehensive checklist of 165 birds that can be seen along the urban James. The checklist tells how abundant each bird is during each of the four seasons. The brochure also lists 31 "accidentals," and has a basic map of the river. What this brochure is not is a field guide to birds. You'll have to take along your Peterson's.

Boating Education
Boating education courses are available from the Boating Education Coordinator, Virginia Department of Game and Inland Fisheries, P.O. Box 11104, Richmond, VA 23230, (804) 367-0267.

BOAT/U.S. Foundation for Boating Safety
880 S. Pickett Street, Alexandria, VA 22304, (703) 823-9550

The Coastal Canoeists Inc.
P.O. Box 566, Richmond, VA 23218-0566

Chesapeake Bay Foundation
162 Prince George Street, Annapolis, MD 21401, (410) 268-8816

Chesapeake Bay Local Assistance
805 East Broad Street, Suite 701, Richmond, VA 23219, (804) 225-3440

"Complete Visitor's Guide to Metropolitan Richmond"
Available from Metropolitan Richmond Convention & Visitors Bureau, 300 East Main Street, Richmond, VA 23219, (800) 365-7272 or (804) 782-2777.

Only a little bit about the James River, but quiet useful for context and perspective.

Divers, Inc. of Richmond
2334 Thousand Oaks Drive, Richmond, VA 23294, (804) 781-0217, Tiny Dawson

"DISASTER ZONE: Ecology of a Floodplain"
Available at the James River Park Visitor's Center, Hillcrest Avenue and Riverside Drive (804) 780-5311

This 12-page brochure presents a self-guided tour beginning at the Visitor's Center. It acquaints the reader with beavers, poison ivy, Sycamores and River Birches. It teaches about the river's flow and how it affects the rocks and the fish and the riverbed. This is a terrific introductory foundation to the urban James.

"EYEBALL ORNITHOLOGY: No Fail Birding for Beginners"
Available at the James River Park Visitor's Center, Hillcrest Avenue and Riverside Drive, (804) 780-5311

This simple single-page brochure, written by Ralph White and illustrated by Cricket White, shows and tells you how and where to identify 10 birds of the urban James: Mourning Dove, Bobwhite, Great Blue Heron, Mallard Duck, Cardinal, Blue Jay, American Crow, Robin, Turkey Vulture, and Mockingbird.

Falls of the James Atlas
Available from Richard A. Davis, VC&NS Sales, Rt. 2, Box 254, Lexington, VA 24450

This 68-page publication of The Virginia Canals & Navigations Society is the most comprehensive look available at the historical remnants of Richmond's canal days. This book has detailed maps of every portion of the river from Bosher's Dam to Great Ship Lock Park, and has a wealth of history about the river. It is a book every Richmonder should read.

"FISHING ACCESS TO THE JAMES RIVER IN RICHMOND"
Available from the Virginia Department of Game and Inland Fisheries

This big-page brochure, written by Ralph White and Tom Gunter, contains absolutely everything you need to know about access areas to the river, parking, types of current, various warnings, and the various species of fish and their habits and habitats. There is also information about size limits, seasons, and boating safety. And, there is a detailed map.

"Fishing is Fun For Everyone"
This elementary and extremely helpful brochure is published by the American Fishing Tackle Manufacturers Association, 1250 Grove Ave., Suite 300, Barrington, Illinois 60010, but is also available from the Virginia Department of Game and Inland Fisheries. The brochure provides all of the basics you need to go fishing: how to rig a fishing pole, line, hook, sinker and bobber; which baits to use; which lures to use; and where to fish. It also gives casting instructions, safety rules, and conservation advice.

Float Fishermen of Virginia
7801 Ruthville Road, Providence Forge, VA 23140, (804) 829-6202

Fly Fishers of Virginia
P.O. Box 29477, Richmond, VA 23242, (804) 782-1986

"Freshwater Fishing Guide"
Available from the Virginia Department of Game and Inland Fisheries, P.O. Box 11104, Richmond, VA 23230-1104, (804) 367-1000.

This 32-page tabloid has everything you want to know about fishing across the state including a listing and descriptions of lakes and streams.

Friends of the Rivers of Virginia
1302 Second Street, S.W., Roanoke, VA 24016-4923, (703) 343-3696

"Guide to Feeding Wild Birds"
Available from the Virginia Department of Game and Inland Fisheries, P.O. Box 11104, Richmond, VA 23230-1104, (804) 367-1000.

This pamphlet has some basic information and 10 beautiful illustrations by Phyllis Saroff.

A Guide to the Works of the James River & Kanawha Company From the City of Richmond
This 36-page booklet is available for $5 from Richard A. Davis, VC&NS Sales, Rt. 2, Box 254, Lexington, VA 24450. This is a carefully-prepared map and guide to the 283 miles of canals and river navigation of the James River & Kanawha Company—all of the canals dry now except for some areas in Richmond. "This guide is for those who

have the imagination to appreciate the past and the cultural treasures which history has left us. There is still much to see of the Canal and Turnpike eras. It is up to each generation to save the best of our past for future generations to enjoy and understand. Only in this way can a society develop its roots and mature gracefully."

James River Association
P.O. Box 110, Richmond, VA 23201, (804) 730-2898

James River Batteau Festival
P.O. Box 10564, Lynchburg, VA 24506

THE JAMES RIVER BATTEAU FESTIVAL TRAIL: A GUIDE TO THE JAMES RIVER AND ITS CANAL, FROM LYNCHBURG TO RICHMOND
Available for $5 from Richard A. Davis, VC&NS Sales, Rt. 2, Box 254, Lexington, VA 24450

This 32-page oversize booklet is one of several publications from VC&NS (Virginia Canals and Navigation Society). It is filled with charts of the river based on official geographical survey maps, along with diagrams, reproductions of historical illustrations, and good information about various dams and rapids, canals and other natural and manmade structures.

"JAMES RIVER PARK: Interpretive Guide to Belle Isle Historic Park"
Available at the James River Park Visitor's Center, Hillcrest Avenue & Riverside Drive
(804) 780-5311

This 12-page brochure is a must for every Richmonder, because every Richmonder should take a self-guided tour of Belle Isle. The brochure gives the history, tells about the rapids and the quarry, identifies beavers and drill holes, even tells you the best places to watch for kayaks. Best of all, the brochure contains a wonderfully complete hand-drawn map.

"JAMES RIVER PARK: Interpretive Guide to the Geology Walk"

Available at the James River Park Visitor's Center, Hillcrest Avenue & Riverside Drive (804) 780-5311

This little eight-page brochure presents an understandable explanation and description of the geology of the urban James—from identifying granite and biotite to explaining potholes and horizontal stress lines. The brochure is meant to accompany the reader on a specific path. The rocks along the James are fascinating, and this is a brochure for the whole family.

"JAMES RIVER PARK: Interpretive Guide to Netherwood Quarry"
Available at the James River Park Visitor's Center, Hillcrest Avenue & Riverside Drive, (804) 780-5311.

This eight-page brochure presents an informative and interesting guided tour (beginning at the 43rd Street parking area of the James River Park System) of the Netherwood Quarry which supplied granite for many purposes in Richmond and beyond. The brochure presents history, descriptions and illustrations of types of rock, maps and historical photos.

"James River Park System: Map and Guide to the woodlands and waters of the James River in Richmond"
Available at the James River Park Visitor's Center, Hillcrest Avenue & Riverside Drive (804) 780-5311

Printed on DuPont Tyvek which is waterproof and won't tear, this is the map everyone needs. It not only provides a well defined map of the river from Bosher's Dam to Ancarrow's Landing, but it also contains lots of information like rules for the James River Park System, the phone number for river level information, and how many cars each of the parking lots holds.

"James River Park System: Saturday NATURE PROGRAMS"
Available from the James River Park Visitor's Center, Hillcrest and Riverside Drive, (804) 780-5311

This seasonal brochure is a must for those who want to fully enjoy the natural aspects of the urban James. It presents a schedule of activities including service projects; tours of plants, birds, butterflies and bees; a map; a list of park rules; a list of publications; and a variety of other information.

"JAMES RIVER RAPIDS in RICHMOND"
Available from the James River Park Visitor's Center, Hillcrest and Riverside Drive, (804) 780-5311

This single-page brochure classifies and describes all the rapids of the urban James, provides rules, warnings and prevention measures, and even provides a brief column of "NATURE NOTES" which identify some trees, snakes, birds, fish and clams. It also presents a basic map of the rapids.

James River Reeling & Rafting
P.O. Box 757, Scottsville, VA 24590, (804) 286-4386
  Canoeing, tubing, camping and fishing trips.

James River Runners Inc.
Rt. 4, Box 106, Scottsville, VA 24590-9721, (804) 286-2338
  Canoeing, tubing, and rafting trips.

"Join us on the James"
Available from the James River Association, P.O. Box 110, Richmond, VA 23201, (804) 730-2898

This is a promotional brochure which tells how to become a member and how to order publications and videotapes from this association dedicated to "conservation of the natural and historic resources of the tidal James River Watershed, consistent with orderly development."

"LATE SUMMER WILDFLOWERS of the James River Park System"
Available from the James River Park Visitor's Center, Hillcrest Ave. and Riverside Drive, (804) 780-5311

This wallet-size, accordian-fold brochure illustrates and describes 10 wildflowers which can be found along the urban James in July and August. Although the brochure's illustrations are not in color, it presents a reason: "Bring along some colored pencils or fine tipped markers and fill in the colors as you spot each flower listed." One word of advice: the illustrations aren't detailed enough for children to match them to the correct flowers, so have an adult to help.

METROPOLITAN RICHMOND VIRGINIA—Map
Available from Metropolitan Richmond Convention and Visitors Bureau, 300 East Main Street, Richmond, VA 23219, (800) 365-7272 or (804) 782-2777

This is a hand-drawn and colored map of the entire Richmond area, including a delightful look at the urban James in the context of its surroundings.

"Monarch Butterflies and Common Milkweed Plants at James River Park"
Available from the James River Park Visitor's Center, Hillcrest and Riverside Drive,
(804) 780-5311

This eight-page pamphlet, prepared by Mark Northam and R.R. Mills of Virginia Commonwealth University's Biology Department, discusses the life cycle of the Monarch Butterfly and describes the host Milkweed plants. These butterflies arrive from Canada to lay eggs from July to September, and then migrate to Mexico.

National Audubon Society
1104 Fernwood Ave., Suite 300, Camp Hill, PA 17011

Natural Wonders of Virginia: A Guide to Parks, Preserves and Wild Places
This book by Garvey and Deane Winegar has a nice three-page section on James River Park.

Old Dominion Adventures, Inc. (kayaking)
10210 Thor Lane, Mechanicsville, VA 23111, (804) 559-5632

Richmond Area Bicycling Association
409-H N. Hamilton Street, Richmond, VA 23221, (804) 230-1632

Richmond Audubon Society
P.O. Box 804, Richmond, VA 23207, (804) 257-0813

Richmond Raft Company
4400 East Main Street, Richmond, VA 23231, (804) 222-RAFT

Richmond Raft Company is right across the alley from the Annabel Lee. "We offer professionally guided paddle raft trips on the Falls of the James. . . Richmond's historic sites and scenic beauty alternate with exciting whitewater to make this outing one you will never forget." You should visit their facilities in person. You'll see that they have everything you need for a rafting experience. Plus they sell their own T-shirts. If you can't visit, at least telephone for their brochures. They offer all sorts of raft trips and will cater custom trips for special requests and needs. Their standard trips—the 5 1/2-hour "Falls of the James" trip and the 3 1/2-hour "The Lower Section" trip—cost $45 and $30 per person and should be reserved in advance. This is probably the best way to experience the entirety of the urban James.

Sierra Club Falls of the James Group,
P.O. Box 25201, Richmond, VA 23260, (804) 353-4747

"Snorkeling in the City: Underwater exploration on the James River in Richmond"

Available from the James River Park System Visitor's Center, Hillcrest & Riverside Drive, Richmond, VA (804) 780-5311

Made from DuPont's waterproof and tearproof Tyvek, this is perhaps the most instructive and delightful of all of the brochures on the urban James—if you enjoy the best part of the river: wading right in. It presents drawings of snails and insects and larvae and various fish. It tells you how and where to snorkel and exactly what to look for and exactly what you're seeing. It also lists some safety rules. The brochure has lots of "Try this:" sections. For example, "Dig your hands into sand bars and fine gravel to find live Oriental Freshwater Clams," or "Look in calm water near the shore or behind boulders. With patience, you can see the male Sunfish flare his fins to show his colors."

"Swallowtail Butterflies and their Host Plants in James River Park"

Available from the James River Park System Visitor's Center, Hillcrest and Riverside Drive, (804) 780-5311.

This eight-page guide was prepared by Harland Patch, Shannon Breeding, Dr. Richard R. Mills and Mark Northam in 1995. It presents drawings and information on four species of butterfly: Eastern Black Swallowtail, Spicebush Swallowtail, Zebra Swallowtail, and Eastern

Tiger Swallowtail. It also provides drawings of their larvae and descriptions of the host plants for the butterflies.

Trout Unlimited
2011 Dresden Road, Richmond, VA 23229, (804) 270-5754

University of Richmond Outings Club
University of Richmond, Richmond, VA 23173, (804) 289-8285

"Virginia Boating Guide"
Available from the Virginia Department of Game and Inland Fisheries, 4010 West Broad Street, Richmond, VA 23230, (804) 367-1000.
   This 12-page tabloid has rules and regulations and an annotated listing of the state's boat access areas.

The Virginia Canals and Navigations Society
Sue Hopper, Treasurer, 1229 Summerfield Drive, Herndon, VA 22070
Dr. William Trout, 35 Towana Road, Richmond, VA 23226, (804) 288-1334
   A $15 annual membership fee entitles members to receive the illustrated quarterly, THE TILLER and other items. The VC&NS was formed in 1977 "to preserve and enhance Virginia's rich inland waterways heritage in all its fascinating aspects."

Virginia Commonwealth University Center for Environmental Studies
(804) 828-7202

Virginia Commonwealth University Outings Club
907 Floyd Avenue, Richmond, VA 23220, (804) 367-6043

Virginia Department of Conservation and Recreation
(804) 786-2064

Virginia Department Of Environmental Quality
(804) 698-4000

Virginia Department of Game and Inland Fisheries
(804) 367-1000

Virginia Department of Health, Water Programs
(804) 786-6278

Virginia Department of Historic Resources
(804) 786-3143

Virginia Division of Tourism
901 East Byrd Street, Richmond, VA 23219, (804) 786-4484

"Virginia Freshwater & Saltwater Fishing Regulations"
Available from the Virginia Department of Game and Inland Fisheries, P.O. Box 11104, Richmond, VA 23230-1104, (804) 367-1000.

This 40-page brochure is exactly what it says, and it gives all the details. All urban James fishers should read it. There are some interesting rules. For example, American shad, hickory shad, and striped bass (rockfish) all have a creel limit of zero above Mayo's (14th Street) Bridge. Another example of a little-known regulation is that bait such as crawfish, hellgrammites, and minnows have a possession limit of 50 in aggregate unless you have a receipt specifying the number of baits—by species—you have purchased.

Virginia Marine Resources Commission
(804) 541-4646

"Virginia Motorboat Owner's Guide"
Available from the Virginia Department of Game and Inland Fisheries, P.O. Box 11528, Richmond, VA 23230-1528, (804) 367-0939

This 34-page brochure has information about registration, regulations, equipment, navigation, safety, and more.

Virginia Native Plant Society
12567 Brook Lane, Chester, VA 23831, (804) 748-2940

Virginia Secretary of Natural Resources
(804) 786-0044

"Virginia Small Craft Handling"
Available from the Virginia Department of Game and Inland Fisheries, P.O. Box 11104, Richmond, VA 23230

This 32-page brochure has wonderful information for anyone who uses a small boat. It contains information about equipment, trailering, waterway markings, safety, first aid and more.

Virginia State Water Control Board
(804) 527-5000

Virginia Wildlife
One-year subscriptions are available for $10 from *Virginia Wildlife* Subscriptions, P.O. Box 7477, Red Oak, Iowa 51591-0477.

This is the colorful monthly magazine on fishing and hunting in Virginia.

"VOLUNTEER PROJECTS IN THE JAMES RIVER PARK"
Available from the James River Park System Visitor's Center, Hillcrest and Riverside Drive, (804) 780-5311

This front/back typed page offers 36 different projects to improve the James River Park System. Many of them are listed as "suitable for Eagle Scout Certification." They include removing the underbrush at the Civil War Cemetery on Belle Isle, constructing benches at Huguenot Woods, picking up litter, planting Red Bud trees, and painting some doors and walls at the Visitor's Center.

"A WALK ON THE WALL: Interpretive Guide to the Richmond Floodwall"
Available from the James River Park System Visitor's Center, Hillcrest and Riverside Drive, Richmond, VA (804) 780-5311

This 12-page brochure presents an easily readable, yet extensive, guide to what you see when you walk along the Floodwall bordering the urban James. It's filled with important bits of history, drawings of 11 of the birds you're liable to see (including the Double-crested Cormorant and the Turkey Vulture), drawings of the Muskrat, River Otter and Beaver, facts and figures and items of interest, and a hand-drawn map of this section of the river with a panoramic photo of downtown Richmond aligned with the map. There is even a nifty little timeline of the history of the urban James—from 1607 until the present.

West View Livery & Outfitters, Inc.
1151 West View Road, P.O. Box 258, Goochland, VA 23063, (804) 457-2744
   Canoeing and tubing trips and rentals.

Wetlands for the Americas
P.O. Box 1770, Manomet, MA 02345

"Wetland Wonders: An Interpretive Guide to the Wetlands Section of the James River Park System"
Available from the James River Park System Visitor's Center, Hillcrest Ave. and Riverside Drive, Richmond, (804) 780-5311
   This 12-page brochure is one of the best the Park System offers, and it guides you through one of the best areas of the James River Park System. The Wetlands area is on the south side of the river behind the Stratford Hills area at the end of Landria Drive. The brochure is not only a guide to all sorts of plants (including trees) and all sorts of animals (including birds), but it is also an educational document about wetlands—how they are formed, what their purposes are, and how to protect them. The brochure was written and designed by S.R. Feaser in 1996.

INDEX

Ailanthus Tree—185
Albemarle Paper Manufacturing Co.—145–147, 252
Alliance for the Chesapeake Bay—279–281
American Canoe Association—81
American Whitewater—67, 69
American Whitewater Affiliation—81
Ancarrow's Landing—14, 25, 30, 74, 105, 118, 119, 177, 233, 277, 299, 301
Ancarrow, Newton—19, 157, 299
Anderson, Joseph Reid—144, 145
Annabel Lee—14, 15, 20, 30, 31, 65, 75, 76, 104, 115, 121, 231, 240–242, 294, 297, 301
Archer's Island—158
Armored Storage Shed—247
Ash-leaf Maple Tree—232, 272
Aster—124
Atkinson, Rick—190, 191
Audubon Guide—163
Bagby, George W.—290
Bald Eagle—23, 65, 67, 70, 78, 95, 120, 137, 157, 160, 165, 228, 293
Baldwin, Whit—161
Ball, Rick—193
Barnes, Michael—277
Barred Owl—148
Batzli, Johathan—277
Bear—157
Bateau—132, 135, 142, 150, 261
Beaver—58, 155, 228, 269, 270, 271, 296, 297
Beech Tree—23, 28, 55, 125, 157–159, 172, 184, 185
Beetle—44
Bell, James—57, 140
Belle Isle—14, 16, 22, 32, 33, 39, 41, 42, 44, 45, 48, 50, 56, 57, 59–61, 71, 72, 88, 91, 97–99, 138, 140, 150, 157, 174, 175, 225, 227, 233, 234, 238, 242, 244, 246, 249, 277, 285, 286, 294, 296, 297, 299
Belle Isle Rolling and Slitting Mill—139
Belt Line Bridge—150
Berkley, Craig—201
Biking—17, 27, 29, 30, 31, 39, 61, 62, 131, 179, 217, 220, 233–237, 242, 244–249, 251, 252, 268, 277, 299
Binford Middle School—16, 96
Biotite—172
Bitternut Hickory Tree—117, 185
Blackberry—46, 272
Blackgum Tree—157
Blackbird—112
Black Duck—86, 161, 163
Black Tern—163
Blem, Charles—160, 164, 166
Bloodroot—169
Bluefish—35, 83
Bluegill—76, 77, 107, 120, 122, 245, 246, 253
Blue Jay—50, 87
Boat Lake—129
Bobcat—270
Bosher's Dam—25, 88, 90, 133, 136, 157, 174, 227, 233, 274, 280, 299
Boulevard Bridge—17, 28, 29, 34, 42, 52, 71, 76, 78, 116, 125, 217, 218, 262, 263, 288
Box Elder Beetle—232
Box Elder Tree—50
Boyle, Robert—275
Brazzell, Austin—285
Brazzell, Chester—285
Broad Rock Island—57, 139
Brown, Mark—291, 292
Brown Creeper—87
Brown's Island—15, 32, 190, 225, 226, 242, 248–252
Brown's Island Dam—72, 226
Bryan, Charles F., Jr.—131
Bryan, Kelly—16, 17, 63, 93, 96, 122, 186, 187, 265
Bryan, Thomas—16, 17, 36, 49, 56, 61–64, 91–98, 122, 133, 152–156, 174, 177–179, 186, 187, 224, 235, 236, 247, 253–260
Buffalo River—265

Bufflehead—160
Bull Thistle—46
Butterfly—44, 46, 47, 50, 112, 157, 232, 248, 252
Buttermilk Trail—234, 238, 239, 285, 286
Butternut Hickory Tree—185, 186
Byrd, William—58, 132, 139, 228, 230
Byrd, William II—138, 139
Byrd, William III—139
Byrd Park—55, 86, 128, 129, 143
Cabell, James Branch—141
Caddis Fly—42, 43, 182, 302
Canada Geese—78, 86, 95, 222
Canal Walk—22, 249
Canoe—28, 36, 58, 81, 89, 90, 135, 211, 227, 249, 250, 264
Cardinal—137, 165, 237
Carp—23, 76, 114, 184, 236, 298
Carter, Molly—199
Carter, Rob—109, 188–216, 262
Catfish—50, 76, 102, 103, 106, 107, 113, 118, 120, 125, 161, 177, 183, 187, 220–222, 265, 297, 298, 301, 302
Cedar Tree—50
Cedar Waxwings—265
Center for Environmental Studies—283, 284
Chappel Island—31, 136
Chattahoochee River—37
Cherry Tree—248
Chickadee—55, 61, 62, 87, 88, 137, 158, 165, 178, 255
Chickweed—169
Choo Choo Rapids—65, 94, 96
Chouinard, Yvon—204
Chub—124, 125, 180, 181, 183
Civil War—22, 44, 48, 50, 57, 59. 60, 68, 72, 133, 135, 138, 140, 141, 144, 149, 174, 226, 227, 229, 285, 290, 294
Clams—47, 58, 180, 297
Clean Water Act—282

Climbing—87, 188–215, 226, 227, 238, 264, 286
Coastal Canoeists—81–84, 89
Combined Sewer Overflow—133, 273, 281, 287
Confederate Soldiers and Sailors Monument—295
Corbett, Roger—72
Cormorant—78, 95, 157, 160, 163, 165, 227, 246, 249
Cottonwood Tree—50, 272
Craggs, Chris—190
Crappie—31, 76, 77, 106–108, 114, 118, 220, 221, 265, 297, 298
Crawfish—183
Crenshaw, Lewis W.—136
Cross Country Skiing—231
Crow—161–164, 227, 244, 246, 249
CSX Corporation—142
Cumberland River—36
Dabney, Virginius—159
Damsel Fly—50, 78, 182, 218
Dandelion—236, 248, 252
Daniel, Thomas—256
Davis, Jefferson—72, 141
Dawson, Ron—190, 191
Deepwater Terminal—145, 147, 241, 242, 277
Deer—51, 157, 159, 294
Devil's Kitchen—228
Di Pasquale, Paul—248
Donnell, Cindy—241, 242
Donovan, Keith—191
Downy Woodpecker—87
Doyle, Howard—203
Dragonfly—182
Driftwood—30, 159, 178, 179, 235, 238, 267, 293, 296
Duck River—49, 266
Dunlop, The Honorable Becky Norton—287, 288
Dwiefel, Michael—285
Eckman, Phil—150
Edwards, Bob—105, 119–121
Edwards, Richard—100
Eel—22, 103, 184
Elliott, Greg—191
Elliott, Suzanne—195
Environmental Education Center—42, 57, 278
Ethyl Corporation—139, 145, 146, 227, 248

The Fall Line—22, 45, 92, 186, 187, 227, 229, 277, 301
The Falls of the James—19, 157, 166, 299
The Falls of the James Atlas—149, 150
The Falls of the James Scenic River Advisory Board—19, 281-283
Feldspar—172, 176
Field Cricket—47
First Break Rapids—14, 59, 71, 97
Floodwall—14, 29, 30, 31, 32, 44, 50, 51, 73, 87, 112, 125, 133, 135, 179, 194, 195, 217, 221, 224, 227-230, 233, 234, 236-239, 285, 289, 295, 301
Fly Fishing—109-111, 123, 298
Footbridge—16, 17, 32, 80, 98, 233, 242, 247, 248, 301
Fort Nashborough—36, 37
Foushee's Mill—52
Fox Elementary School—258
Frederick, Phil—293
Freeman, Douglas Southall—141
Frog—45, 137, 169
Gallego Mills—133, 251
Gamble's Hill—136
Gar—23, 50, 76, 107, 114, 184, 262, 298
Garman, Greg C.—283
Geology—44, 45
Gilmore-Bryan, Janet—36, 61, 96, 98, 130, 153, 186, 187, 219, 223, 260
Glasgow, Ellen—141
Goat Islands—271, 272, 273, 286
Goldenrod—46, 112
Gordon, Bill—92
Grackle—88, 112, 161, 246, 248, 249, 251
Granite—48, 50, 58, 59, 72, 139, 141, 172, 174-176, 226, 227, 229, 274, 297
Great Basin—250, 251
Great Blue Heron—23, 45, 53, 73, 78, 87, 95, 108, 126-129, 164, 227, 235, 237, 262, 268, 298
Great Falls—69
Great Horned Owl—148
Great Shiplock Park—22, 30, 31, 74, 76, 108, 136, 218, 220, 221, 234, 253, 286
Green Ash Tree—50, 272
Green Briar Tree—47
Green Heron—164
Grey Fox—50, 157
Grove, Ed—72
Hackberry Tree—148
Hall, Keith—191
Halsey, Brenton S.—19, 138, 289-90
Hambrick, Ralph—88
Harpeth River—265
Harris, Ruth—150
Haxall, Richard B.—136
Haxall Canal—133, 226, 251, 282
Haxall-Crenshaw Flour Mill—136, 251
The Headman—248
Hellgrammite—182
Henry, Patrick—92
Herring—69, 82, 103, 104, 106, 113, 114, 122, 161, 220, 221, 227, 234, 236, 274, 296-298
Herring Gull—160, 164
Hickory Tree—28, 158, 185
Hicks, Bob—19
Hiking/Walking—30, 31, 34, 39, 131, 156, 237, 245, 246, 268, 277, 302
Hiravama, Yuji—203
Holly Tree—141, 185, 265, 298
Hollywood Cemetery—14, 17, 33, 48, 59, 138, 141, 143, 163, 238, 246, 295, 298
Hollywood Dam—71
Hollywood Paper Mill—132, 138, 145, 146
Hollywood Rapids—14, 44, 58, 65, 72, 75, 77, 79, 89, 95, 97, 98, 245, 295, 298, 300
Hornblende—172
Hornet—50
Horse Chestnut—265
Hudson River—35, 82, 83, 275

Huguenot Bridge—14, 25, 65, 75
Huguenot Woods—14, 25, 26, 65, 69, 70, 88, 90, 103, 234, 238, 285, 301
Hummingbird—164, 297
Hurricane Agnes—133, 224, 298
Hurricane Camille—57, 68, 69, 133, 140
Hutcheson, Mike—191
Hylton, Lawrence—139
Iceland Gull—160
Igel, Charles—196
Igneous Rock—171
Indians—20, 37, 47, 56, 58, 68, 131, 132, 139, 158, 159, 180, 229, 276, 295
In River Time: The Way of the James—275, 276
Intermediate Terminal—231
I-95 Bridge—30, 108, 114, 120, 121, 126, 177, 179, 187, 222, 225, 230, 235, 236, 253–255, 257
James, Brian—277
James River Association—278, 279, 300
James River Corporation—17, 72, 138, 140, 141, 142, 144–147, 238, 247, 290
James River Corridor Planning District—281
James River Park System—16, 17, 19, 23, 26–29, 34, 36, 39, 41, 43, 48–51, 56, 70, 71, 74, 78, 84, 86, 116, 132, 133, 140, 148, 150, 158, 159, 166, 170, 177, 180, 192, 217, 224, 227, 234, 238, 239, 246, 269, 276, 281, 282, 285, 289, 294–297, 300, 302
Jet Skiing—233, 299
Jogging—29, 217, 218, 227, 234, 237, 238, 277
Johnson's Island—251, 252
Junco—61, 87
Kalman, Marc—75
Kanawha Canal—22, 54, 68, 76, 133–136, 138, 141, 143, 222, 227, 253, 256, 282

Kayak—22, 32, 36, 58, 59, 63, 79, 81, 90, 95, 218, 227, 244, 249, 250, 264, 278, 279, 289, 291
Kite Flying—217
Knoop, Chris—285
Krohn, Hank—91–98, 152–156, 177–179, 236
Lady Bug—46
Largemouth Bass—22, 23, 38, 76, 77, 106, 107, 113, 119, 120, 122, 129, 218, 220, 221, 237, 245, 250, 253, 297, 298
Latrobe, Benjamin—139, 141
Lee Bridge—17, 29, 35, 37, 48, 52, 56, 59, 77, 80, 97, 117, 140, 170, 225, 236–238, 242, 244, 247, 275, 281, 286, 301
Lee, Light Horse Harry—139
Lee, Robert E.—139
Lichen—158, 173
Little Falls—69
Little Pigeon River—217, 218
Lizard—179
Lockkeepers House—54, 55
Locust Tree—54
Lord Chesterfield—261
Madison River—111
Malarkey, Michael—277
Mallard Duck—45, 49, 78, 86, 95, 160, 161, 163, 237, 248–250, 262
Maloney, John—52
Manchester Bridge—14, 29, 48, 73, 87, 224–227, 230, 237, 239, 240, 248, 252
Manchester Canal—228
Manchester Dam—57, 73, 87, 228
Manchester Wall—188–216, 264, 286
Marshall, Chief Justice John—142
Mather Gorge—69
Maury, Matthew Fontaine—141
Maury Street—30, 177, 226, 230, 236
Mayfly—182, 302
Maymont—34, 52, 263, 290

Mayo's Bridge, 14th Street Bridge—14, 22, 29, 30, 73, 81, 92, 99, 104, 106, 108, 112, 113, 118, 125, 126, 131-133, 176, 186, 225-227, 229, 233-236, 239, 276, 277, 291, 294, 296-298, 300, 301
Mayo's Island—20, 73, 174, 225, 227, 229, 242, 278, 282, 291, 292, 299
McGrath, Jamie—188-216
McKenna, Barry—191
Metamorphic Rock—171
Milkweed—46, 237
Mitchel's Gut—65
Mockingbird—247
Monroe, James—141, 298
Moore, James III—149, 150
Mourning Dove—248
Mullet—113, 265
Murray, Fred—117, 118
Muskrat—51, 122, 157, 228, 296
Mussel—47, 50, 58, 159, 180
Newman, Les—190, 191
Newport, Christopher—19, 21, 131, 138, 139, 158, 295, 297, 299
Nickel Bridge—See Boulevard Bridge
Northbank—34, 51, 52, 239, 285
Nuthatch—87
Oak Tree—49, 55, 125, 148, 157, 185
Ohoopee River—123, 217, 218, 265
Old Dominion Iron and Nail Works—140
Old Dominion Iron and Steel—44, 48, 57, 60
Old Dominion Railway Museum—226
Oregon Hill—33
Osprey—67, 70, 120, 122, 124, 228
Otter—50, 157, 228, 263, 296
Owl—50
Packet Boat—135, 142, 249, 251
Passages—264
Perch—113, 114
Peregrine Falcon—160, 165

Peterson, Roger Tory—163, 165
Pickerel—265
Picket, George—72
Pie-billed Grebe—86
Piersol, Carol—260
Piersol, Morrie—253, 255-260, 295
Piersol, Trevor—253-260
Pileated Woodpecker—88
Picnic—28, 29
Pipeline—15, 32, 65, 70, 72, 73, 75, 80, 81, 89, 225, 228, 239, 240, 250, 300
Pluton—171, 174, 175
Poetry—48, 217
Poison Ivy—47, 49, 53, 297
Poison Oak—49
Pony Pasture—26, 27, 40, 42, 52, 65, 69, 70, 76, 86-89, 91, 137, 148, 238, 285, 286, 300-302
Poplar Tree—125, 158
Potomac River—37, 69
Powhatan, Chief—132, 159
Princess Tree—47
Pump House, City—136, 138, 142, 143
Pumphouse Park—22, 34, 52-54, 108, 134, 150, 153, 290, 291
Purple Martin—230
Quarry Pond, Belle Isle—14, 44, 48, 58, 59, 61, 122, 245, 246, 285, 297, 298, 30
Quartz—172
Rabbit—51
Raccoon—51, 53, 88
Ramsey, George—150
Randolph, Edmund—142
Rappelling—264
Rawls, George D.—149
Redbreast—22, 50, 100, 123, 124, 180, 262, 297
Red Bud Tree—286
Red Fox—157, 296
Red Maple Tree—137
Reedy Creek—28, 49, 65, 70, 71, 86, 88, 89, 160, 239, 269, 277
Reynolds Metals Co.—135, 136
Reynolds Take-Out—33, 73

Richmond Audubon Society—166
Richmond Raft Company—30, 74–77, 79, 81, 298
Richmond Renaissance—140
Richmond Riverfront Development Corporation—149, 289, 290
Ring-billed Gull—160
River Birch Tree—23, 45, 49, 158, 184–186, 246, 247, 272
Riverside Mill—147
Riverview Cemetery—3
Robin—112, 249, 251
Rockfish—See Striper
Rollerblade—301
Ross's Mill Race—251
Rowe, Mossy—191
Rowing—120, 122, 240–242, 299
Royal Paulownia Tree—185
Ryan, David—19, 157, 166, 299
Saw Mill Island—269
Saxifrage—169
Schwartz, Susan—191
SCI, Inc.—146
Second Break Rapids—73, 228
Shad—82, 103, 104, 106, 120–122, 124, 157, 161, 218, 220, 227, 229, 274, 289, 302
Shelby Park—36
Shields Lake—55
Simon, Michael—61
Slippery Elm Tree—137
Smallmouth Bass—22, 23, 36, 38, 63, 82, 100–102, 107, 108, 113, 116–118, 123, 124, 159, 183, 187, 218, 247, 262, 265, 288, 289, 296, 297
Smith, John—20, 132, 138, 139, 279
Snail—47, 181
Snake—23, 43, 50, 77, 159, 178, 218, 230, 267, 270, 293, 300
Snorkeling—42, 180
Southern States—30, 229
Southside Rapids—73, 228
Sparrow—61, 62

Specialty Paperboard, Inc.—146
Spicebush—137, 169
Spider—43, 112
Spring Beauty—169
Squirrel—51, 120
Starling—88, 237
Stephens, Jason—285
St. John's Church—92
Stonefly—182, 232
Strawberry Street Festival—258
Striper—22, 35, 69, 76, 82, 83, 104–108, 111, 113, 118–122, 125–127, 129, 130, 157, 161, 220, 221, 227, 229, 295, 297, 298, 302
Stuart, J.E.B.—141
Stucke, Peter—197
Sturgeon—23, 107, 132, 299
STYLE Weekly—52, 291
Swallow—164
Sweetgum Tree—157
Swimming—27–29, 45, 95, 97, 158, 217, 293, 294, 301
Swinburn, Noel—191
Sycamore Tree—23, 47, 49, 54, 88, 125, 157–159, 218, 247, 272
Texas Beach—See Northbank
Three Mile Locks—53, 285, 290
Tickseed Sunflower—124
Toothwart—169
Tredegar Iron Works—68, 72, 132, 138, 144, 145, 149, 227, 290
Triple Drop Rapids—73
Tropical Storm Juan—133
Trout—23, 35, 37, 55, 107, 111, 218, 301
Trout, W.E., III—149, 150, 261, 293
Tubing—19, 22, 36, 50, 244, 275, 296
Turkey—120
Turkey Creek—123
Turkey Vulture—45
Turtle—43, 49, 50, 54
Twight, Marc—194
Tyler, John—141, 298
Valentine, Edward—141
Valentine Bike Trail—220

325

Valentine Riverside—145, 242, 290
Variation Rapids—72
Vauxall Island—150
Vepco Levee—72, 73, 226
Violet—169
Virginia Boat Club—240–242, 299
Virginia Canals and Navigation Society—149, 150, 250, 290
Virginia Commonwealth University—160, 162, 166, 278, 283, 284
Virginia Creeper—53
Virginia Department of Game and Inland Fisheries—61, 70, 122, 287, 295
Virginia Department of Historic Resources—149, 287
Virginia Department of Natural Resources—287, 288
Virginia Historical Society—131, 290
Virginia State Water Control Board—280
Virginia Wildlife Federation—282
Visitor's Center, James River Park System—16, 28, 41–43, 48–50, 71, 86–88, 112, 137, 157, 217, 231, 232, 269, 274, 285, 286
Wade, Ed—191
Wlaker's Dam—220
Walleye—23, 107, 118, 124, 125, 187, 218
Ware, Charles V.—67, 70, 81
Washington, Bushrod—139
Washington's Island—139
Washington, George—68, 139, 141, 142
Water Skiing—233
Water Willow Tree—184
Waybright, Tyler—191, 194
Weatherford, Greg—291
Weevil—46
Westham Gauge—41, 65, 70–72, 74, 293, 300
Wetlands—27, 87, 88, 137, 148, 169, 234, 238
Wheelchair Access—14, 15, 29, 32, 44, 51, 122, 226

White, Ralph—15, 19, 39, 42, 45, 46, 53, 56, 86, 112, 132, 137, 148, 157, 169, 170, 180, 217, 224, 231–235, 267, 269, 276, 293, 295, 302
White Perch—76, 82, 104, 105, 115, 120–122, 220–222, 234, 265, 297, 298
Whitlock, Dave—109
Wildflower—27, 30, 33, 39, 42, 43, 46, 51, 157, 169, 179, 184, 232, 236, 237, 267, 285, 286, 293, 296, 299, 301
Wild Grape—47
Wild Rose—46
Wilhelm, Robin—285
Willey Bridge—227
Williams, James—112–115
Williams Dam—65, 70, 88, 89, 133
Williams Island—70, 88, 294
Willow Tree—49, 53, 265
Wise, H. Alexander, Jr.—149
Witch Hazel Tree—148
Woodlief, Ann—275, 276
Xenolith—171, 176
Yellow Perch—298
Young, R. B.—19, 281, 282

NOW—From Charles Creek Publishing—
A Newsletter for Those Who Want Their Lives
Continually Enriched by Richmond's James River:

The Urban James Letter

A Newsletter Dedicated to Enjoying, Appreciating and Caring for the James River in Richmond

A Full Year—6 Issues—Only $9.95

- Features and Tips On Fishing, Hiking, Paddling, & More ...
- Nature, History, Volunteer Projects
- Latest Updates On River Improvements: James River Park System, Richmond Riverfront Development Corporation, Combined Sewer Overflow Project, Fish Passages

The Urban James Letter is your ongoing source of fresh information from experts and insiders.

Families Will Also Want:

The Urban James Kidsletter

A Special Insert For Kids From 6 To 16

• Prizes • Giveaways • Projects • Activities •

The Urban James Kidsletter is your children's guide to safely enjoying and taking care of Richmond's most important natural resource.

The Urban James Letter Plus *The Urban James Kidsletter*
A Full Year of BOTH For Only $14.95

- Order Form For -
The Urban James Letter *and* The Urban James Kidsletter

☐ Send me a full year—six issues—of *The Urban James Letter* for only $9.95.

☐ Send me a full year of *The Urban James Letter* PLUS *The Urban James Kidsletter*, Both for only $14.95.

My name, address and phone:

_____

_____

_____

_____

Share Our River with Your Friends in Richmond and Beyond—Order Gift Subscriptions for Birthdays, Special Days, and Special Friends.

☐ Yes, I have written gift subscription information on the back of this order form.

Make Checks Payable to **Charles Creek Publishing**, and send to: **Charles Creek Publishing, P.O. Box 26746, Richmond, VA 23261**

GIFT SUBSCRIPTIONS

☐ Send *The Urban James Letter* ($9.95) to:

Name _____
Address _____
City, State, Zip _____

☐ Please enclose a free gift card with the following note:

_____
_____
_____

☐ Send *The Urban James Letter* ($9.95) to:

Name _____
Address _____
City, State, Zip _____

☐ Please enclose a free gift card with the following note:

_____
_____
_____

☐ Send *The Urban James Letter* plus *The Urban James Kidsletter* (both $14.95) to:

Name _____
Address _____
City, State, Zip _____

☐ Please enclose a free gift card with the following note:

_____
_____
_____

☐ Send *The Urban James Letter* plus *The Urban James Kidsletter* (both $14.95) to:

Name _____
Address _____
City, State, Zip _____

☐ Please enclose a free gift card with the following note:

_____
_____
_____

BOOK ORDER FORM

Postal Orders: Charles Creek Publishing, P.O. Box 26746, Richmond, VA 23261

Urban Bassing in Richmond (1994)—$12
The James River In Richmond: Your Guide To Enjoying America's Best Urban Waterway (1997)—$19.95

Please send the following books:
(All books can be returned for a full refund for any reason.)

_____

_____

_____

_____

My name, address and phone:

_____

_____

_____

Shipping/handling:
Book rate (three to four weeks): $2.00 for the first book and 75 cents for each additional book.
Priority mail (two to three days): $4.00 for the first book and $1 for each additional book.

Payment:
Make checks payable to Charles Creek Publishing and send to Charles Creek Publishing, Post Office Box 26746, Richmond, VA 23261.